ERASED FROM SPACE AND CONSCIOUSNESS

ERASED FROM SPACE AND CONSCIOUSNESS

Israel and the Depopulated Palestinian Villages of 1948

Noga Kadman

Foreword by Oren Yiftachel

Translation from Hebrew: Dimi Reider
Translation consultant: Ofer Neiman

Indiana University Press

Bloomington and Indianapolis

This book is a publication of

Indiana University Press
Office of Scholarly Publishing
Herman B Wells Library 350
1320 East 10th Street
Bloomington, Indiana 47405 USA

iupress.indiana.edu

Manufactured in the United States of America

Library of Congress Cataloging-in-Publication Data

Kadman, Noga, author.
  [Be-tside ha-derekh uve-shule ha-toda'ah. English]
  Erased from space and consciousness : Israel and the depopulated Palestinian villages of 1948 / Noga Kadman ; translation from Hebrew, Dimi Reider ; translation consultant, Ofer Neiman.
    pages cm
  Includes bibliographical references and index.
    ISBN 978-0-253-01670-6 (cl : alk. paper) — ISBN 978-0-253-01676-8 (pb : alk. paper) — ISBN 978-0-253-01682-9 (eb)   1. Israel—Rural conditions. 2. Israel—Rural conditions.   3. Villages—Israel—History—20th century. 4. Palestinian Arabs—Israel.   5. Israel-Arab War, 1948–1949—Destruction and pillage.   6. Palestine—History—1917–1948.   I. Reider, Dimi, translator. II. Title.
    HN660.A8K3315 2015
    307.72095694—dc23
                                                                    2015009101

1 2 3 4 5   20 19 18 17 16 15

To my family

Look at the landscape around you, and carve it onto your memory. You must change it, so that it does not resemble what was here before you. You must leave your mark on it. The mountains, the hills, the forests and the meadows—they must all bear your name and reflect the light of your face. . . . You must mercilessly destroy anything in the landscape which is not directly related to you. . . . Tell everyone that you were here first. They will believe you. Tell them there was nothing before you—no mountain, forest, hill or meadow. Say this with complete objectivity.

—Amos Kenan, "The First"

Contents

Foreword: On Erasure, Research, and Reconciliation

—"Please stop at Masmiyya."

—"Where is it?"

—"You know, the junction where you can turn left to Be'er Sheva or right to Tel Aviv."

—"No, this place is called Re'em junction . . . what was that weird name you just used?"

—"Masmiyya. You haven't heard about it? This is what the people from the south call this junction."

—"Okay, I'm from Jerusalem, but I drive here every once in a while, and I don't know the name . . . You should know: this place is called Re'em junction, and it's even on the map, look . . ."

This recent conversation I had with a cabdriver from Jerusalem, a person of Russian origin, demonstrates well the act of erasure and its long-lasting influence. Those who were born in the 1950s, like me, still carry with them fragments of memories of the Palestinian localities demolished by Israel, mainly retained from the landscapes we traveled through, in which we frequently brushed against the ruins of the demolished sites. Those ruins had names, and of course were connected to systems of roads and tracks, as well as remains of orchards, groves, hedges, and fields. These crumbs of memory have also survived in spoken, everyday language, which refers to the country's places, vegetation, and customs. But the new generations, and especially the new immigrants who have arrived over the last few decades, already have no connection to this disappearing geography.

This, of course, is no coincidence. The act of erasure has been guided for decades by the mechanisms of the Jewish state, which seek to expunge the remains of the Arab-Palestinian society living in the country until 1948, as well as deny the tragedy visited on this people by Zionism. The act of erasure, which followed the violence, the flight, the expulsion, and the demolition of villages, is prominent in most major discursive arenas—in school textbooks, in the history that Zionist society recounts itself, in the political discourse, in the media, in official maps, and now also in the names of communities, roads, and junctions. Palestine, which underlies Israel, is continuously being erased from the Israeli-Jewish body and speech. The remains of Arabness left in the Israeli landscape are perceived by the Jewish majority as the communities of "Israel's Arabs"—some sort of Arab islands scattered around, unrelated to the Palestinian space that existed here before 1948.

At the same time, Palestinian society is going through an opposite process: it makes an ever-growing effort to document, map, revive, and glorify the memory of the pre-1948 Palestinian society. For the refugee population who still live in camps or in "temporary" host countries, the pre-1948 reality continues to sizzle as a self-evident, daily matter, which casts meaning into their personal and communal identity. In the last few years the general documentation effort has also grown, as well as Arab-Palestinian research and media discourse, both of which try to revive a society that has disappeared. The Nakba—the "disaster" of the defeat of 1948—turns from a historical event and a low point in a still-bleeding conflict, into a basic value, through which many Palestinians try to rebuild their nation through memory, return, and political resistance.

Therefore, the two national movements have created opposing discourses, resembling photographic negatives, in which the same land—sacred to both peoples—embodies opposite images. Zionism draws a Jewish, Western, and democratic country, rooted in the Hebrew biblical space while erasing the Arab-Palestinian past. Palestinian society, on the other hand, portrays a romantic image of a lost paradise and (in part) refuses to recognize the millions of Jews who settled in Israel and created a new vibrant society on the same ruined Palestinian space. These polarized discourses—held by considerable groups within each nation—reject any possibility of reconciliation.

However, other groups and approaches exist to challenge this dualism. Noga Kadman's research, in the book you are holding, seeks to break out of this polarized discourse. It documents in detail the spatial practices of erasure and manufactured oblivion by Zionist institutions as well as by Jewish residents who settled the lands, and sometimes even the houses, of Palestinians. Her research is pioneering and important in several ways. First, it explores a fascinating geographical, political, and psychological phenomenon that sheds light on the mechanisms through which one ethnic space is being erased and replaced by another. The understanding of these processes has consequences for many conflict areas in the world in which similar phenomena have taken place. Too little has been written about this colonial geography, focusing on both institutional and cultural practices of dispossession. In her research, Kadman adds an important aspect that seeks to open the State of Israel's supposedly self-evident framework of legitimacy ("It's our territory and our business!") in order to document and analyze the takeover act.

No less important is the attempt to understand (even if not to support) the acts of the Jewish residents. Kadman approaches the practices of manufactured oblivion in a critical way, but the practitioners in the book are flesh and blood: not only the vanguard of a national historical enterprise, but also refugees themselves who seek a safe haven in a world full of dangers and discuss the morality of their deeds among themselves. By day they are loyal soldiers of the Zionist frontier project, but at night they still live under the terrifying shadow of the Holocaust of the European Jews and the aftermath of a war of survival, forced—according to their view—on the Jewish community in 1948. Kadman "opens" and "fragments" the internal Jewish colonial act and presents it as it is—a human deed with all its complexities.

Kadman's research joins a small number of studies that courageously seek to remove the mask of daily denial of the Palestinian exile, which grips not only Jewish society at large and its consensus-seeking leaders but also its academic and research institutions, which are supposed to pursue historical truth. The act of denial was already described with painful accuracy in 1949, by novelist S. Yizhar in his book *Khirbet Khizeh*:

> To be knowingly led astray and join the great general mass of liars—that mass compounded of crass ignorance, utilitarian indifference, and shameless self-interest—and exchange a single great truth for a cynical shrug of a hardened sinner.[1]

Nearly seven decades later, a discussion about the Nakba and its consequences opens another small hatch toward the possibility of reconciliation between the peoples. Kadman's book brings the depopulated villages back into discussion and places them again on Hebrew maps and discourse. This is an essential step for opening "our" history and geography here, in the homeland, intertwined with Palestinian history and geography. Only this approach—which sees the place as the homeland of both peoples and seeks to know and acknowledge the complex of this homeland's periods, spaces, and residents—can open a space for discussion between the two peoples on the most important issue of all: their joint and secure future on this tortured land.

Oren Yiftachel
Professor, Geography Department
Ben-Gurion University

Acknowledgments

I AM GRATEFUL TO Professor Oren Yiftachel of the Department of Geography and Environmental Development at Ben-Gurion University for his insightful supervision, which greatly complemented and enriched the research, and for introducing me to fields of knowledge that had been unknown to me.

Many others invested time and resources to assist me in my research and in the writing of this work. I wish to thank the archivists who hosted me and allowed me access to documents and publications of the State Archive; Yad Tabenkin; Yad Ya'ari; and the kibbutzim of Beit Ha'Emek, Beit Guvrin, Megiddo, Sasa, and Yiron, as well as moshav Kfar Daniel. I am also grateful to members of many other kibbutzim and moshavim for responding to my queries and sending me additional materials. I also wish to thank Yehuda Ziv for sharing some of his writings and his experiences as a member in the Government Names Committee, the Zochrot organization for sharing information, and Yishai Menuhin and November Books for publishing the original Hebrew edition of this book. Rebecca Tolen at Indiana University Press has my gratitude for her interest in and support of the publication of the translated book and making it available to English-speaking readers.

I am grateful to my family, friends, and acquaintances for assisting me in so many different ways in the course of the research and its transformation into a book. Special thanks go to Shelly Cohen, who painstakingly edited the Hebrew text, for her sharp and clear eyes and invaluable advice; to Ofer Neiman and Tony Nugent for carefully proofreading and editing the English text; to Shira Ramer Wittlin for the meticulous work of preparing the footnotes and bibliography; to Tamari Kadman for her work on the last bits and pieces of the manuscript; and to Yuval Drier Shilo for the vital assistance with the maps.

Despite striving for maximal accuracy in my data, some inaccuracies may arise, due to contradictions between different sources or human error. The responsibility for everything written here is my own.

Note on Transliteration

THE ARABIC TRANSLITERATION of the names of all the depopulated Palestinian villages is taken from Khalidi, *All That Remains.*

The transliteration of Hebrew terms is based on the rules of simple transliteration, fixed by the Academy of the Hebrew Language in Israel, except when the official English spelling of names of people, places, and institutions is different.

Abbreviations

GNC	Government Names Committee
IDF	Israel Defense Forces
ILA	Israel Land Administration (from 2013: Israel Land Authority)
INPA	Israel Nature and Parks Authority
ISA	Israel State Archives
ITC	Israel Trails Committee
JA	Jewish Agency
JNF	Jewish National Fund
KAA	Kibbutz Artzi Archive
SPNI	Society for the Protection of Nature in Israel
SOI	Survey of Israel
UKA	United Kibbutz Archive
UKM	United Kibbutz Movement
UNRWA	United Nations Relief and Works Agency for Palestine Refugees in the Near East
YT	Yad Tabenkin (the Research and Documentation Center of the UKM)
YY	Yad Ya'ari (the Research and Documentation Center of HaShomer HaTza'ir and Kibbutz Artzi)

ERASED FROM SPACE
AND CONSCIOUSNESS

Introduction

WHEN ONE TRAVELS in Israel, it is almost impossible to avoid seeing piles of stones, ruins, collapsing walls and structures overgrown with uncultivated almond and fig trees, rolling terraces crumbling with disuse, and long hedges of prickly cactuses. These integral parts of the Israeli landscape are all that remain of Palestinian villages that existed before the War of 1948.

After the war, the newly created State of Israel contained within its borders over four hundred depopulated villages and eleven cities emptied of all or most of their Arab-Palestinian residents. Israel prevented these residents, who had escaped or been expelled across the border, from returning home, making the majority of Palestinians refugees.

Most of the villages were demolished by Israel either during the war or in its aftermath. Today, many offer nothing but scant remains, and many more were razed to the ground, leaving no trace in the landscape. Israel confiscated the vast lands of the villages and the belongings left by the refugees in their flight. The state established hundreds of new Jewish communities on the confiscated lands and granted existing Jewish agricultural communities extensive tracts of expropriated grounds. The depopulated Palestinian cities and dozens of depopulated villages were repopulated with Jews, many of whom were refugees in their own right—survivors of the war in Europe or displaced people from Arab countries. The State of Israel, to a large extent, has been built and developed on the ruins of Palestinian villages and cities.

Growing up in Jerusalem in the 1980s, I was taken on many tours by my school and youth group to Lifta, the partly ruined, empty Palestinian village near the main entrance to the city. A spring still flows there among the ruined homes into a small pool. The visits left me with the vague impression that Lifta was an ancient place, a ruin that had always been as I had encountered it—desolate, beautiful, slightly mysterious, and, in some way, intimidating, with its eerie silence and narrow paths winding among the imposing houses and walls.

Later on, I spent several years working at B'Tselem, an Israeli human rights organization, documenting violations of human rights of Palestinians in the territories occupied by Israel in 1967. This work exposed me to knowledge about the conflict that had never gotten through to me before. I understood that many of the residents of the territories, who suffer today the restrictions imposed by Israel's military rule, lost their entire world in 1948; that the Palestinians in Lebanon are not just another ethnic group in that divided northern country, but also refugees who had lived here, where I live, until the Israeli triumph in the War of 1948; that Lifta is not just a picturesque ruin from a bygone age, but a home recently taken from people, from families, from children. These realizations made me want to understand more deeply the roots of the adversity facing Palestinians, as well as Israelis, today.

In the many walks and journeys I undertook across Israel over the years, all the while gaining a growing awareness of the history of the land and its two peoples, I came across these ruins time after time: in an anemone-sprinkled hill near Jerusalem, on a mountain ridge in the Galilee, by a steep path down to the Tabor stream. By then, I was already able to try to imagine how lively the place must have been but a few short decades ago: the bustling daily life, full of voices and colors, children, housework, livestock, water drawn from the well—all replaced today by emptiness and silence. And there is no commemoration or even reference to the world that has been lost and the circumstances of its disappearance. This troubling contrast was the impetus for the present work.

This book is about the way in which Israel deals with the preceding layer of its existence, a layer that it has erased and on which it has been built. It examines Israeli views and representations of the depopulated Palestinian villages and looks at the place they occupy in Israeli consciousness after they were, for the most part, removed from the landscape. It focuses on the most ordinary, everyday encounters of Israelis with the memory of the villages and their physical remains: using place names, looking at a map, traveling around the country, and residing in rural communities. As far as the first three experiences are concerned, I examine the shaping of Israeli consciousness by the authorities who mediate between Israelis and the villages: whether the villages were given official names and mapped, and whether the authorities responsible for tourism and recreation sites provide information on the depopulated villages located within those sites' boundaries. As for the fourth, I also describe firsthand encounters between Israeli communities and the villages whose sites they have come to inhabit, by examining the new inhabitants' writings.

My research drew on a variety of sources, including official documents, maps, academic works, and observations during excursions I made to the sites of some 230 villages between November 2006 and May 2007.[1] Different sources cite different estimates of the total number of villages depopulated in 1948; I have chosen to use the list of 418 villages compiled by Walid Khalidi in his extensive 1992 work *All That Remains*.[2] Khalidi's book is the result of years of cooperation among three Palestinian research institutions, located in Israel, the West Bank, and the United States. Their research is based on official Ottoman and British data, maps, and information from other sources and extensive field work carried out in the early 1990s. Khalidi's list includes villages and hamlets with a core of permanent structures, emptied of their Palestinian inhabitants during the War of 1948 or in its immediate aftermath, situated within Israel's pre-1967 borders.

Using these sources in conjunction with the atlases of Salman Abu Sitta, I have located all 418 villages and placed them on up-to-date maps of the country, comparing their locations to the present-day geographical and demographic layouts.[3] Appendix A includes a map of the 418 villages and basic information about each one.

The list of 418 villages compiled by Khalidi does not include Bedouin communities in the south of the country, from which, according to Khalidi, some ninety-eight thousand people were uprooted in 1948.[4] Consequently, the research in this book also does not reflect the Israeli approach to these places in naming, mapping, the provision of information at touristic resorts, or the establishment of new communities on formerly Bedouin sites. It focuses on Palestinian villages and does not look in depth at Israeli policy and attitudes toward the depopulated Palestinian cities.[5] Also largely excluded are the villages depopulated and razed after the 1967 war—predominantly in the Golan Heights and near Latrun on the West Bank.[6]

The book begins by providing the historical and theoretical contexts for understanding the depopulated villages and Israeli attitudes toward them. Chapter 1 presents the cataclysmic events that resulted in hundreds of depopulated villages within Israel: the progression of the 1948 war, the reasons for and circumstances of the mass uprooting of the land's Palestinian residents, and the Israeli decision to prohibit their return. I describe the means by which Israel gained physical and legal control of the refugees' lands, villages, and property; the deliberate destruction of numerous villages; and the establishment of Jewish communities on village lands and village sites. Finally, I discuss the present-day remains of the villages.

In chapter 2, Israeli actions with regard to the refugees and their villages are viewed in relation to the Zionist ideology that drove the pre-state Jewish leadership and has driven the State of Israel to the present day. I discuss this as an instance of the creation and fortification of national identity, focusing on both time and space as expressions of such an identity and as arenas of national conflict. In the context of the Israeli-Zionist national movement, I focus on the basic Zionist ideal of "Judaization"—the intentional process of turning something non-Jewish into something Jewish—a term frequently and positively employed

Houses still standing in the depopulated village of Lifta, near the entrance to Jerusalem, February 22, 2007. Courtesy of Noga Kadman.

in official Israeli terminology to this day. I review the way in which the Judaization ideal has affected the overall creation of Israeli space, including the eradication of depopulated Palestinian villages and the construction of a selective collective memory that stresses the land's Jewish past and suppresses the many centuries of its Arab past. Ignoring and sidelining Arabness in time and in space represents yet another Israeli victory in another arena of the Israeli-Palestinian conflict, made possible through the Israeli military conquest of the territory and the making of most of its Palestinian residents into refugees beyond the state's borders.

Chapter 3 looks more closely at the process of Judaization through an examination of references to depopulated villages in documents and publications from twenty-five rural Jewish communities settled on or next to village ruins after 1948, mainly in the early 1950s.

Chapter 4 explores the official representation of the demolished villages through an examination of the processes of renaming village sites and their presentation on maps. Using documents of the Government Names Committee (GNC), I examine whether village sites were given official names, how many of these were the original names of villages, and what characteristics are shared by the new names given to such sites. I also review trail maps produced by the Survey of Israel (SOI; the government agency for mapping), in order to investigate which of the village sites and names are featured on official, up-to-date maps in current use in the country, and in what way.

Chapter 5 examines the Israeli encounter with the physical remains of the villages—the "visible tip of an iceberg"—focusing on village sites whose previously built-up areas are accessible and visible to the general Israeli public.[7] Such villages are mostly located today either within tourist sites and resorts or within Jewish-Israeli rural or urban communities. Israeli views of the former are analyzed through texts produced by official bodies that control tourist sites today. An overview of signs and publications by the Jewish National Fund (JNF) and the Israel Nature and Parks Authority (INPA) focuses on whether these organizations inform the public of the existence of the ruined villages in the nature reserves and tourist resorts they are responsible for and examines the content and extent of the information provided.

The concluding chapter provides a summary of the book as well as discussion of an emerging alternative discourse about these villages in Israel.

The Judaization of space and memory is apparent in a pattern of marginalization of the Palestinian depopulated villages, in every aspect of Israeli discourse examined in this research: the erasure or Hebraization of the villages' names; the elimination of many villages from the map and the blurring of the identity of others; JNF's and INPA's disregard for the majority of the villages and the suppression of the identity, history, and circumstances of depopulation of those that are acknowledged by these organizations; and the acceptance of Palestinian dispossession by Jewish communities established on depopulated Palestinian village sites or lands, while minimizing the interaction with the villages' history, the circumstances of their depopulation, and the moral dilemmas arising from the use of refugee homes and properties.

As in many other national conflicts, one of the Israeli-Palestinian conflict's most poignant and persistent features is the utter unwillingness of either side to listen to the other's perception of the disputed territory and its version of the history of the conflict, to understand the distress and the losses suffered by the other, and to accept responsibility for complicity in causing them. Without a change in these attitudes, there can be no reconciliation, and therefore no realistic, comprehensive, and long-term resolution of a national conflict. The ongoing Israeli-Palestinian conflict has been shaped, to a great extent, by the events of 1948—termed by the Palestinians "al-Nakba" ("the catastrophe")—when the Palestinians lost most of their land, while the Jews used the same land to establish their nation-state. Therefore, the importance of examining the Israeli approach to the Palestinian villages depopulated in 1948 goes beyond the subject matter itself, since this approach can serve as an indicator of Israeli readiness to achieve a sustainable resolution of the conflict.

Until quite recently, there was little research on this topic. The handful of books that touched on it include *Sacred Landscapes* by Meron Benvenisti; *The Object of Memory* by Susan Slyomovics, which analyzes the residents of 'Ein Hod's accounts of the past of the village of 'Ayn Hawd, in whose houses they reside to this day; and *The Present Absentees* by Hillel Cohen, which deals, among other matters, with Israeli communities established atop depopulated villages.[8]

The last few years, however, have witnessed an awakening of interest among Israeli scholars in the depopulated Palestinian villages and the publication of a series of essays and books on related matters, such as the erasure of memory of the Nakba; information provided by the JNF to visitors in the forests planted over the ruins of Palestinian villages; the role of national parks in silencing Palestinian history; the connection between nature preservation and the eradication of Palestinian landscapes; the conversion of a depopulated Palestinian village into a Jewish neighborhood; and Jewish residents' opposition to the expansion of their rural community over the site of a ruined Palestinian village.[9] Publications on adjacent issues deal with the Israeli approach to the preservation of Palestinian structures and villages; the attitude of early Israeli archaeology toward the Palestinian depopulated villages; book looting and the eradication of Palestinian culture; and the Judaization of urban landscapes in Haifa and Jaffa.[10]

These works are referenced throughout this book, which joins other scholarship that seeks to scrutinize Israeli awareness of the country's Palestinian past and the dispossession of its Palestinian population. This approach, in turn, is based on, is inspired by, and makes ample use of the work of "the new historians": In the late 1980s, a small number of scholars began presenting a more balanced and critical picture of the events of 1948, which up until then were described in Israel in exclusive adherence to the dominant Zionist narrative.[11] For information about the circumstances of depopulation of the villages, I draw primarily on the works of Benny Morris, one of the most important in the group of "new historians" and the author of this very term, whose research was based mainly on official Israeli sources.

Another important source for detailed information on the villages is Walid Khalidi's *All That Remains*, written to "breathe a life into a name," to "be a kind of 'in memoriam,'" and to rescue the 418 villages from oblivion.[12] Trying to document the world inhabited by the refugees prior to their uprooting and its physical destruction, Khalidi outlines the history of each village, its architectural and economic characteristics, the circumstances of its conquest and depopulation, and the physical remains still visible forty years after the depopulation.

The growth of Israeli academic interest in the price paid by the Palestinians in 1948 and its place in Israeli consciousness is a part of a wider process of awakening to these issues in Israeli society, however marginal. Like any society, Israel is not a monolith, and beyond the dominant narrative are a wide range of opinions. In the conclusion of the book, I describe the beginnings of alternative narratives of the shaping of memory and space in Israel, which has been growing in Jewish-Israeli society, and includes voices who call for bringing the depopulated villages into public awareness.

This book focuses on discourses within Jewish-Israeli society and its institutions, and these are the entities alluded to by general terms like "Israel," "Israeli society," and "Israeli discourse." Historical memory surrounding the depopulated villages among Palestinian citizens of Israel is entirely different and will not be discussed here. It is important to note, however, that in recent years there has been an extensive effort within Palestinian society in Israel to publicly commemorate the Nakba and to preserve mosques, churches, and cemeteries belonging to depopulated villages, in order to prevent their destruction and desecration and to begin using them again.[13]

I use the term "depopulated" to describe the villages, rather than the term more frequently heard in Israel—"abandoned." The latter suggests that their departure was at the villagers' own initiative, while "depopulated" implies an external agent or circumstance—as indeed was the case, with villages emptying out in response to attacks against them or against nearby targets, rather than spontaneous abandonment.

I use the terms "Palestine" and "Land of Israel" interchangeably, to refer to the complete territory of the British Mandate of Palestine, from the Mediterranean Sea in the west to the Jordan valley in the east. The terms "Arabs" and "Palestinians" are also used interchangeably, to describe the Arab-Palestinian residents and villages of Israel-Palestine. The sequence of events known to Israelis as the "War of Independence" and to Palestinians as the "Nakba" is described by the more neutral term "War of 1948."

1 Depopulation, Demolition, and Repopulation of the Village Sites

On THE EVE of the violent events of 1948, the Arab population of British Mandatory Palestine amounted to 1.2 million, of them 850,000 within the borders of what is today recognized as the State of Israel proper; they constituted the great majority of the population of that area. Arab-Palestinian society of the time was largely agricultural, with some two-thirds of the Palestinian population before the war living in villages. Most of the Arab workforce in 1947 in Palestine worked in agriculture.[1] On their land the Arab villagers cultivated nearly ten thousand acres of orchards, mostly citrus fruit (on the coastal plain) and olives (in the mountainous areas), as well as figs, grapes, deciduous fruits, and bananas. In the rest of the cultivated area the villagers grew vegetables, legumes, and grains.[2]

Most of the residents of Arab villages in Palestine were Sunni Muslim, with Christian, Druze, and Shi'ite minorities present. The majority of the villages stood on hilltops, often built on top of, or in continuation of, much older settlements. In the mountain areas the houses were usually made of stone, and in the coastal plain houses were often constructed of mud.[3] In the twentieth century, with the citrus boom, quality of life in the plain improved, and more modern houses began to appear. Every village typically had public structures for religious and social purposes, and later on schools were set up, usually in the largest building in the village.[4]

It is difficult to determine exactly how many Palestinians became refugees in 1948, and estimates vary: Israeli official sources maintain the number of 520,000, while official Arab sources insist it was 900,000. Benny Morris concludes that the number of Palestinian refugees displaced was between 600,000 and 760,000.[5] There is still a debate as to the circumstances and factors that played a role in these Palestinians becoming refugees. According to Morris, the residents of approximately half of the villages and towns that were depopulated fled because of military attacks; the rest were deported or fled out of fear of an attack, due to Israeli conquest of a nearby community, as a result of Israeli psychological warfare, or for reasons presently unknown. In a handful of villages, residents were ordered to leave by various Arab leaders.[6]

Whether they fled, were attacked, or were deported, few Palestinians who found themselves beyond the Israeli borders that were determined at the end of the war were allowed to return to their country and their homes, and these people have remained refugees to this day. Some four hundred thousand of the refugees came from several hundred villages that remained in Israeli hands after the war, ravaged and empty. The Palestinian refugees were made to leave their lands and their homes, as well as all of their possessions, except what they could carry off when they left. Israel took over refugee property, reallocated their lands to existing Jewish communities, built new communities on the appropriated land, settled Jews in emptied Palestinian houses in cities and some villages, and razed most of the depopulated villages altogether.[7]

Approximately twenty thousand Palestinians who were displaced from sixty of the depopulated villages settled in other Arab communities within Israel and received Israeli citizenship. These internally displaced persons are known in Israel as "internal refugees" or "present absentees," and the property they left behind was expropriated all the same.[8]

Meanwhile, over two thousand Jews living in twenty rural communities in the Jerusalem area, the Jordan valley, the southern coastal plain, and the Galilee were also forced to leave their homes when their communities were attacked and demolished by Jordanian, Egyptian, or Iraqi forces. Eighteen thousand Jews were also displaced from the Jaffa area during the fighting in 1948 and settled in and around Tel Aviv, while some two thousand Jewish residents of the Jewish quarter and other neighborhoods of Jerusalem were deported from their homes and settled in the western part of the city.

The Palestinians displaced beyond Israel's borders, as well as their descendants, are still recognized as refugees by the United Nations Relief and Works Agency for Palestine Refugees in the Near East (UNRWA), established in 1950. By late 2012 they numbered almost five million. Most Palestinian refugees reside today in Jordan, Lebanon, Syria, the Gaza Strip, and the West Bank, 1.5 million of them still living in refugee camps.[9]

The Making of the Palestinian Refugees

> The Arabs of the land of Israel have only one function left—to run away.
>
> —David Ben-Gurion [Israel's first prime minister]
> October 21, 1948 (Morris, *The Birth of the Palestinian Refugee Problem Revisited*)

On November 29, 1947, the UN General Assembly endorsed a call to partition Palestine into two states, Jewish and Arab. The next day Arab residents began

attacking Jews in cities and on the roads. In January 1948 units of volunteer ir-
regulars began arriving from Arab states in a bid to join the fighting. The Arab
military force was inferior to the Jewish one in numbers, munitions, coordination, and professionalism. The Haganah militia—the bulk of the Jewish fighting
force—adopted a policy of defense and counterattack. Up to March 1948, most
Haganah attacks—conducted by its fighting force, the Palmach—were retaliatory
actions, limited to areas where Arab attacks had occurred earlier.[10]

As the conflict flared, Arab residents began leaving their cities—Haifa, Jaffa,
and Jerusalem—following shooting and bombing attacks by the Haganah and
the more radical militias of the Irgun (Etzel) and the Stern Gang (Lehi). The
departure was also due to threats and fear of retaliatory assaults by Jewish paramilitaries. This exodus can in part also be attributed to food shortages, unemployment, robberies committed by Arab forces, and general fear of the aftermath
of the British mandate's approaching end.[11]

Villagers began to flee at around the same time, usually in direct response
to attacks by Jewish forces or fear of such attacks. In some villages the Haganah
expelled the residents, while in others residents left on the instructions of Arab
combatants.[12] Yossef Weitz, head of the land department of the Jewish National
Fund (JNF) at the time, took a direct and active part in forcing Arab sharecrop-
pers living on lands acquired by JNF in the Menashe hills to flee; later on, Weitz
ensured the demolition of their dwellings and successfully lobbied the Haganah
to evict Arabs from other places, especially the Bedouin of the northern Jordan
valley.[13] By March 1948, some hundred thousand Palestinian Arabs, mostly city
dwellers, had left for Lebanon, Jordan, and the Jordan-occupied West Bank.[14]

In March 1948 attacks by Arabs and resultant Jewish casualties escalated,
and in many areas Arabs began blockading roads to Jewish communities. In
response, the Haganah prepared Plan D, meant to prevent armed Arab forces
from operating in Palestinian communities adjacent to Jewish ones.[15] The plan
stipulated that as the need arose, the Jewish forces should disarm combatants,
occupy communities, expel the residents, and raze the villages—especially those
that could not be permanently held.[16]

The implementation of the plan began in April 1948 in a sequence of offen-
sives by the Haganah, meant to purge entire areas of Palestinian villages before
May 15, 1948, the end date of the British Mandate, when it was widely anticipated
that war would begin. In most cases, villages found themselves facing sustained,
coordinated, and well-organized attacks by the Haganah, with no organized
military defense of their own or coordination with other villages. Most of the
residents fled during the attacks or as the attacks loomed.[17]

The attacks soon whipped up the sporadic incidents of flight into a tidal wave.
On April 9, Irgun and Stern Gang paramilitaries killed more than a hundred
residents of the village of Dayr Yasin, most of them noncombatants, including

women and children. Based on the accounts of witnesses, both Palestinians and Jews, Israeli historian Ilan Pappé concludes that later, on the night between May 22 and 23, Israel carried out a massacre in the village of al-Tantura on the shore under Mount Carmel, which was "far worse than the infamous case of that at Dayr Yasin." He describes how 200–250 residents were killed there, in a raging spree by the Israeli forces after they occupied the village and also by a systematic summary execution of boys and men on the beach.[18]

Salman Abu Sitta lists ten more villages in which massacres by Israeli forces took place around the same time, including Balad al-Shaykh near Haifa and 'Ayn al-Zaytun near Safad.[19] News of the massacres, especially in Dayr Yasin, increased the fear among Palestinian villagers and contributed to their flight, as did the Haganah's custom of spreading rumors of impending attacks and advising residents to evacuate.

The villages fell one by one. When fighting died down in a village, the occupying forces would usually chase out the remaining residents. In some villages standing by important roads, especially in the Jerusalem corridor and around kibbutz Mishmar Ha'Emek at the mouth of the Jezreel Valley, the Haganah conducted premeditated expulsions.[20]

The depopulation of the villages was influenced by, and influenced in its turn, the flight of the Palestinian city dwellers. The flight from the cities continued also owing to the collapse of law and order there, the escape of the local leaders, and the poverty and overcrowding created by the arrival of refugees from other areas. In some places, cities were forcibly depopulated of their remaining Palestinian residents by the Haganah militia.[21]

On May 15, 1948, the British Mandate ended and the State of Israel was established. The next day, military units from five Arab countries joined the fray, and this phase lasted until the cease-fire on June 11. The period between April and June 1948 saw the greatest exodus of Arabs from Palestine: 250,000–300,000 from the center and north of the country became refugees in the West Bank, Egypt-occupied Gaza, and neighboring states. The scale of the flight of the Arab residents took the Jewish leadership by surprise in the beginning but was soon perceived as something desirable that should be encouraged. Military commanders were increasingly acting accordingly, by intimidation, attacks, and deliberate expulsions.[22]

In spring 1948 the Palestinian refugees, encouraged and supported by the Arab States, began lobbying for a return to their homes. On the other side, the leadership of the Jewish community in Palestine—and later, the leadership of the State of Israel—tried rallying support against the return of the refugees. At a cabinet meeting in June, Prime Minister David Ben-Gurion and Foreign Minister Moshe Shertok (later Sharet) spoke forcefully against allowing the return. Ben-Gurion declared, "I believe we should prevent their return. . . . I will be for them not returning also after the war," and Shertok said, "This is our policy: that they are not returning." Members of the left-leaning Mapam party, a part of the governing coalition, opposed that view, objected to the expulsion of Arab residents from the newly founded state, and spoke in favor of allowing the refugees to return after the war. As the first cease-fire of the war came into force in June 1948, growing international pressure was put on Israel to resolve the problem of the Palestinian refugees. In July Israel announced that no refugees would be allowed to return while the war continued, and that any decision on the matter would have to come within the framework of a peace agreement with the Arab States.[23]

The Haganah, Irgun, and Stern Gang militias were amalgamated into one force, the IDF (Israel Defense Forces), which was boosted by new recruits. On July 9, 1948, fighting resumed and the IDF launched assaults on several fronts. By July 18, Israel had conquered vast swaths of territory across the entire country, some well outside the area allocated to it by the UN in the 1947 partition plan. The occupied area was dense with Palestinian villages. As the occupation of villages in the north progressed, most Muslim residents there took flight. Some of those who remained were expelled during the following months, but others surrendered without resistance and were allowed to remain. Residents of Christian and Druze villages remained in their villages and generally were not deported. After Nazareth fell, the Lower Galilee villagers also took flight, fearing that a further assault was imminent. In the center of the country the IDF brought heavy shelling down on the cities of Ramla and Lydda (Lod) ahead of their occupation and in hope of making their residents flee; many did flee, and Ramla soon surrendered. The occupation of Lydda on July 12 resulted in several casualties for the Israeli forces; the IDF was then ordered to shoot at everyone found in the streets, killing 250. Later the IDF expelled the residents of Ramla and Lydda eastward, with many, between scores and hundreds, dying along the way of exhaustion, dehydration, and disease. Most of the villages in the Jerusalem corridor and the south of the country were already empty when taken; in others, residents fled as the army approached. The handful of residents who chose to remain were expelled by IDF troops as soon as their villages were occupied.[24]

During the second cease-fire of July 18 to October 15, the IDF conducted several attacks and expulsions meant to remove Palestinian populations from certain areas, such as the "little triangle" of the villages of Jaba', Ijzim, and 'Ayn Ghazal. The "Ten Days Battles" of July 1948 and the activities of the second cease-fire added a hundred thousand more Palestinian refugees to the toll. Most ended up in the West Bank, and the rest in the Upper Galilee, Lebanon, and the Gaza Strip.[25]

At an August 18 meeting of senior cabinet members, from which the Mapam leadership was excluded, complete unanimity prevailed regarding opposition to the refugees' return and the means to this end: demolishing villages, expropriating lands, and settling them with Jews. An order was issued on the same day to all forces on all fronts to prevent the return of refugees—"infiltrators," as they were dubbed—"with all means."[26] Individual requests by refugees seeking to return were overwhelmingly refused.[27] In late August the Transfer Committee, chaired by Yossef Weitz of the JNF land department, was set up and tasked with composing a plan for the permanent resettlement of the refugees in the Arab States.[28]

In October and November 1948, the IDF conquered the southern coastal plain, the northern Negev, the southern slopes of Mount Hebron, the Jerusalem corridor, and the Upper Galilee. Some 100,000 to 150,000 Palestinians in these areas fled, mostly to the Gaza Strip, the West Bank, and Lebanon, becoming refugees. Although no deliberate policy was articulated by the IDF regarding the effect of expelling Palestinian residents from these areas, many commanders acted to bring about their flight, directly or indirectly. In October 1948 IDF forces turned south to defeat the Egyptian army and reach the encircled Jewish communities of the Negev. The IDF engaged the Egyptian army with aerial bombardment and tank shelling of Palestinian villages and cities, sending many residents fleeing to Gaza and the Hebron hills. The pattern of expelling those few residents that remained reasserted itself here also. In the village of al-Dawayima, west of Hebron, IDF troops massacred some eighty residents, despite the village's surrender with no resistance. The villages and towns of the south, which were entirely Muslim, were nearly completely emptied of their residents.[29] During the occupation of the Upper Galilee, tens of thousands of Palestinians became refugees after fleeing or being expelled. The IDF carried out a number of massacres here as well, and news of the atrocities contributed to the decision to flee from other villages. Abu Sitta lists nine massacres conducted by the IDF in that period, on top of al-Dawayima, including in the villages of Saliha and Safsaf in the Upper Galilee.[30]

On November 8, 1948, Israel conducted a door-to-door census. Anyone located within the boundaries of the state on that day, Arabs as well as Jews, got Israeli citizenship and an Israeli ID. Palestinians displaced beyond Israeli borders were not recognized as Israelis, and the state soon expropriated the property they left behind—just as it expropriated the property of the internal refugees.

After the fighting had ended, Israel turned to evicting villages that still remained in the newly established border areas. This time the initiative came from the IDF, which made strategic and security arguments, but the move was also fueled by a broader desire to reduce the number of Palestinians within Israel. In November 1948 residents from villages along the northern border were expelled. After the war many Palestinian refugees tried to reenter Israel, usually to collect items from their homes or to harvest their crops. In 1949 two more waves of expulsion took place, from half-empty villages now occupied by these "infiltrators," the lands of whom were now being coveted by neighboring Jewish communities. Some of the residents of these villages were expelled to Lebanon or the West

Bank, and some to other Arab villages in Israel, becoming internally displaced. Israeli pressure, manifest in harassment and financial stimuli, led the residents of several more villages along the Syrian border to go across by 1956.[31]

In the south of the country, over a period of several months, IDF units harassed villagers around al-Faluja (near the town of Kiryat Gat today) by intimidation, shootings, and beatings. These took place in early 1949, in violation of the cease-fire agreement signed only recently with Egypt. In response, all Palestinian residents of the area left for the West Bank by April 1949. Bedouins remaining in the Negev desert were then expelled to the West Bank or the Sinai Peninsula. In 1950 the Palestinian population of the town of al-Majdal (Ashkelon of today) was expelled, mostly to the Gaza Strip, and residents of villages along the Jordanian border were driven east. On top of that, the villagers of Zakariyya, near Beit Shemesh, were expelled to Ramla (inside Israel) and to Jordan. All told, some twenty-five thousand Palestinians were expelled in raids after the war.[32]

The Dispossession of the Palestinian Refugees

> We tend to regard all of the abandoned property as property of the
> State of Israel, with which the State of Israel can do as it wishes.
>
> —Foreign Minister Moshe Shertok at the Knesset
> (the Israeli Parliament), May 2, 1949 (Benziman and Mansour, *Subtenants*)

The Palestinian refugees left their homes and their lands on the assumption they would be able to return after the fighting was over. As such a return was never allowed; they lost nearly everything they had—lands, orchards, homes, and personal property. Beyond possessions, the refugees lost the stable, familiar lives they had led and the communal-economic web in which they had dwelled.

There is a wide range of estimates of the material property left by the refugees in the wake of their flight. Atif Kubursi, who investigated the matter and examined the different estimates, concludes that the lost Palestinian property amounted to 743,000,000 pounds sterling.[33] In 1951 the Israeli foreign minister, Moshe Shertok, estimated the total worth of the refugee property at one billion U.S. dollars.[34]

In 1948 the Palestinians lost most of the land they owned. In 1947, only 7 percent of Mandate-era Palestine (some 440,000 acres) was owned by Jews, whether publicly or privately.[35] After the war, Israel held a general territory of over five million acres, of which less than nine hundred thousand acres (17 percent) were Jewish-owned land and state land handed over by the Mandate government.[36] Nearly all the rest were lands left behind by Palestinian refugees, mostly in the Negev. The Israeli Ministry of Agriculture estimated in 1949 that refugee-owned lands amounted to 80 percent, or 4.1 million acres of the territory of the entire state.[37] Later estimates were more modest, as they excluded Negev lands where

Bedouins had used to live: an Israeli survey estimated the lands of the absentees at just over one million acres.[38] Summing up Khalidi's data on the precise territory of every village and its land brings the total up to a similar number—smaller by some twelve thousand acres.[39] Abu Sitta suggests that the land of the Bedouin refugees of the Negev—absent from Khalidi's count—amounts to some three million acres.[40] In 1962, the Israeli Justice Ministry estimated the worth of the refugee land at over 140,000,000 pounds sterling.[41]

Palestinian refugees also left their homes in eleven cities—six of these Arab, and five mixed Arab-Jewish. Vast parts of ninety-four other towns that continued to exist after the war were also emptied of their Arab residents.[42] Estimates of the overall number of depopulated Palestinian communities range between 356 (Kimmerling) and 531 (Abu Sitta).[43] Abu Sitta includes in his count residency sites of Bedouin tribes, mostly in the Be'er Sheva governorate, whose population, he asserts, amounted in 1948 to ninety thousand—the equivalent of 125 average-sized villages.[44] Throughout this book I use Walid Khalidi's list of 418 depopulated villages.

The real estate assets left behind by Palestinian refugees included houses, schools, clinics, mosques, and churches, and in the cities also commercial centers, banks, hospitals, and public parks.[45] According to lists compiled by the Israeli Custodian of Absentee Property in February 1950, the urban properties of the Palestinian refugees included some 94,000 residential rooms, 9,700 shops and 1,200 offices, worth in total some 11,800,000 pounds sterling. In the villages, the Palestinian refugees left tens of thousands of buildings, used primarily for residence;[46] according to one estimate, real estate assets belonging to refugees amounted to nearly a quarter of all buildings in the country at the time.[47]

In addition to the real estate, the villages, towns, and neighborhoods left by the refugees retained most of their inhabitants' personal possessions, including the contents of entire households; nearly a million head of cattle, sheep, and goats; vehicles; and agricultural and industrial equipment.[48] The UN Conciliation Commission for Palestine estimated this portion of Palestinian property at twenty million pounds sterling.[49] Looting of Arab property by Jews was extremely common during and in the immediate aftermath of the war. Soldiers and civilians alike helped themselves to furniture, household items, money, vehicles, herds, and other property; the phenomenon soon swelled to "robbery on a massive scale," to use Ben-Gurion's own words.[50]

In March 1948 the Haganah set up the Committee on Arab Property in the Villages, tasked with expropriating refugee property commandeered by Israeli forces. Local committees of a similar kind were set up in Arab cities as they fell. In July 1948 a ministerial committee was established and charged with "abandoned property," and later that month it was awarded custodianship of the depopulated villages.[51]

The contradiction between the temporary nature of property seizure by the custodian and the desire and need of the state to put refugee property to regular use for its settlement and development needs soon came to the fore. In December 1948, following UN Resolution 194 and its call for the return of the Palestinian refugees, Israel took up the policy of transferring refugee land and property from Arab ownership to permanent public Jewish ownership and using them for national Jewish needs, especially Jewish settlement across the country.[52] The main instrument for that was legislation, which, to quote then-JNF chairman Avraham Granot, was based on a "legalist illusion": it allowed the state to use the money it received for refugee property without owning that property, a phenomenon that could potentially draw international scrutiny.[53] This situation was achieved in phases, through a combination of military and legislative steps:[54]

- Prevention of land cultivation by Palestinian refugees who were attempting to return, by gunfire and/or by setting their fields ablaze.
- Leasing out the refugee land to Jewish communities for the purpose of cultivation.
- Setting up new Jewish communities on the refugee land and populating refugee homes with Jews.
- Installing temporary emergency regulations that allowed the state to take hold of any private property without legal or administrative due process.
- Seizing property—including thousands of structures, apartments, and rooms—by military decree, without legal authorization from the state.
- Applying laws that retroactively legitimized expropriations of Arab property by military units during the war and allowed for further such expropriations in the future.
- Using the British Defense (Emergency) Regulations that allowed the declaration of closed military zones for security needs. Twelve villages whose residents were internally displaced were kept empty through such decrees, including the village of Kafr Bir'im.[55]
- The enactment of the Absentee Property Law of 1950, which transferred ownership rights of refugee property to the Custodian of Absentee Property. The term "absentee" was defined in the law as applying to all Palestinian refugees, including those internally displaced, who were termed "present absentees." The law transferred to the custodian some one million acres of refugee land, of which some six hundred thousand acres were already being cultivated by Jews. Bank accounts belonging to refugees, in the total sum of several million pounds, were impounded by the custodian in 1948.[56] On top of that, in 1951 the custodian's storerooms held refugee property worth over four million pounds sterling.[57]
- The enactment of the Development Authority Law (Transfer of Property) of 1950, which established the only authority licensed to buy refugee

property from the custodian, for national needs like settlement and development. This authority comprised representatives from the government, the JNF, and the Jewish Agency, and was allowed to sell property to national institutions only, with strong preference for the JNF. Through this law, the custodian sold all the lands he held to the Development Authority, which in turn sold some six hundred thousand acres of agricultural land to the JNF. The JNF then leased out much of this land to Jewish communities.

- The enactment of the Land Purchases Law (Authorizing Activities and Compensations) of 1953, which transferred legal ownership of refugee property to the Development Authority. Based on that law, over three hundred thousand acres, including the land of some 250 depopulated villages, were transferred to the authority. The Development Authority then granted right of use of that land to Jewish communities, who had been using it already without legal permit.

In 1961 the Israel Land Administration (ILA) was established, with the aim of administrating all state lands and Jewish-owned land in Israel, including lands hitherto administrated by the JNF. Since its establishment, the ILA has been in charge of 93 percent of the territory of the entire country. According to an agreement signed by Israel with the JNF, the ILA is composed of state representatives (51 percent) and JNF representatives (49 percent), with the result that the JNF—an extranational organization whose declared aim is to work exclusively for the Jewish people rather than for all citizens of Israel—is still responsible, to a large extent, for most state land.[58]

Establishing Jewish Communities on Refugee Villages and Lands

> Now the villages stood empty, orphaned, mute. The horror of the void peeked out in myriad eyes from every corner. It demanded its own destruction, it asked to be instilled with life.
>
> —Levi Eshkol [head of the Settlement Department of the Jewish Agency and later the third prime minister of Israel] November 1948 (Eshkol, *Land Bond*)

On the eve of the War of 1948, Palestine contained 279 Jewish communities—cities, towns, kibbutzim, and moshavim (collective or cooperative agricultural communities). From that year to late 1951 the Jewish population in Israel nearly doubled, due to the arrival of some seven hundred thousand immigrants. Most were refugees, either Holocaust survivors from Europe or Jews from Arab countries who had to leave without their property. After the exodus of the populations of entire Palestinian villages from within the boundaries of the newly established state, a strong desire was expressed in Israel to use their lands for the establishment of new communities—for security purposes, for the accommodation of newly arrived immigrants, and to prevent the return of Palestinian refugees. In August 1948 Mapam proposed the "surplus land formula," according to which Jews would settle Arab lands, while reserving a portion of them for the original owners; upon the latter's return, the former would help them improve their agriculture so that it would produce greater crops from a smaller share of land. The leaders of the Jewish community endorsed that formula, which enabled a consensus on settling Arab lands.[59]

Later that month Israel approved the construction of new Jewish communities on Arab lands occupied by the IDF outside the borders allocated to Israel by the UN partition plan.[60] Israel feared it would be required to give these areas up or allow the return of refugees to them, and, hoping to prevent either outcome, rushed to populate these newly seized lands with dozens of new communities. The Settlement Department of the Jewish Agency took the lead and coordinated all other authorities involved, such as the JNF and the different ministries. In December 1948, after the UN endorsed Resolution 194 and its call for the return of Palestinian refugees, Israel accelerated its settlement activity in those areas. That same month Ben-Gurion retired the surplus land formula, which was never implemented. Three hundred fifty out of the 370 new communities established across the country between 1948 and 1953 were set up on refugee land, and in 1954 more than a third of Israel's Jewish population was living on land belonging to refugees, whose return no one intended to allow.[61]

After the war Israel retained most of the Palestinian citrus orchards, packed into some thirty-four thousand acres, mostly in the central and southern coastal plains. Only a third of these orchards were cultivated by Jews; the rest fell into neglect, whether for bureaucratic, financial, or political reasons, and were eventually uprooted and destroyed. The Palestinian refugees were also forced to leave behind over forty thousand acres of olive groves, mostly in the north of the country. Jewish attempts to cultivate olive groves they seized usually did not fare well, for lack of workers and profits; Jewish farmers often preferred to neglect the trees or uproot them altogether. Geographer Arnon Golan notes that the olive was identified with "enemy" Arab agriculture, seen as primitive and conservative, and was thus marginalized in Israel, which sought to develop advanced, modern agriculture.[62]

The Jewish settlement network set up after the war largely overlapped that of the communities of origin of the Palestinian refugees, which had grown organically over hundreds of years. The political impetus for that was the creation of a reality in which refugees would have nowhere to come back to. In turn, it was hoped, this would reduce international pressure on Israel to allow the return and prevent refugees from "infiltrating" their old communities.[63] The establishment of Jewish communities in depopulated Palestinian villages in border areas and near important junctions had a further strategic significance. Another reason

Jewish children, immigrants from Kurdistan, in moshav Elkosh, established in the houses of the depopulated village of al-Ras al-Ahmar, July 1, 1949. Courtesy of Zoltan Kluger, Government Press Office, Israel.

Jewish immigrants arriving at Yehud, established in the depopulated village of al-Yahudiyya, October 1, 1948. Courtesy of Zoltan Kluger, Government Press Office, Israel.

stemmed from the economic needs of a state that absorbed hundreds of thousands of immigrants in a mere two years: refugee property was the main accommodation and employment reserve for the immigrants. Palestinian refugee lands, orchards, water reservoirs, and many of the homes were given to Jewish refugees and immigrants.[64] Mapam opposed "settling the Jewish 'Oleh [immigrant] in the house of the expelled Arab," but its position had little influence in practice.[65]

Settling Jews in emptied Palestinian homes in the cities began in the summer of 1948, and by 1954 nearly a third of the new Jewish immigrants—some 250,000 people—were living in urban areas inhabited by Arabs before the war.[66] As early as September 1948, voices in the Israeli leadership began calling for settling Jews in the empty Palestinian villages as well.[67] Levi Eshkol, head of the Settlement Department of the Jewish Agency (and future prime minister), was the main driver of the move. In his writings, Eshkol recalled how he came by the idea, in November 1948: "We were passing by the village of al-Barriyya . . . an idea flashed through my mind . . . I believed by intuition that the neglect and emptiness carry within them solutions for the ingathering of the [Jewish] exiles."[68]

Eshkol found scores of habitable buildings still standing in the village. He concluded the situation would be similar in other depopulated villages, and decided: "We should storm these [villages], and prepare them for the coming winter, transfer to each dozens of families with instructors . . . and start working the fields."[69]

On that same day Eshkol began realizing his vision by contacting the settlement movements and consulting engineers. Ben-Gurion endorsed Eshkol's plan and urged him to carry it out with haste.[70] In December 1948 the Jewish Agency began resettling the depopulated villages; the Settlement Department of the agency located villages, prepared them for repopulation, and assisted the settlers, while its Immigrant Absorption Department settled immigrants in new Jewish urban centers set up in depopulated villages. All in all, the Jewish Agency spent some eight million U.S. dollars on repopulating Palestinian villages.[71] The Moshavim Movement organized groups of immigrants for settling in new moshavim set up on depopulated village sites; the Jewish Agency employed these immigrants to repair the houses and demolish those that were beyond repair.[72]

In total, just less than a fifth of Jewish communities set up in the first years of the state were established on the actual built-up sites of depopulated Palestinian villages. The limited use of these sites for the establishment of new communities, despite the acute housing shortage, stemmed largely from planning and financial considerations. The structure of an Arab village—crowded houses, narrow alleyways, few public structures, small plots of land, and often the absence of modern infrastructure—were all very different from the European model on which the Moshavim Movement and the Jewish Agency wanted to base a Jewish agricultural community: identical houses built along streets, a plot of land adjacent to each household, modern infrastructure. Altering a Palestinian village to match the needs of such a community required the demolition of most of the village and the construction of new infrastructure, which necessitated a great investment of money and effort. Therefore, the Jewish Agency and the Moshavim Movement decided in August 1949 to desist from using depopulated village sites for settlement, and instead started building new communities from scratch. Of the over forty-five moshavim set up in the winter of 1949–1950 on depopulated village sites according to Levi Eshkol, only thirteen remained in their original locations. The others were moved a few kilometers away and rebuilt as new, thoroughly planned communities.[73] Members of the moshavim who moved away from the villages often continued using the village structures for public needs and for storage.[74]

Several kibbutzim were also set up on depopulated village sites, as was an artists' village ('Ein Hod). All in all, the Jewish Agency conducted restoration work in some seventy depopulated villages, only half of which were intended for permanent repopulation.[75] By the end of 1952, forty thousand Jewish immigrants had been settled in depopulated Palestinian villages.[76]

Depopulated Palestinian villages close to large Jewish cities were usually quickly populated with Jews and later annexed to the municipality of the nearest city. In mid-1948 Jews from Jerusalem settled in the depopulated Palestinian village of al-Maliha, and later that year immigrants were settled in the village of 'Ayn Karim. In the summer of 1949 Jews settled in Dayr Yasin, despite protest by public intellectuals against settling in a village where a vicious massacre had been carried out only the year before.[77] These villages were later incorporated into Jerusalem and became neighborhoods of the city (Manaḥat, 'Ein Kerem, and Givʿat Shaʾul, respectively).

In February 1948 the Tel Aviv municipality and the Jewish Agency began housing Jews in the nearby depopulated villages still intact. Shortly after their occupation, these villages—al-Jammasin al-Gharbi, Summayl, al-Shaykh Muwannis, and al-Salama—were populated with three thousand Jews who left their homes in Jaffa and in the south of Tel Aviv during the fighting; later, they were joined by newly arrived immigrants. The Jewish Agency paid the new residents to repair the village homes, and the villages were later incorporated into Tel Aviv. New neighborhoods in Tel Aviv and nearby Ramat Gan were built on these villages' lands (for example, Ramat Chen neighborhood in Ramat Gan, built on Salama's land.[78]

Some forty additional villages in the greater Tel Aviv area were populated with Jewish refugees and immigrants, after the authorities had run out of empty houses in Jaffa and villages near Tel Aviv ran out. These villages (such as al-'Abbasiyya (al-Yahudiyya), Saqiya, Kafr 'Ana, Yazur, and Bayt Dajan) became urban Jewish centers (Yehud, Or Yehuda, Azor, and Beit Dagan, respectively), and their lands were seized largely by nearby, expansion-eager Jewish communities.[79]

Depopulated Palestinian villages elsewhere in the country were also re-populated with immigrants and made into towns. For example, the Palestinian village of al-Tira became the Jewish town of Tirat Carmel; the northern city of Kiryat Shmona was built over the village of al-Khalisa.[80] Other villages were in-corporated into the new cities that emerged in Israel over the years: The urban community of El'ad, set up in 1998, has expanded over the site of the village of al-Muzayri'a; the sites of the villages of Barfiliya and al-Burj lie underneath the present-day city of Modi'in (established in 1993); and so on.[81]

The Demolition of Depopulated Villages

Most of the depopulated villages were partly or entirely demolished by mid-1949. Most of the demolition took place in the immediate aftermath of the fighting and the occupation. In most cases the destruction was deliberate, carried out either by the forces that took over the village or by neighboring Jewish communities. The demolition was driven by a combination of military needs, political reasons, and economic motives, and in most cases it would be difficult to tell which factor was the decisive one for the demolition of a specific village.[82]

Demolition for Military and Strategic Purposes

The demolition of houses and entire sections of villages was part of the arsenal of retaliatory attacks by the Haganah as early as December 1947. This was done in response to Arab attacks on Jews, against nearby villages suspected of shelter-ing or supporting Arab paramilitaries who had supposedly carried out those at-tacks. These demolitions often triggered the departure of entire families. During the implementation of Plan D, which commenced in March 1948, entire villages were destroyed in order to prevent Arab forces from using them as bases for at-tacks, and when manpower shortages prevented the posting of Jewish guards to recently occupied and depopulated villages. Some of these villages were razed entirely, others only in part. The first villages to be razed as part of Plan D were the ones that served as departure points for Arab attacks on Jewish communities and their access roads, in the Jerusalem Corridor and around kibbutz Mishmar Ha'Emek.[83]

On some occasions the demolitions were driven both by a military need and a desire to punish the villagers. Meron Benvenisti describes, for instance, the or-der to demolish Palestinian villages taken in the Upper Galilee in 1948—mostly al-Kabri and al-Zib—as motivated by military need, but also a desire to punish the villagers for the killing of forty-nine Jewish combatants in the attack on the convoy to isolated kibbutz Yeḥiʿam, which had occurred two months earlier, near al-Kabri.[84]

Another example of demolition for strategic purposes was the razing of ninety villages in the north of the country during May 1948: fifty villages were demolished in the east of the Galilee to improve home-front security in the case of an attack from Syria or Lebanon; forty additional villages were razed in border areas in the east of Lower Galilee, near the Sea of Galilee, and in the northern Jordan valley. In the latter area the demolition was carried out by military units and volunteers from local Jewish communities, who pressed the authorities for permission to expand and settle over the lands of their erstwhile Arab neighbors. Benvenisti notes that this was one of the first areas in which the motives for occupation and demolition shifted from military needs to settlement needs and "redemption of the land"—bringing it into Jewish hands.[85]

Most of the official authorities—on both the national and local community level—supported the policy of demolishing the depopulated villages. However, other voices were also heard: In May 1948 the leaders of Mapam protested against the policy of what they described as the "intentional evacuation" of the Palestinian population, and of the demolition of villages for political rather than mere military needs. Another political leader who expressed his opposition to the demolition was Minority Affairs Minister Bechor Shitrit, concerned by other state organizations intruding on what he believed was his purview.[86]

In July 1948, following criticism by Mapam and several cabinet members on the demolition policy, the IDF issued an order prohibiting the demolition of Palestinian villages and the expulsion of their residents when not in battle, unless authorized directly by the minister of defense. The army then proceeded to raze villages in disregard of its own order. Later that month, further outcries prompted the appointment of the Ministerial Committee on Abandoned Property as custodian of the depopulated villages. The committee decided that the demolition of villages would be carried out only with its permission, but it failed to prevent the destruction and pillaging that went on at the hands of military units and civilians. The military continued blowing up villages for months after fighting had officially ceased, as well as during the second ceasefire of July to October 1948. The pretext for these demolitions was usually "military need."[87]

After the war and throughout the 1950s the IDF took to using depopulated villages as training sites for urban warfare and sapper squads, which naturally resulted in the demolition of many more homes.[88] Thus, during a training exercise in 1955, a paratrooper platoon conducted experimental explosions in five houses in al-Ghabisiyya in the west of the Galilee, razing them to the ground; the site of the village of Sataf served in the 1950s as "a site for the training of Unit 101 and for paratroopers," according to the JNF; and so on.[89]

Explosion of the village of Bayt Nattif, following its occupation by the IDF, October 1, 1948.
Courtesy of unknown photographer, Government Press Office, Israel.

Prickly pear cacti cover the site of depopulated al-Mazar, in southern Mt. Carmel, March 2,
2007. Courtesy of Noga Kadman.

Demolition for Political Purposes

In May 1948 the demolition of depopulated villages also began serving as a means to a political end that was becoming increasingly popular among the leaders of the Jewish community—making the absence of the refugees permanent and preventing any possibility of their return. In the following month the JNF began carrying out demolitions with the support of most of its board, under the pretext of Ben-Gurion's own ratification of a recommendation by the Transfer Committee to destroy the villages. Having demolished eight villages, the committee stopped working in early July, for lack of official recognition and technical resources.[90]

In the fall of 1948 the state began the systematic demolition of depopulated villages in the Galilee, with the aim of preventing the return of their original inhabitants. In May 1949 the UN Conciliation Commission for Palestine facilitated meetings between representatives of Israel and the Arab States in Lausanne, Switzerland. At these meetings, Israel was pressured—primarily by the United States—to make concessions on the refugee issue. The pressure caused Israel to accelerate the demolition of the villages instead. In July 1949 the Public Works Department, relying in all probability on the instructions of Ben-Gurion, issued directives for the demolition of mud structures in forty-one villages in the Jerusalem Corridor and in the south of the country—areas meant to be included in the Arab state under the partition plan. Stone structures were designated for future Jewish settlement, and therefore were not demolished.[91]

The demolition operation of summer 1949 provoked a number of protests, for different reasons: a plan to house internally displaced Palestinians in villages slated for demolition, a desire to use them to house Jewish immigrants presently staying in transit camps, the risks of having ruins left unattended, and the damage to the landscape and to the geographic and historical legacy of the country.[92]

The official policy of village demolition went on through 1949 and the beginning of 1950 throughout the country, after buildings were inspected regarding their suitability for the housing of Jews. The overall tendency of this erasure project was to avoid the destruction of mosques, churches, and tombs of Muslim saints, but there are reports of mosques being deliberately destroyed as a matter of policy. That was the fate of mosques in al-Majdal (Ashkelon), Yibna (Yavne), and Isdud (Ashdod).[93] In villages where bulldozer access proved to be difficult (such as Lifta near Jerusalem), many buildings remained standing for many years.

In the early 1950s there were over ten thousand registered incidents of Palestinian refugees entering Israel. Once they entered, many took refuge and stayed overnight in the remains of the depopulated villages. In response, IDF units demolished many of the villages in border areas in 1949 and the early 1950s.[94] Raz Kletter quotes the book of Yehezkel Sahar, the first commissioner-general of the

Israel Police, who asked the government to give orders to demolish houses in some fifty villages. The request was granted and the demolition, Sahar observes, greatly facilitated the fight against the "infiltrators."[95]

A number of villages whose inhabitants continued to live within Israel in adjacent villages after they had been internally displaced were destroyed by the authorities to prevent the return of the villagers to their original homes. In some cases, demolitions were carried out in direct disregard of Supreme Court rulings in favor of the villagers: the village of Iqrit was razed in December 1951, five months after the Supreme Court recognized the right of its inhabitants to return to it; Ben-Gurion claimed the demolition was required for security reasons. Two years later, Kafr Bir'im was largely flattened by aerial bombardment and artillery shelling, after the Supreme Court upheld the appeal of its residents against the prohibition on their return.[96] Internally displaced villagers from al-Ghabisiyya also petitioned the Supreme Court to be allowed to return to their village. The Supreme Court agreed in 1951, but the state ignored the ruling, expropriated the village land, and blew up its houses in 1955.[97]

In August 1957 the Ministry of Labor was asked by then–foreign minister Golda Meir to ensure the clearing of the ruins of Palestinian neighborhoods and villages. Priority was given in the request to "getting rid of ruins" in villages whose inhabitants remained in the country, such as al-Birwa in the western Galilee and Saffuriyya in the Lower Galilee.[98]

Demolition for the Benefit of Jewish Communities

On various occasions kibbutzim members demanded that the authorities demolish depopulated villages of their former Arab neighbors, and sometimes they razed nearby villages themselves, in order to seize the village lands and prevent the return of the original owners. This type of destruction took place mostly in the Jordan and Jezreel valleys. The Transfer Committee encouraged Jewish communities to follow suit in the summer and fall of 1948. Later, with the return of refugees increasingly unlikely, the demolitions were aimed less at preventing their return and more at leveling fields for construction or agriculture. In some cases kibbutzim were eager to demolish villages because they feared these would be used to house immigrants, who would then take lands the kibbutzim wanted for themselves.[99]

A number of Jewish communities opposed the demolition of nearby villages with which, before the war, they had established good neighborly relations. Other voices protested the demolition on economic grounds, arguing that it was better to use the refugee property than destroy it. In the fall of 1948, with a rising tide of Jewish immigration and growing housing shortages, more and more began calling for restoring the villages instead of destroying them and using them to house the newly arrived Jews.[100]

In depopulated villages chosen to become Jewish agricultural communities, many buildings were demolished to alter the Palestinian village and adjust it to the desired model of a Jewish moshav. In some cases the settlement department of the Jewish Agency demolished unused sections of a village in order to prevent the creation of an urban center around the site. The Jewish settlers themselves often demolished buildings they did not need in the area allocated to them. After the decision was made to stop using depopulated villages for Jewish settlements, many empty homes fell into disuse and disrepair and left only remains, even if they were not deliberately demolished.[101]

Many Palestinian houses were casually destroyed in a disorganized, spontaneous manner. Jews looted stones, roof tiles, doors, windows, and other construction elements. Other houses were demolished for the sake of vandalism, or in revenge, or out of general hostility toward remains and reminders of the Arab past.[102] "Commissioned demolitions" by construction contractors also took place, largely for the masonry.[103]

Demolition for "Cleaning Up" the Landscape and Erasing the Memory of the Villages

In the 1950s and 1960s the demolition's emphasis shifted from military and utilitarian needs to those of landscape architecture and erasure of the ruins, which stood as constant reminders of the refugee problem that Israel strongly preferred to ignore. Statements from leaders of the time convey their unease at the presence of the villages in the landscape, which they felt to be aesthetically wrong and politically embarrassing. In 1952, Ben-Gurion said: "I think one should have removed all the ruins left in the south of the Negev . . . they still stand because a lot of money is needed to explode them and clean them up, but why should they stand at all? People pass in the vicinity of Julis and other places and see empty ruins. Who needs that?"[104]

Foreign minister Golda Meir used a similar argument in her 1957 order to clear out the remains of Palestinian homes: "The ruins of Arab villages and Arab neighborhoods, or clusters of buildings standing desolate and empty since 1948, bring up harsh associations that cause considerable diplomatic damage. In the last nine years many ruins were cleared out . . . but the ones that remain stand out in a sharper contrast with the new landscape."[105]

In that same order, priority was given to "getting rid of ruins" in areas exposed to the public eye, such as in the centers of Jewish communities, in sight of major transport routes and on tourist sites—such as the remains of Qisarya, the Bosnian village near the Roman site of Caesarea, which still stood desolate. The Ministry of Labor was asked to use caution while carrying out the demolitions, since "diplomatically, it was preferable for the operation to be carried out without anyone discerning its political significance."[106]

In early 1959 the Company for Landscape Improvement, a subsidiary of the Governmental Tourism Company (later the Israel National Parks Authority), was handed a plan to beautify the road to Jerusalem. As part of the plan, JNF was asked to demolish the village of Qalunya and plant trees over the remains, in order to "prevent passersby on the Jerusalem road the pleasure of seeing a desolate landscape, which elicits various questions among tourists."[107]

In the 1960s, buildings in many depopulated villages were still standing in Israel. In the spring of 1965 the ILA launched an operation to destroy more than a hundred such villages. The operation began in the middle of that year and continued up until the aftermath of the 1967 war.[108] The ILA argued that the villages mar the landscape, create the impression of desolation, and constitute a sanitary and safety hazard. When asked in parliament whether the demolition was necessary, Prime Minister Levi Eshkol replied that "not destroying the abandoned villages would be contrary to the policy of development and revitalization of wasteland, which every state is obliged to implement."[109] Presenting the demolition as an act aimed at cleaning up the landscape and development created the semblance of a neutral administrative action, motivated by nothing but the state's concern for the well-being of its citizens and the aesthetics of the land; nevertheless, the political arguments cited previously and the desire for a "quiet" operation indicate that this was a sensitive issue with political ramifications: it seems that the demolition was predicated on a desire to erase from sight any memory of the refugee problem.

Archaeologist Aron Shai writes that the demolition initiative of the 1960s could be seen as the continuation of the demolition activities around the War of 1948, and that both were aimed at preventing the return of refugees to their homes. He quotes a senior official in the ILA, who argued that the goal of the operation was to prevent a situation of former villagers coming and saying, "This is my tree. This was my village."[110] Some in the ILA even voiced the opinion that leveling the villages would reduce the distress caused to Palestinian citizens of Israel as they pass by the longed-for villages where they were born. The decision on the demolition operation was made jointly by different state organs who had sought to demolish the villages for years, including the Ministry of Foreign Affairs and the Landscape Improvement Company. They thought only architecturally appealing buildings should be spared, as in the northern ancient site of Achziv.[111]

The ILA's plan was to level the country north to south and leave no hill or hillock "uncleaned." The plan was intended to be quiet and gradual, out of the assumption that demolishing many villages at once would create great resonance and attract equally great criticism. A list of 131 villages slated for "leveling" included Lubya and Saffuriyya in the Lower Galilee, Zakariyya in the Beit Shemesh region, al-Qubab and Tall al-Safi in the Judea plain, and many others.[112] The villages were demolished following an archaeological survey conducted in each of them, in which archaeologists approved the demolition except for what they defined as ancient structures. In some cases, even such ancient structures were demolished.[113]

According to Meron Benvenisti, after the War of 1967 and the occupation of the West Bank and the Gaza Strip by Israel, the demolition of depopulated villages in Israel was sped up to deter the 1948 refugees living in the newly occupied territories from pilgrimage to their original homes.[114] Shai believes that the demolition of villages depopulated in the War of 1967 itself, near Latrun and on the Golan Heights, should be seen not only as an incident of war but also as related to the ILA's village demolition spree, which was taking place around that time. That way or another, the demolition operation of the mid 1960s did not provoke resistance from the Jewish public, except for a few voices distraught by the destruction of places that they knew and loved.[115]

The Remains of the Villages, Decades Later

> Everywhere you see almond trees or fig trees or olive trees, there used to be a village. People lived there. Now they dwell in refugee camps, in the Territories, or in other villages across the country, or across the border.
>
> —Ilan Pappé, "The Green Lungs and the Blue Box"

Using a field study conducted between 1987 and 1990, Walid Khalidi classified the 418 depopulated villages according to their degree of destruction and what remained of them forty years after the depopulation had taken place. His study found that most villages—nearly three hundred—were totally destroyed, and over a hundred more were mostly destroyed. Only in fifteen villages did most of the structures survive, and some of the latter were populated by Jews.[116]

Based on a field study conducted between 1987 and 1991, geographer Ghazi Falah established the degree of destruction in the villages, as well as the use made of the remaining structures.[117] He concludes that forty years after their occupation and depopulation, two-thirds of the villages suffered high levels of destruction, and nearly a third were destroyed to a significant degree and were partly repopulated by Jews. However, Falah found that most of the villages still have some kind of reminder in the landscape—a cluster of ruins, remains of walls or parts of structures. Falah details the different categories of destruction:

- Eighty-one villages that were razed to the ground and completely erased from the landscape used to stand in the plains or near the shore; they were small and were built from less durable materials, such as wood or mud bricks. Falah found new landscapes where these once stood, usually an agricultural one. Thus, for example, the sites of al-Ashrafiyya and Masil al-Jizl in the Jordan valley are today fields and fishing ponds.

- In one hundred forty demolished villages, the piles of masonry that remained from their houses are clearly visible across the entire country, especially in the Galilee mountains, near Mt. Carmel and just south of it, in the Menashe hills. Some of the villages are concealed by trees planted on the ruins, and in many of them prickly pear cacti and olive groves grown wild still remain. The cactus hedges, which originally divided the land plots of the village, are often the only visible reminder that remains from a village.[118]
- Freestanding walls with no roofs to cover them have been preserved among the piles of stones in sixty small villages, which stood far enough from Jewish communities so as not to be perceived as a threat, or on mountains and hill slopes too steep for bulldozers to climb. Other walls were protected by trees planted among them after the original demolition and prevented the return of the bulldozers; this was the case, for instance, in the village of 'Aqqur in the Jerusalem hills.
- Falah found intact but unpopulated homes in seventy-four villages across the country. Some of these homes housed Jews in the immediate aftermath of 1948, until they were abandoned or converted to storage; others stood well outside the main built-up area of the village, and others were particularly large, which contributed to their being spared. Nonresidential buildings that survived were usually historical-cultural sites, such as khans (roadside inns) and taverns (as in Khirbat al-Burj east of Caesarea); forts and castles (as in al-Qastal in the Jerusalem hills); community sites such as schools, diwans (hospices), or coffee shops (as in Salama in Tel Aviv); mills or artificial pools; and service centers, including train stations ('Atlit) and police stations (Isdud). These buildings survived, as their demolition was deemed to be of low priority under a policy aimed primarily at destroying residential homes to prevent their residents' return. It is also possible that some of them were spared because of the potential use to which they could be put to by the Israeli authorities, though Falah observed that most of these surviving buildings were crumbling from neglect.

Falah found that religious sites survived in sixty-eight villages. He observed that convents were often allowed to remain and to continue operating, probably out of respect for the Western Christian world and because their residents were often not Arab. Muslim shrines and tombs of prominent sheikhs were usually left unharmed, but the lack of a preservation effort by the state has led to their deteriorating over the years; churches and mosques that survived were also mostly neglected and are in a dilapidated state today.

Meron Benvenisti adds that of the 140 mosques that served Arab villages before 1948, only 40 remain. Half are in various degrees of erosion and collapse; six are used as residential rooms, sheep pens, stables, carpentries, or storerooms; six

Remnants of Khirbat al-Duhayriyya, today within JNF's Ben-Shemen Forest, January 23, 2007. Courtesy of Noga Kadman.

Remains of the cemetery of al-Lajjun, today near kibbutz Megiddo, March 3, 2007. Courtesy of Noga Kadman.

serve as museums, bars, or other tourist sites; and four are now synagogues. Two more were restored by Palestinians for the resumption of worship services there, but those services were prohibited or constrained. Many of the village churches were untouched, and some belong today to non-Arab organizations. Six village churches stand empty and crumbling. Of the hundreds of cemeteries of the depopulated villages, the remains of only forty can still be seen, according to Benvenisti.[119]

In a few cases, sites holy to Muslim worshipers were "adopted" by Jews, who created new traditions of pilgrimage to the same places. In the village of al-Nabi Rubin on the southern coastal plain, for example, where a large structure survived over a holy tomb, Jewish pilgrimages appeared in the 1990s in the place of the Muslim pilgrimages who had frequented the place before 1948.[120] Yitzhak Laor claims that the Israeli Ministry of Religious Affairs is manufacturing "tombs of saints" for Jewish pilgrimage in the actual burial sites of Arab sheikhs. He illustrates his argument by the case of the tomb identified as belonging to Shim'on Bar Yoḥai, the Jewish religious leader of the Roman era, in the depopulated Palestinian village of Mirun.[121]

The Judaization of the tombs is another manifestation of the Judaization of the land, which is also the underlying motive for encouraging the flight of the Arab residents of the country during the war, the prevention of the return of the Palestinian refugees, the demolition of the villages, and the widespread use by Israel of their lands and remaining buildings for the housing of Jews. The value of Judaization is fundamental to the Zionist ideology of Israel, and we turn next to the different manners of its instillment.

2 National Identity, National Conflict, Space, and Memory

Nᴀᴛɪᴏɴᴀʟ ɪᴅᴇɴᴛɪᴛʏ ᴀᴛᴛᴀᴄʜᴇs its bearer to a "nationality"—a defined political community driven by an ideology of social and territorial exclusivity. National identity evolves and consolidates through a prolonged and intricate process, involving a host of cultural and political forces grappling to shape its character. Part of the process is the creation of a hegemonic narrative that describes the history of the nation, establishes the link between the nation and the territory that it claims, stresses its uniqueness and unity, charts out its shared goals and mission, and cultivates the values and norms by which this nation abides. The national ideas expressed in the narrative are communicated to society through art (literature, painting, poetry), mass media, the education system (especially in the subjects of history and geography), and holidays and rituals. These fields of discourse and practice are performed by different institutions—governmental, social, political, and cultural—that bring nationalism into daily life, thus cultivating the individual's identification with national ideas and reinforcing his or her national identity.[1]

Territory is an essential component of national identity. It provides the nation with boundaries and habitat, it is perceived as the nation's homeland, and it therefore gives the latter historical roots. Spatial socialization is the process through which individuals are socialized as members of a territorially defined nationality. This process is performed through narratives and imagery of the territory, and it instills in the members of a certain nationality a sense of identification with a given territory, including both its material and symbolic elements.[2]

The territorial aspect of national identity carries both inclusive and exclusive meanings. In the national narrative territories are represented as "our" homogeneous homes, and as a source of identification for "us" in contrast to the "other," who may be located inside or outside the territory.[3] David Sibley dubs this "spatial purification" and argues that it constitutes a key element in the organization of social space: on the global scale this is manifest in the existence of robust borders intended to ensure cultural homogeny; on the local scale, it is expressed in hostility toward the "outsider" population, such as ethnic minorities, or even by removing them altogether.[4]

Many national conflicts are characterized by struggles over a territory contested by two different national groups. In these cases the two groups have parallel historical claims to the same region that they inhabited at different times in the past. Examples include Germans and Poles, Albanians and Serbs, and Jews and Palestinians. In each such case, the overlap between national identity and control over territory prevents both groups from compromising and recognizing the full rights of the other group for the contested space.[5] The dominant group controls the territory and pushes the other group outside it, physically and symbolically, sometimes while declaring the state to be its own exclusive homeland. In extreme cases the dominant group physically "cleanses" the contested territory of members of the other group, by expulsion or annihilation. In less extreme cases the dominant group invests efforts into marginalizing the members of the other group, territorially as well as socially.

In some cases a regime is established to serve the interests of the dominant national group, such as facilitating its spread across the contested space. Oren Yiftachel has coined the term "ethnocracy" for such a regime: one that promotes the spatial, economic, political, and cultural goals of the dominant nationality while constraining marginalized groups and minorities. Examples of ethnocratic states can be found in Estonia, Serbia, Malaysia, Greece, Sri Lanka, and Israel. One of the main characteristics of ethnocratic regimes is the spatial-territorial control practiced by the dominant group and its activity of shaping national geography: members of this group enjoy privileged access to land, they control the planning system, and they often enact laws that allow for the expropriation of land from the weaker groups. Another important element of ethnocracy is the project of ethnic settlement, aimed at strengthening the control of the dominant group over different areas of the country. Under that project the settler society remains "pure" and does not merge with other local group; the "locals" are excluded from the creation of the new society, they remain isolated on its margins and are pushed down to the lowest strata of society and economy alike.[6]

In the process of forming a national identity, a single collective memory is gradually consolidated out of all the groups constituting the nationality. That memory is structured into the national narrative as a story that presents the shared past of the nation's members, legitimizes and justifies the present, and validates the members' aspirations for a shared future.[7] "Sites of memory," such as monuments, symbols, rituals, and books, create a sense of collective identity in the present by materializing the memories of the group.[8]

The choice of what to commemorate—and therefore, what to remember—is a cultural-political one. The dominant ideological-political system reconstructs the story of the past in order to serve its own interests, advance its political agenda, and reinforce its ideological stance. This narrative makes selective use of history, and it often changes in response to the society's changing needs. Some past events are emphasized; some are infused with political meaning and are reinterpreted, deconstructed, or altered. Other aspects of the past, seen as marginal or obstructive to the narrative flow and delivery of the ideological message, are marginalized, repressed, and actively forgotten.[9] Marginalized groups sometimes create alternative narratives of memory, which contradict the hegemonic one, deny its validity, and represent a claim for a more accurate and fairer representation of history.[10]

The two sides of a national territorial conflict tend to shape their collective memories through suppression, marginalization, and erasure of aspects and past events that are seen as supportive of the narrative that links the other group to the contested territory. According to Maurice Halbwachs, when constituents of the past are forgotten, it is due to the disappearance of the groups that fostered the corresponding memories.[11]

The suppression of the past of competing groups is achieved through a variety of means. Historical research tends to eschew documentation of the competing group's past in the contested territory, archaeologists neglect findings that could substantiate the bond other groups have to the territory in question, and textbooks used by the education system reflect these trends of disregard.

On occasion, in the aftermath of wars, the victorious nation launches a campaign against the architecture and structures of the defeated people and "cleanses" the landscape of the cultural marks left on it by "the others." Thus, for example, in the former Yugoslavia, in addition to massacres and expulsions, the Serbs blew up mosques and Muslim villages to create a manifestly Serbian national landscape. Beyond the immediate effect of preventing the physical return of the defeated population, the destruction is wrought to erase the memories, history, and identity associated with the architecture and the place.[12] According to Ghazi Falah, groups leave their ideological mark on the landscape, so when one group takes over places inhabited by another group, a complete or partial replacement of these landmarks takes place.[13] The demolition of structures—and, conversely, the conservation of structures—plays a role in the construction of collective memory, because structures that no longer exist in the landscape are condemned to be forgotten, while the conservation of other structures communicates that they need to be remembered.[14]

Other symbolic arenas for national-territorial struggles include the naming and mapping of locations in the contested space. Mapping and naming are some of the mechanisms through which national identity is made and sustained. The naming process reflects the power dynamics between the parties to the conflict, since the dominant national group has the ability to impose on the terrain whatever names it chooses. Thus, in Alto Adige, annexed to Italy after World War I, Italy introduced new Italian names for some eight thousand previously German locales; in post–World War II Czechoslovakia, local German names were banned, and signs carrying them were removed.[15] Naming creates a link between the places and the nation that names them and amounts to a statement of exclusive ownership over them.

Names of communities and places appear on street signs, on maps, in newspaper articles, in everyday conversations, and so on. The daily use of place names makes it difficult to detect the political meaning with which they are charged, but names are often given in the service of national ideological goals and used to instill national values into everyday life.[16]

The presence of national groups challenging the authority of an ethnic group can also be silenced by dropping them off the map. This was the case in Weimar-era Germany, whose maps depicted the Sudetenland in Czechoslovakia as a purely German region.[17]

Throughout the colonial era, mapping served as a component in the process of securing material ownership over peoples and places, a process manifest on the ground via settlement and expeditions "over a page that was far from blank," in the words of Jane Jacobs.[18] Jacobs presents Australia as an example of "cartographic possession," guided by the perception of the continent as empty, and expressed both in the mapping practices and in the genocide and dispossession of the aborigines.[19] John Harley refers to "silence on maps"—which means dropping objects off the maps—and regards it in the context of colonialism as a practice of discrimination against local populations.[20]

The perception of the map as a scientific tool makes it a powerful instrument of persuasion, manipulated by those who wield power in society. Maps are often assumed to offer an unbiased reflection of reality, but in fact they are influenced by the ideologies and interests of their makers.[21] Harley defined maps as "value-laden images"; he argues that mapmakers define power dynamics in society and record the manifestations of these dynamics in the visible landscape. He also maintains that often the decisions made in the process of mapping are loaded with political meaning, including the decision about which objects are to be left off the map and which are to be depicted on it, which objects are to be described, which objects are to be named, which items are to be emphasized, and which symbols and styles are to represent the objects on the map.[22]

Space and Memory in Zionist Ideology and Practice

> There is a country which happens to be named the Land of Israel, and it has no people, and then there is the Jewish people who has no country—so what is amiss . . . , to match that people to this land?!
>
> —Chaim Weizman, 1914 (Quoted in Hertzberg, *The Zionist Idea*)

The Zionist movement came into being in an attempt to find a solution for the increasingly precarious existence of Jewish minorities in Europe. These minorities were excluded from the nationalities that had evolved across the continent and had frequently suffered from discrimination and anti-Semitic persecution, which reached its murderous apogee in the Holocaust. Zionism argued that the Jews were a nation that needed a territory in which it could develop normally, and for that purpose it supported the gathering of Jews from their exile to their ancient homeland—the Land of Israel. The Zionist ideology was realized through the establishment of a separatist Jewish state in the Land of Israel, which gained control of that territory through the physical, social, and symbolic pushing-out of the land's Arab residents, in a bid to create a Jewish space across the country.

In the Israeli-Palestinian conflict, each party has created its own ideological narrative, stressing its continued bond to the land and downplaying the bond asserted by the other party. The dominant Palestinian narrative describes the Palestinians as a nation that had inhabited Palestine continuously for centuries until it was expelled and dispossessed by Zionism. The core Israeli-Zionist narrative is that of return from involuntary exile to an ancient homeland, in order to find there a shelter from persecution and in order to develop the land.[23] Edward Said describes this as an "intense conflict of two memories, two sorts of historical invention, two sorts of geographical imagination."[24]

The return of the Jews to the Land of Israel has been constructed by Zionism as a two-sided metaphor: not only do the Jews yearn to return to Zion, but the land itself—Jewish since time immemorial—longs for its exiled Jewish sons and daughters. Thus, the delivery of the land into Jewish hands—dubbed "redemption of the land"—was perceived as a key goal of the Zionist ideology, and its implementation was supposed to take place through Jewish presence, ownership of the land, and sovereignty within it.[25]

"Redemption of the land" had another meaning in Zionism—the resuscitation of nature and environment in the country, which, it was argued, had been both neglected and devastated by the previous inhabitants. This mission was named "making the desert bloom" or "conquering the wasteland." Ben-Gurion explained this as a need to "reconstruct the ruins of poor and decrepit land . . . which has become desolate during hundreds of years, and has been standing in desolation for nigh two thousand years."[26]

While depicting the land as having its own desires and needs, Zionism initially ignored the Arabs, who at that time were an overwhelming majority of the population of the land. The use of the word "desolate" with regard to the land implies that it was perceived by the Zionist pioneers as empty and unpopulated. This was reflected in the famous slogan coined by Zionist activist Yisrael Zangwil: "A land without a people for a people without a land." Later, as Jewish immigration and settlement increased, it was no longer possible to ignore the existing Arab population, yet their presence was perceived as part of the natural, picturesque landscape or as a living testament to the way of life of the ancient Hebrews, and as such it served as evidence of the bond between the Jewish people and their land.[27] The Arab residents were perceived as devoid of any political or national aspirations, and as a backward society that Zionism would introduce to modernity.

The pattern of Jewish settlement in the land was one of separation from the Arab population through construction of separate economic, political, social, and cultural systems. The agricultural communities and the towns established by the Zionists were settled with Jews only, the Zionist political institutions were established to promote Jewish interests, and most of the developing Jewish economy was sealed off to Arab workers.[28]

This process of "Judaization," which began in the pre-state era, was accelerated after the War of 1948, when most of the Arab residents of the country were made into refugees beyond the borders of the newly established state because of Israel's refusal to allow them to return to their homes. Israel thus actively created a new demographic map, closer to the original Zionist imagery of an "empty land."[29] Judaization and de-Arabization of the space were also carried out in the course of the war and in its aftermath; this was done physically by populating empty Palestinian homes with Jews, demolishing depopulated Palestinian villages, and razing Palestinian olive groves, and legally through legislation that transferred most of the Palestinian lands and property into Jewish hands. Ghazi Falah describes this as "war aimed against the 'enemy's' former places, i.e., the 418 depopulated villages left behind." He argues that by removing the cultural tracks of the Palestinians' past from the landscape, Israel eliminated their attachment to the land and weakened their claim to it. By doing that Israel also removed the Palestinians from the collective memory of the country: "Places that were the loci for Palestinian culture and national identity . . . were obliterated."[30] Meron Benvenisti introduced the metaphor of the "white spots" on the mental map of the Jews, which cover the Palestinian communities and their members in the physical space as well as the historical continuum.[31]

The developing conflict with the Arabs introduced to the Zionist narrative the idea of an "Arab problem" that had to be resolved. The disregard for the Arab residents of the land that typified the Zionist narrative in its inception took in Israel the form of renouncing responsibility for their displacement. The conflict with the Arab states is described in the Israeli national narrative as the result of Arab hostility, accused also of turning most of the Palestinians into refugees. As far as Israel is concerned, these states are now also responsible for the rehabilitation of the refugees. The refugees themselves must also accept responsibility for their own fate, by virtue of having "chosen" to flee: their flight is seen as proof of their weak connection to the land, unlike the deeper and more solid bond between the Jews and the same land.[32] Israeli-Jewish collective memory remains in denial of the catastrophe experienced by the Palestinian population as a result of the establishment of the Israeli state; it does not treat that catastrophe as a key fact in the history of the country and the Zionist enterprise, ignores the drastic changes in the landscape and the lives of the Palestinian residents after the war, and eschews any responsibility for the fate of the refugees. According to Raz-Krakotzkin, this denial is one of the key cultural characteristics of Israel, and it stems from suppressed guilt or a desire to preserve the myths of the Zionist narrative.[33] In the words of Oren Yiftachel, the "dark sides" of the Zionist enterprise have been all but totally concealed in the process of constructing the narrative of the return of the Jews to their land.[34]

The Zionist narrative of the Jewish past, present, and future is well expressed in the Declaration of Independence of the nascent Israeli state, which remained faithful to the Zionist ideology. After the state was in place, different systems were created to retain Jewish control over many realms of public life, at the expense of the remaining Palestinian minority, which was discriminated against or ignored. Numerous examples include the Law of Return, which allows immigration to Israel only to Jews; the decision to prevent the return of the Palestinian refugees; development and education budget allocation that blatantly discriminates against the Palestinian minority; and land confiscation from Palestinian citizens of Israel and in order to build Jewish towns on them. The Judaization project is still a key political value in Israel, and thus, according to Yiftachel, Israel can be defined as an ethnocracy.[35]

Beyond the political and military appropriation of the land, one of the goals of Zionism, before and after the establishment of the state, is appropriating the Land of Israel for the benefit of the Jews also in the sense of emotional belonging and making that space a meaningful "home" for them. This spatial socialization is obtained through a complex process that includes endorsing a particular version of collective memory that makes the space, in past and present, "ours" rather than "theirs."[36] The message of Judaization is communicated to the residents of Israel by various channels and agents, governmental and others.

The Establishment of Agricultural Communities

Pastoral landscapes and agriculture hold particular importance in the construction of national identity, since they serve as a link between the nation, its land, and its shared past.[37] Zionist ideology is no exception and upholds the establishment of agricultural settlements and the cultivation of the land as fundamental and meaningful values.[38]

New Jewish settlements were set up by the Zionist movement, and later by the state, for security and political purposes, on top of the immediate goal of providing accommodation, and were intended to serve as shields against security risks posed by Arabs.[39] Their construction was also seen as a strategy for establishing Jewish presence in areas where it was found lacking, and for seizing Arab land in order to "Judaize it," "create facts on the ground," and claim sovereignty over it.[40] In the early days of the Zionist movement, agricultural settlements were also meant to transform the urban Jewish communities of Europe and into a pioneering, agricultural society working the soil of its ancient homeland.[41] The popular term for the establishment of new communities was *'Aliyah 'al HaKarka'*, meaning "ascending the land": an expression evocative of fulfilling a religious commandment, portraying the act as a part of the broader process of *'Aliyah*—"ascending"—the immigration to the Land of Israel.

The establishment of new Jewish communities has been seen as a process of redemption of "uninhabited" and "empty" land from historical oblivion and from a social and geographical void.[42] According to Dan Rabinowitz, the new communities, most of which were set up on lands belonging to Palestinian refugees, were intended to create environmental change by "erasing old landscapes and their cultural content, and turning the land into 'Israeli' territory." These communities were perceived to be "incarnations of progress" in "an otherwise wild and primitive Middle East."[43]

JNF's Carmel Coast Forest, on the site of depopulated 'Ayn Ghazal. The prickly pear cacti of the village can still be seen among the planted trees, March 30, 2007. Courtesy of Noga Kadman.

"Judaizing" entire areas through settlement is still being carried out by the state, even decades after its establishment. As part of the "Judaization of the Galilee" project, undertaken by the Israeli government, the Jewish Agency, and the Jewish National Fund (JNF), new Jewish communities were set up in the Galilee in the 1970s and 1980s. The plan aimed at increasing the Jewish population in an area where there was (and is) a Palestinian majority.[44] The communities established under that program were built on Palestinian land, much of it confiscated from Palestinian citizens of Israel. More recently, Israel has been allocating vast swaths of land in the Negev for Jewish settlement in "lone farms," in a bid to obstruct Bedouins from accessing the lands they had used before 1948, which have been defined as "state lands" ever since.

One example of how the message of Judaizing the land through settlement was popularized is the song "Come with Me to the Galilee," which well captures Jewish exclusivism in Israeli perception of the landscape in populated areas; the song lists many names of Jewish communities in the Galilee but fails to mention even a single Palestinian one, even though Palestinians constitute a clear majority in this area.[45]

Planting Trees and Forestation

> A JNF forest, a green spot on an empty land . . . forests that set facts on the ground . . . forests that are a political value, . . . an arid land that became the land of dew and picnic for the entire family.
>
> —Cha'im Hefer [poet] (Quoted in Shkolnik, *Such Fun! Guidebook to Hikes and Active Recreation in* JNF *Forests*

Tree planting is one of the ways in which Israeli collective identity has been shaped. Planting trees symbolizes the bond with the land and serves as a practical way of "striking root" in the soil. The Yishuv—the emerging Jewish community in Palestine—began planting trees in the Land of Israel almost as soon as Zionist immigration began, mostly through the JNF. The JNF was established in 1901 by the Fifth Zionist Congress and tasked with purchasing territory in the Land of Israel through collecting donations from Jews in the Diaspora. Later the JNF began also planting trees, assisting in settlement, and encouraging Jewish immigration to the country. After the establishment of the state in 1948, the JNF dealt with forestation, immigration absorption, preparing lands for settlement and agriculture, and development. All this was carried out on land it had bought and on expropriated refugee land sold to it by the state. In 1961, the JNF and the state signed a covenant that defined the goals of the organization, including "redeeming land from desolation." The covenant entrusted the JNF with complete authority over forestation and forestry across the country, as well as authority over preparing lands for settlement, Zionist education activities in Israel and abroad, and the development of ties between the Jewish Diaspora and the State of Israel.[46]

The large-scale forestation carried out by the JNF changed the landscape of Israel. On the eve of 1948, forests covered less than 20,000 acres of the country, half of which had been planted by the British and half by the JNF and other Jewish organizations; by 2013, over 240 million trees were planted by the JNF on a territory of approximately 230,000 acres. In addition to its authority over this territory, the JNF forestation department is also responsible today for some 100,000 acres of natural woodland in Israel and the development of an additional 100,000 acres of grazing grounds. The forests managed by the JNF include mostly planted pines and other coniferous trees (58 percent), as well as eucalyptus and other non-native broad-leaved trees (17 percent). Only in the remaining 25 percent of the planted land does the JNF plant local species. All this is an implementation of its stated policy of endowing Israel with a European landscape.[47]

In addition to providing shade, the JNF plants trees for various purposes and in pursuit of various declared and undeclared goals, all of which are related to the bond between the Jewish people and the Land of Israel, stemming directly from the organization's Zionist ideology. The main goal of planting in the 1950s was to provide employment for immigrants settled in the periphery. This contributed to immigration absorption and to the settlement project, as well as advancing the goal of spreading the population across the country. On more than one occasion, the sites of depopulated and demolished Palestinian villages were covered by trees as part of this forestation effort. This was the case with the forestation project of the southern slope of *Dayr Yasin* near Jerusalem, initiated in 1950 to provide employment for the Jewish immigrants who settled there. Agricultural needs also motivated tree planting by the JNF, since the trees improve the soil, prevent erosion and desertification, and block the wind.[48]

JNF plantings also create, preserve, and demonstrate presence on the ground, and to use the words of the JNF's own forestation director at the time, Mordechai Ru'ach, trees are "the best guards of the land."[49] In the early days of Zionism, trees were planted to block Arabs from accessing land bought by Jews and using it for grazing. After the founding of the state, trees were planted on "absentee land" to prevent its use by internally displaced Palestinian refugees. To this day, forests are used as wedges that block the expansion of agricultural or built-up areas of Palestinian villages and towns in many areas of the Galilee, the Triangle, and Jerusalem.[50]

Since the beginning of the forestation enterprise, the JNF has set itself the goal of "making the desolate environment friendlier," viewing the European forest as its role model: thick and wide, with coniferous trees. The planting custom is also intended "to tie a rooted, stable bond between the Jews returning to their homeland—and their land."[51] This is also expressed in the celebrations of the Tu

BiShvat holiday (the Jewish New Year of Trees), in which children plant trees as a national ritual of "putting down roots."[52] The forestation enterprise is also used for strengthening the bond between Israel and Jewish communities around the world, through a tradition of tree donation by individual Diaspora Jews and Jewish communities, and the dedication of forests to the donors by the JNF.[53]

Another custom of the JNF is planting commemorative forests, usually for individuals or communities who perished in the Holocaust or for fallen Israeli soldiers.[54] Carol Bardenstein sees the planting as a statement of Jewish rootedness in Israel, linking those in whose memory the trees are planted to the country as a Jewish land.[55]

Beyond its roles in demonstrating Jewish presence and creating Jewish memory, the forestation project of the JNF has been used for covering the remains of destroyed Palestinian villages and therefore as a way of deliberately casting them into oblivion.[56] Michal Katorza, a JNF official who is responsible for putting signs in JNF parks, has stated explicitly, "In fact, a large portion of JNF parks are on lands where Palestinian villages used to stand, and the forests are intended to camouflage this."[57]

Susan Slyomovics sees this action as the uprooting of the Arab-Palestinian heritage by the insertion of new shapes into the landscape, presented as natural but in fact ideologically charged.[58] Planting on sites of depopulated and demolished villages is intended to symbolize how Israel is "making the desolate land bloom" in these sites. Maoz Azaryahu wrote of the ceremony of forest planting on the sites of two depopulated villages near Jaffa, which "symbolized the new life rooted in the site of the former Arab village."[59] In some cases, forests were planted to conceal the remaining walls of village houses. The trees ended up protecting the walls from further destruction, and they still stand within the forests.[60]

In the 1970s the JNF began developing tourism in its forests and setting up picnic sites with tables, benches, restrooms, water taps, trash cans, and signs. The JNF made walking paths across the sites, paved scenic roads, marked routes, and set up observatories and children's playgrounds. In the early 1990s the tourism activity in the forests expanded and became a key activity for the JNF. By 2013 the JNF had developed more than a thousand resorts and parks in forests and open grounds. Some of these include archaeological and historical sites: some are declared as national parks, and some are developed by the JNF together with the Antiquities Authority.[61] The JNF is interested in attracting visitors to the sites and conveying Zionist messages through them:

> In hidden nooks between the forest trees and on open grounds managed by the JNF, alongside the roots of the trees and the plants, other roots, historical ones, sprout: scores of archeological sites that tell us the story of our land's past

and remind us we have been here since Biblical times. In recent years, the JNF developed . . . many sites such as these, preparing them for visitors to reinforce the affinity of the public for the country's soil and its landscapes through the connection to roots and to history.[62]

Alongside the physical development of the resorts, the JNF is investing resources in educational and informational services at the sites, tours and hikes with JNF guides, family activities during the holidays, and the production of publications. The JNF also uses the development of tourism and leisure in the forests to advance its other stated objectives—developing the land, improving the environment, and cultivating the values of Zionism. This is done by bringing visitors to the sites for leisure purposes, exposing them to JNF ideology, mobilizing public support, and improving the organization's public standing.[63]

Nature Preservation

Israel's location at the juncture of three continents and four climatic zones gives it a rich diversity of landscapes and flora. In its early days the Zionist movement raised the flag of "conquest of wasteland," regarding open grounds, desert landscapes, marshlands, sands, and rocky terrain as lands worthy of settlement and cultivation. Over the years population growth, accelerated development, and the rising standard of living have led to increased pollution of water sources, the destruction of natural habitats, damaged landscapes, and the extinction of dozens of species of plants and animals. This was accompanied by growing awareness in Israel of the importance of preserving natural environment, biodiversity, and open areas.[64]

The environmental movement that came into being in Israel in the 1950s, organized as the Society for the Protection of Nature in Israel (SPNI), did not have room for the Palestinian residents of the land, and they were not offered participation in defining the environment and how it should be cared for.[65] The protest actions of SPNI accepted the premises of Zionism; they concentrated on environmental issues and protection of the flora and fauna and avoided engaging with the political and economic interests that often underpin environmental damage.

In 1964 two environmental protection authorities were set up. One was charged with maintaining natural reserves and the other with national parks and "heritage sites." They were merged in 1998 into one body called the Israel Nature and Parks Authority (INPA) and charged with the protection of nature and heritage in Israel, at sites where natural reserves and national parks had been declared. By 2009 this authority, operating under the aegis of the Environmental Protection Ministry, was in charge of 255 reserves, spread across over 1.1 million acres, and 81 national parks, spread across another 154,000 acres.[66]

Dedication stones to JNF donors, in the site of depopulated Bayt Thul, today within JNF's Kfira Forest, May 16, 2007. Courtesy of Noga Kadman.

The remaining buildings of depopulated Qisarya, today part of Caesarea National Park, November 29, 2006. Courtesy of Noga Kadman.

Natural reserves are areas in which the natural environment, including flora, fauna, and landscapes are being preserved. National parks are declared for "public leisure in nature" or for "preserving values of historical, archeological, architectural, natural or scenic importance."[67] Of all the national parks in Israel, only a handful were declared to be on sites without a history predating the Arab era, with the exception of Crusader sites.

The INPA's main goals are the preservation of biodiversity and landscapes and the nurturing of "heritage sites" in national parks and nature reserves, as well as public education on "values of nature, landscape and heritage."[68] The INPA carries out informational and educational activities at the sites themselves, as well as in schools, youth movements, IDF bases, and the media.

While environmental protection activities in Israel are grounded in concern for the preservation of the landscape, flora, and fauna, they are not devoid of other influences, including Zionist ideology. Although the great enemies of biodiversity and open landscapes, in Israel as elsewhere, are industrialization, technological development, and "progress" in general, the common notion in Israel is that the Arabs neglected the land in the years prior to the establishment of the state, while Israel has the scientific means and the environmental awareness to mend the damage. This has been expressed in Israeli school textbooks, which present the Arabs as responsible for the ecological disaster that befell the land.[69] Naama Meishar argues that according to the Israeli perception, in order to recover the original natural ecosystem, nature needs to overcome the damage caused by the Palestinians in their own environment, and also to cover the Palestinian space that the Israeli army destroyed in 1948. Nature also needs to be protected from the Palestinians who remain within the country, and it is therefore preserved by marking tight boundaries for Arab local councils, restricting Arab villages within and next to nature reserves to small densely populated areas (unlike comparable Jewish communities), and limiting Palestinian use of lands for grazing. According to Meishar, environmental protection is also used in this way as an instrument for reducing the space afforded to Palestinian citizens of Israel. She suggests that the basis for environmental protection in Israel is ethnocentric, and Israeli Jews are trying to establish their positive local identity through this, vis-à-vis the negative local Palestinian identity—all while destroying Palestinian links to the environment and giving priority to the Jewish national landscape, environmental development, and visitor convenience.[70]

An example is the "Green Patrol," an INPA department tasked with "guarding state land in open areas from invaders and trespassers, on behalf of the Agriculture Ministry, the Defense Ministry, the Israel Land Administration and the Jewish National Fund."[71] The "invaders" are usually Bedouins herding livestock in areas of the Negev where they once made their living and that they lost to expropriation after 1948. From time to time, the Green Patrol uses force to evict Bedouin from these "state lands."[72]

Preservation of Antiquities and Historical Sites

Archaeological research and preservation of historical sites in Israel are also affected by Zionist ideology and its preference for Jewish history, while marginalizing periods in which Jewish presence in the country was meager. By emphasizing the ancient roots of the Hebrew nation and its bond to the Land of Israel, Zionist collective memory suppresses the memories and experience of groups that lived in the country after most of the Jews had left it. This includes marginalizing centuries of Arabness and neglecting historical Arab sites, including those within the depopulated villages. In focusing on the Jewish past, Israel uses archaeology for national goals, just like any other national movement; this also reflects the natural interest of researchers in what they perceive to be their own culture.[73]

Israeli and Zionist researchers of antiquity focus almost exclusively on the entity of "Ancient Israel," which in reality was only one component of the area's rich and complex history. The history of the great variety of peoples who inhabited the country over the millennia is largely ignored.[74] Most Israeli archaeologists in the 1950s stressed the importance of ancient Jewish sites, such as synagogues, and ignored later periods, especially the Muslim one.[75]

After the War of 1948, Israel demolished most visible remains of the Arab past, since they were not ascribed archaeological value and contrasted with the "Hebrew look" the young state sought to impose on the landscape. Thus, Arab quarters—some of them ancient—were destroyed in the cities of Lod, Tiberias, Jaffa, Haifa, and Acre. Individual initiatives, largely on the part of officials at the Antiquities Department (later the Antiquities Authority), stalled wholesale demolition in a handful of cases, such as the old cities of Jaffa and Acre.[76] The head of the Israeli Antiquities Department, Shmuel Yevin, cried out as early as September 1948 against the demolition in Arab cities and villages being carried out in disregard of important historical monuments. He cited the case of the detonation of the houses of the village of Qisarya, with no regard for the antiquities there. However, he did not protest the wider demolition of the built-up Arab culture and did not call for the new state to end this process. In 1957, when the Foreign Ministry pushed to demolish what was still standing of the depopulated Palestinian villages and neighborhoods, the Antiquities Authority spoke out against demolishing the remains of villages built on ancient sites but demonstrated a distinct lack of interest in the fate of the villages themselves. It remained completely indifferent to their destruction, certainly in the case of more recently built villages. For example, the Palestinian village of Kafr Bir'im was demolished to better expose the ancient and reconstructed synagogue. The move was supported by the Antiquities Authority.[77]

The archaeological establishment in Israel took part in the broad demolition actions conducted across depopulated villages in the 1960s. The Israeli Archaeological Survey Society, established in 1964 and working closely with the Antiquities Authority, was charged with authorizing the demolition of village structures, after conducting archaeological surveys and recording the findings. The Israel Land Administration (ILA) commissioned the society to conduct surveys of over one hundred villages the ILA sought to raze. The surveyors were asked to say whether the village was built atop an ancient site, from which period was the site, and what could and could not be demolished in it. They were also asked to describe the Arab village, which was also destined to become archaeological as time went by. Here, too, there was a basic consensus around the demolition of built-up Arab culture. The buildings of the Arab village were not seen as worthy of preservation in their own right.[78]

Meron Benvenisti, an expert on history of the Crusades in Israel, notes that in depopulated Arab villages where Crusader remains survived, those remains were restored after being "cleansed" of the identity of their Arab residents. The Arab structures that were of no interest to the Israelis were demolished, except those that were converted to tourist use, such as in the national parks of Kokhav HaYarden (Kawkab al-Hawa) and Caesarea (Qisarya). He argues that in some places the "Crusader remains" are actually structures built during the Muslim period and reused by the Crusaders (as in Kafr Lam), structures whose dating to the Crusader period is dubitable (Bayt 'Itab, Suba), or sites with marginal Crusader remains (Khirbat Jiddin). The "Crusader" structures that were preserved often predate the Crusaders themselves and had been used by Arabs before the Europeans took them over and renovated them. They reverted back to Arab use after the end of the Crusader occupation. Benvenisti sees Israel's willingness to reconstruct Crusader structures as an expression of its view of the history of the land after the departure of the Jews as a sequence of foreign conquests, while disregarding the local population. In his opinion, the fact that the Crusaders were seen as "neutral" in the context of the Israeli-Palestinian conflict also contributes to Israel's inclination to maintain their remains.[79]

The British definition of "antiquity," introduced in 1917 and applied to Mandatory Palestine, was "any construction or any product of human activity before the year 1700 A.D." Later the British expanded the definition to include all past eras.[80] Israel, by contrast, retained the earlier definition, and the 1978 Israeli Antiquities Law, which replaced the British regulations, defined antiquities in Israel as human-made remains from the era prior to 1700, or later items declared to be of historical significance by the minister of education and culture. The immediate implication was that the remains of Palestinian villages built in the previous two to three centuries were not defined as "antiquities" and were not deemed worthy of preservation.

Over the years, a growing awareness of the need to preserve buildings that were not old enough to be protected by the Antiquities Law has developed in Israel. In 1984, the Society for Preservation of Israel Heritage Sites was established. The society tends to focus on Jewish-Israeli memorial and heritage sites and ignore Palestinian cultural built-up heritage in Israel.[81] Ghazi Falah, who surveyed all the depopulated village sites in the early 1990s, found that most of the buildings still standing were crumbling with neglect. He argues that this neglect stems from the lack of interest in the history and significance of the villages on the part of the present regime and serves the political goal of belittling the Palestinian past and weakening Palestinian claims to the land.[82] Geographer Tovi Fenster stresses that the Israeli official preservation policy focuses on the commemoration priorities of Israeli Jews, ignoring the Palestinian sense of belonging and memory.[83]

National parks were declared in Israel, among other reasons, in order to nurture "heritage sites" and educate the public on "values of heritage." According to Joel Bauman, national parks and archaeological sites in Israel serve as a tool for creating a collective memory and an "imagined national identity," they attempt to "conscript the past in service to the state and nation," and they have a significant role in the physical and symbolic process of displacement of Palestinians in Israel.[84]

As a rule, Arab-built heritage was neglected or destroyed. However, some Arab buildings and quarters in Israel were preserved. According to several researchers who analyzed the matter, the preservation of Arab construction in these cases amounts to the appropriation of the Arab past while neutralizing the original character of the place and severing its link to its original Arab inhabitants. According to Smadar Sharon, the conservation approach to Arab construction that prevailed in the 1950s among planners who opposed, for example, the demolition of stone structures, reflected an orientalist approach: the discovery of scenic, biblical, and "exotic" value in the native landscape and the desire to make that landscape into a museum exhibit of a society that froze in time or ceased to exist.[85] One example of this approach can be found in the 1949 proposals to make the entire Old City of Acre into a museum, removing the remaining Palestinian residents or at least preventing the return and entry of others.[86] Haim Yacobi writes that the Israeli approach is one of erasing the native landscape and preserving a small part of it, with a view to "domesticating" it and preserving its "authentic" aesthetics while emptying it of its original content, neutralizing its political meaning, and co-opting it for constructing the hegemonic narrative. Yacobi demonstrates this by describing the Arab city of Lydda (Lod), largely demolished in a bid to turn it into a Judaized, clean, and modern city, but with some isolated remains preserved as a tourist attraction.[87]

A more recent example of the same approach can be found in a plan, jointly drafted by the ILA and the Jerusalem municipality in 2004, to turn the remains of the village of Lifta near Jerusalem into an upscale neighborhood and tourism center, including the preservation and reconstruction of the village spring and fifty of the village homes. According to Kobi Peled, the preservation of the traditional construction, as far as the planners are concerned, is merely an instrument to increase the quality and financial value of the envisioned luxurious neighborhood. Peled argues that the plan "erases the Palestinian link to the village and the land and obfuscates it under the pretense of conservation."[88] In the planning objections it submitted against the plan, the nonprofit Israeli organization Bimkom—Planners for Human Rights—argues that the preservation of the village remains is offered only in order to add architectural character to the new neighborhood, while ignoring the Palestinian community that inhabited the village in the past.

"Knowing the Land"

> We were taught that by hiking in the desert we, with our very own feet, were conquering its mountains and valleys. The desert roads and paths will become Jewish as a Jewish vehicle travels along them.
>
> —Meron Benvenisti, *The Sling and the Club*

The bond to the land is a key value in Zionist ideology, and one of its most meaningful expressions is the project of "knowing the land" (*Yedi'at HaHa'aretz*). As most Israelis immigrated to Israel from other countries and did not know the land at all, the project was designed with a view to bridging the gap: acquainting Israelis, from a young age, with the landscapes, history, flora, geography, and geology of the Land of Israel, both through learning and by physically traveling across the country. The goal is to get them to know the land as well as their ancestors knew it in the past.[89] For the first generation of Israelis born in the country, specializing in "knowing the land" was an ideological status symbol: it secured their superiority over their parents' generation and immigrants alike and expressed their belonging to the land and their bonding with it.[90]

Knowledge of the land is instilled in Israelis through the education system, youth movements, the IDF, and independent organizations, as well as books and guidebooks written from an ideological perspective that creates identification with the land and the Zionist enterprise. This was also the case in other settler-migrant societies, with the physical conquest of the space being accompanied by an "emotional conquest."[91]

This knowledge is usually imparted in what are called "homeland" classes in schools. Schools and youth movements engage in field trips across the country, in a bid to provide students with immediate and intimate knowledge of the homeland, in addition to their theoretical knowledge. Such trips would include walking across mountains and streams, as well as visiting sites of importance to ancient Jewish history or the history of Zionism and the state.[92]

"Knowing the land" is an entire subculture with a key role in shaping Israeli national identity. It includes ceremonies that bind Israelis to the land, such as the aforementioned field trips, which carry the message of ownership of the land and conquering it by walking it.[93] Hikes across the land, sometimes in adverse physical conditions, were deemed essential for the development of the "new" Jew, the one who is strong in body and spirit, in contrast to the Diaspora Jew.[94]

The landmarks of Arab existence in the landscape are not perceived as a part of the land that an Israeli should "know." According to Meron Benvenisti, the education system has instilled in Jewish youths "disregard for the Arab landscape and a sense of its foreignness," and "had taught them to erase it from their mental map." He argues that Arabs have been presented in textbooks as "part of the natural fauna, objects rather than subjects."[95] School and youth movement trips do not usually include familiarization with the Arab part of Israel, although their routes often pass by Palestinian communities. Guidebooks describe Palestinian villages only rarely, and sometimes present the landscape as virginal and unpopulated before the arrival of the Jews.[96]

* * *

Following the War of 1948, Israel carried out a demographic Judaization of the state: its adamant refusal to allow most of the Palestinian residents of the country to return to their homes, and condemnation of the latter to refugee status beyond the boundaries of the state, completely altered the population makeup, enabling the existence of a state with a clear Jewish majority. Later on, Israel appropriated the Arab space and Judaized it through the confiscation of Arab lands, the establishment of new Jewish communities on them, and the housing of Jews in emptied Arab homes. The demolition of depopulated Palestinian villages and quarters and the planting of forests on their sites were aimed at erasing from the landscape the traces left by the earlier inhabitants. Alongside the physical Judaization, spatial socialization is taking place, binding Israelis to the space in which they live, one that is structured and imparted to them as an almost exclusively Jewish space. This process includes, inter alia, the ignoring and marginalization of the depopulated villages in Israel, which complement their erasure from the ground. Symbolic sidelining of the villages is carried out when their names are being erased or when they are being marginally represented in maps. A more essential erasure is carried out in texts that introduce places across the land to Israelis—signs, information leaflets, and publications by rural communities—while ignoring the villages and pushing them to the margins of consciousness and memory.

3   The Depopulated Villages as Viewed by Jewish Inhabitants

> Families came from a house of 'Olim [new Jewish immigrants] / to the abandoned village—true pioneers / demolished the houses, repaired the wrecks / cut paths through the prickly pear cacti growth.
>
> —Segal, *Kerem Maharal 1949–1979: 30 Years to the Moshav*

In the first few years of its existence, Israel carried out a large-scale settlement project, establishing hundreds of Jewish communities on lands of depopulated Palestinian villages, dozens of them in the built-up area of the villages. Research done for this book suggests that the previously built-up area of 108 depopulated villages—over a quarter of the total number of villages—is partly or completely located within Jewish communities nowadays. In 25 villages, Jewish agricultural communities were established within the built-up area of the villages, some using the actual village homes and buildings and some built on top of the ruins. In 19 other villages, Jewish agricultural communities occupy part of the villages' built-up area. Some were originally established on parts of the village site, and others have been expanded to include it over the year; an additional 64 depopulated villages lie today within Jewish towns or cities. In addition, 23 depopulated villages border on Jewish agricultural communities, of which 19 were built after the villages were depopulated. The lists of all those villages and the Jewish communities that include them can be found in appendix A, along with a map presenting their locations across the country.

Depopulated Palestinian village sites within the jurisdiction of Jewish communities retain considerable remains of the original villages: whole or partially demolished structures are still standing in 84 out of 108. In comparison, such remains can be found in only a third of the villages left unsettled.

In fifty-nine (71 percent) of the villages that still contain Palestinian buildings standing intact within the jurisdiction of present-day Jewish communities, these buildings are used by Jewish residents: eighteen Israeli communities of the twenty-five built on sites of depopulated villages still use original Palestinian buildings, as do nine communities of the nineteen that were partially built on sites of nearby depopulated villages. Original Palestinian buildings are also still used by Jewish residents in around half of the sixty-four villages located within present-day Israeli cities.

Israelis living today in these communities, mostly second and third generation, encounter on a daily basis the remains of the village past, such as Palestinian homes repaired and populated by Jews, empty or partially ruined structures, prickly pear cactus thickets, and orchard trees. For the founding generation, who settled there shortly after the villages were depopulated, the encounter was considerably more direct and significant: an overwhelming majority of rural communities atop or beside depopulated village sites were established between 1948 and 1950, shortly after the villages were depopulated. At that time, many village homes were still standing, often with property inside. In some places the newcomers even came across the village refugees, who were trying to return to their homes to collect their belongings or harvest their fields and orchards. As members of their generation, most were probably aware of, if not party to, the wartime processes that led to the depopulation and demolition of the villages.

This chapter examines the encounter between Jews who settled and grew up in rural communities on the one hand, and the depopulated Palestinian villages in which they settled, their former residents, and the circumstances of Jews settling these villages—on the other hand. I focus on the writings of rural communities rather than documents of Israeli cities that annexed village sites into their jurisdictions, since community life is stronger in rural communities, public debates are more frequent, and their content is more readily available.[1] Moreover, the presence of depopulated villages is felt more strongly in small communities than in cities, in which the villages have often been swallowed into sprawling neighborhoods.

In my field research I found no rural community that today makes a physical reference—in signage, for example—to the fact that it was established on the site of a depopulated village. For this reason, the research focuses on the public discussion conducted within the communities over the years, as reflected in their writings and publications.

Only a few studies to date have focused on the attitudes of Israelis inhabiting depopulated Palestinian villages. The most important one is Susan Slyomovics's *The Object of Memory*, examining the Jewish artists' colony of 'Ein Hod, established using the houses of depopulated 'Ayn Hawd on the southern slopes of Mt. Carmel.[2] 'Ein Hod was created on the initiative of Israeli artist Marcel Yanko, who protested against the state's intention to demolish the Palestinian village and in favor of turning it into an artists' colony. Slyomovics examines how the artists described their encounters with the depopulated village in catalogs of their exhibitions and in personal interviews. She also documents how the village is remembered by those displaced from it, some of whom have resettled a mere mile away, still living as internally displaced persons, in a village bearing the name of their original abode.[3]

Another publication on the matter is an article by Shlomit Benjamin, who traced the process through which the village of al-Qubayba became the Jewish neighborhood of Kfar Gvirol in the town of Reḥovot, populated mainly by Yemenite Jews.[4] Meron Benvenisti, too, had referred to 'Ayn Hawd and other villages and elaborated on the response of Jewish communities to repair work carried out by Palestinians in nearby village ruins.[5]

Ronnie Kochavi-Nehab analyzed fiftieth-anniversary books published in 190 kibbutzim. She suggests that these books are part of the establishment of a local collective memory and a myth, "seeking to bequeath an authorized written legacy of the community's history and values to future generations."[6] This study touches briefly on the attitudes toward Arabs throughout the years, mentioning that the kibbutzim publications only rarely referred to lands of depopulated Arab villages appropriated by kibbutzim and entirely ignored the fate of the Arab residents of those villages.[7]

Anniversary books and other publications by kibbutzim and moshavim established on depopulated Palestinian villages are part of the legacies of these communities; my purpose is to examine the manner in which the authors chose to refer to the villages, if at all, and to look into the role the village plays in the community's collective memory.

I reviewed documents from twenty-five rural communities—more than a third of the sixty-seven Jewish rural communities established next to or directly atop depopulated Palestinian villages.[8] Among those, fifteen communities granted me access to their archives or publications. Additional material regarding these fifteen communities, along with material on eight other kibbutzim and one moshav, were found in the archives of kibbutz Artzi and the United Kibbutz Movement and in the Israeli National Library. I also reviewed community websites, where I found additional relevant material, including that of two communities not documented by the aforementioned archives.

The communities studied comprise fourteen kibbutzim, nine moshavim, and two other rural communities, spread across the country and established by different settlement movements. Most of the communities were established after the declaration of the State of Israel in May 1948 during, or shortly after, the 1948 war and the depopulation of the Palestinian villages: five in 1948; seventeen in 1949; and one in 1950. Exceptions include one established in 1954 ('Ein Hod) and one in 1974 (Ya'ad).

Of the twenty-five communities, sixteen comprised only recently arrived immigrants, five comprised pre-1948 Jews, and four comprised a mixture of immigrants and pre-1948 Jewish inhabitants. Seven of the communities were established by members of the Palmach or other military units, mostly pre-1948

Jews. The newcomers' communities represented different countries and cultures: Eastern Europe, including many Holocaust survivors (fourteen communities); Turkey and the Arab countries, including North Africa (nine communities); English-speaking countries (four communities); Western Europe (three communities); and Russia (one community).

Among the twenty-five communities, eleven were established on formerly built-up areas of the depopulated villages and ten on parts of such areas, while using the Palestinian houses that were still standing; an additional four communities were established next to the formerly built-up area of the village. Palestinian buildings in fourteen of the communities are still in use.

It is noteworthy that twenty-one of the villages on which the twenty-five communities were established were depopulated after being attacked by Jewish or Israeli forces—as were most of the depopulated villages in 1948.[9] In seven of these twenty-one attacked villages, residents were deported following the attack (Ijzim, Kuwaykat, Safsaf, Saffuriyya, Saliha, Sa'sa', and al-Tantura); in at least two of these, unarmed civilians had been subjected to massacres by Israeli forces (Safsaf, Saliha), and a claim for a third such case (al-Tantura) still remains disputed.[10] The attacks on four of the villages were conducted after Arab militias carried out attacks against Jewish targets from these villages (Ijzim, Kuwaykat, Saffuriyya, Suba). The depopulation of four other villages was due to various circumstances: the residents of Khirbat Bayt Lid and al-Jalama were ordered to leave in April 1948 and in 1950, respectively. The residents of the villages of Wadi 'Ara left because they feared a Jewish attack, and the causes for the exodus from al-Safiriyya remain uncertain. Inhabitants of five depopulated villages have remained in Israel after being internally displaced, acquiring Israeli citizenship ('Ayn Hawd, al-Jalama, al-Lajjun, Mi'ar, and Saffuriyya).[11]

The selection of communities was influenced by the existence of documents and other records available to the public through archives, libraries, and the web. Nevertheless, the diverse circumstances of depopulation and settlement, the different political settlement movements, and the varied geographical locations and social compositions of the communities included in this study make up a representative sample that can serve as the basis for generalizing about other rural Jewish communities established atop or near depopulated villages.

The archive material includes internal newsletters from the early and latest years of the community, anniversary publications, and general publications about the communities. The publications were written and edited by the community members themselves and include personal notes alongside more "representative" materials regarding the community. Quotes from the first printed publications of a community were often used in later ones. Community websites as well as personal memoirs by moshavim members and by their instructors from the Moshavim Movement, published by the latter, were also examined.[12] Unlike publications by the GNC, the JNF, and the INPA (reviewed later in this book), the community publications are less formal and institutional. Therefore, they often reflect feelings and firsthand experiences of the encounter with the villages, and their narratives are not monolithic.

The documents reflect the difficulties encountered by the Jews who settled the depopulated village sites: nearly all were immigrants from other countries who had just arrived in a land with an unfamiliar climate, culture, and language. Many were refugees—Holocaust survivors from Europe or forced emigrants from Arab countries who had lost their assets and property and needed shelter and a new home. For many, the depopulated village was the first permanent residence they were offered in Israel. Beyond the universal predicament of having to adapt to a new country and a new environment, the settlers in the depopulated villages often suffered from further difficulties: habitable houses were scarce, many of them dilapidated and without doors or windows; in some villages, debris and waste were rolling in the unpaved alleys and many villages lacked running water, sewage, or electricity; and many villages were remote from Jewish social and economic centers, and their new residents suffered from acute and chronic unemployment and financial difficulties, including in some cases a shortage of basic provisions. In some areas the new settlers endured thefts and even attacks by Palestinian refugees who were trying to return to their own villages or to neighboring villages to pick up food and items they had left behind.[13]

All the communities mention in both their early and later publications the fact that they were established on a depopulated Palestinian village. This fact is presented quite naturally, as a part of the community's history. It follows that these communities do not seem to want to entirely suppress the memory of the village or to eject it from their collective memory. However, aside from the regular mentions of the village as the physical birthplace of the new Jewish community, the writings of most of the communities make no reference to the history of the village itself prior to the takeover, or to the manner of its depopulation. The documents hardly ever mention attacks, expulsions, and killings carried out by Jewish and Israeli forces against the villagers. The Jewish communities have few words to spare for the lives of the original villagers before 1948, the fate they had encountered in the war, and where they have settled afterward.

Agricultural communities are a key element of Zionist ideology. They symbolize and embody the link between the Jewish people and its land, the people's return to places and ways of life they inhabited in the past, the Judaization of the country, and the glorified acts of making it bloom and endowing it with progress. These ideas are also evident in the writings of kibbutzim and moshavim set up on top of depopulated villages: some of the writers express their desire to make the village a Jewish one, to restore its ancient Jewish past, and to minimize its Arab identity, since the period in which Arabs inhabited the place is perceived as a negative, fleeting episode, no matter its length. The newly established Jewish communities also spoke of the aspiration to advance the place from backwardness to modernity, to "make the desert bloom," to demolish the old and to build up the new in its stead.

The community documents record time and again the benefits reaped from the remains of the depopulated village and the physical components of the village being used: homes, construction materials, groves and orchards, building materials collected from ruins, and household artifacts. Even when some authors voice unease about living in houses where others had lived until not so long ago, or express sadness at the sight of the depopulated village, seldom do they articulate any feeling of guilt or moral dilemmas in this regard. The only community that tried to confront questions and contradictions, provide some answers, and justify its choices, was kibbutz Sasa, established in the homes of the depopulated village of Sa'sa' by Jewish American immigrants. In several publications Sasa members have expressed empathy for the pain of the refugees, acknowledged responsibility for their uprooting, and showed awareness of the contradiction between the depopulation and the ideals they themselves professed for creating a new, equitable society. Nevertheless, they decided to stay in the village and pay the moral price for realizing the Zionist idea, the national struggle, and the Judaization of the land.

Manners of Reference to the Village, Its History, and Its Depopulation

> Name: Kibbutz Sasa. Birthplace: The abandoned village of Sa'sa'
> —Sasa, *Sasa I.D.*

The moshavim publications refer to the fact that the moshav was built above or next to a depopulated Palestinian village. The same applies to kibbutzim newsletters in their early years and in most later-day kibbutzim publications. Thus, the opening sentence in a brochure about moshav Kerem Ben Zimra in Upper Galilee states that the community was "built on the ruins of the Palestinian village of 'Ras Al-Ahmar'"; kibbutz Karmia sent out invitations to its foundation ceremony, which was to be held "in Hiribya"—the name of the Palestinian village on which the kibbutz was built.[14] Another example is the description of the beginnings of the Ḥasidic village of Kfar Chabad:

> The village of Safiriyya, near Tel Aviv, was found to be the best place for a new Chabad community . . . this was the summer of 1949. In the dead of night, in pitch black darkness, the Chabad 'Olim [immigrant] families invaded Safiriyya village. They came from the transit camps on trucks, entire families with all their belongings. Within a few hours all the stone and mud houses in Safiriyya, which had been empty, were occupied . . . the hold upon the houses became a solid fact.[15]

It would seem that knowledge of the Jewish community having been built on a depopulated Palestinian village is also passed to the community's younger generation, since it appears in texts for children and texts written by children: *Sasa Stories,* a collection of children's stories from the kibbutz life, mentions this fact several times, for instance: "In the early years of the kibbutz there were many Arab homes here, remnants of the village of Sa'sa', which stood here before us."[16] A book written in 2001 by the children of moshav Sifsufa, established on part of the village site of Safsaf, includes an "identity card" of the community, in which they describe "a still standing old Arab house from before the foundation of the state and the conquest of the Galilee, since, as it is well known, Arabs used to live in our moshav back then."[17] Children writing to celebrate the thirtieth anniversary of Kerem Maharal mention the Palestinian village on which their moshav was founded: "Before the War of Liberation, a large Arab village by the name of 'Ijzim' stood here."[18]

By contrast, the Palestinian village that not only stands but has been preserved, restored, and used by Jews is notably absent from the description of the Jewish community it hosts today. The website of the artists of 'Ein Hod, the artists' colony founded in the houses of the depopulated village of 'Ayn Hawd, describes the unique architecture of the homes and mentions the orchards, but does not refer even once to the Palestinian village to which all these had belonged, nor to its residents. The latter's culture is dubbed "Mediterranean," the period in which their homes were built is "Ottoman," and the village's environment is described as "ancient Israelite." There is not a hint in the text to the fact that this is a Palestinian village.[19]

Susan Slyomovics notes that the residents of 'Ein Hod speak of the depopulated village itself as an ancient place of biblical character. They see the buildings of 'Ayn Hawd, she says, as "picturesque antiquity" and describe it as full of "scenes of Biblical desolation." They credit the architecture and the ruins to biblical or Crusader sources, rather than to "the work of named, known, often living Palestinian stone-masons and master-builders."[20] Similarly, Meron Benvenisti claims that an extravagant and non-Arab history was invented for particularly impressive structures still standing in depopulated villages.[21]

Most of the community publications find it sufficient to mention the site of the village as the location of the Jewish community and do not go on to describe the village itself or its history. One example is an article in a newsletter of kibbutz Kabri that reviews ancient ruins and remains within a few miles of the kibbutz. It lists sites dating to the Roman, Byzantine, and Crusader periods but does not mention the Palestinian village of al-Kabri, which stood directly next to the kibbutz before its destruction.[22] A publication by kibbutz Lehavot Ḥaviva mentions the village of al-Jalama, on a part of which it stands, but focuses on the site's ancient history: "Before the establishment of the state, an Arab village by the name of Hirbat Jalami was located here, but . . . when the place was established, much older traces of settlement were discovered."[23] This paragraph is followed by an extensive survey of local archaeology.

Two exceptions to the rule are moshav Ya'ad and kibbutz Erez. Moshav Ya'ad provides on its website extensive information quoted from exiles of the nearby village of Mi'ar, covering the village history and the circumstances of its demolition. Kibbutz Erez quotes an impression by French geologist Victor Guerin, who visited the village of Dimra in the nineteenth century, as well as conversations with the village's refugees, who relate its history.[24] In both cases, these are late publications, from the 1990s onward, emanating from communities whose Jewish residents have made links with refugees who live nearby (inside Israel in the case of Mi'ar and in the Gaza Strip in the case of Dimra).

Other publications do not detail the village history but contain photographs from the time when the village still existed. Sasa's *Identity Card* features two aerial photographs, one of kibbutz Sasa and one of the village of Sa'sa'; an aerial photograph of the village of Hiribya can be found in the collection published by kibbutz Karmia on its thirty-fifth anniversary; and in an encyclopedia of moshav terminology, moshav HaBonim published an old photograph of the village of Kafr Lam, on whose site it stands.[25]

References to the lives of the villagers prior to their depopulation are rare. Moshav HaBonim specified the number of villagers of Kafr Lam, noting that they worked in agriculture; the Kerem Maharal book describes the "Arabic and Druze folklore," which alludes to the original people of Ijzim as "dumb" because of the poor quality of the village's water. The editor soothes his readers: "Obviously, the matter of the water and its impact on the residents does not refer to its Jewish residents at all."[26] In these descriptions, the villagers are mentioned without stating they have become refugees. By contrast, publications by the kibbutzim Sasa and Yir'on describe the lives of the villagers in Sa'sa' and Saliha until 1948 in the context of the guilt felt by kibbutz members for violating the pastoral life of the villagers through settling on their site: "The men worked their plots and tended their flocks while women busied themselves with baking their bread. The cries and tears of children of others were heard in Sasa one year ago."[27] And the newsletter of kibbutz Yir'on reports: "Only a year ago, simple, primitive people lived here, working their land with an ox and a donkey and a plough, drinking water from the rain cisterns and living off the figs, the smuggling and the mountain air."[28]

The book published by moshav Kerem Maharal for its thirtieth anniversary assigns several pages to the site's prehistory. However, the only historical fact mentioned about the village of Ijzim, in the houses of which the moshav had been founded, is that its residents had taken part in hostile activity against the Jewish population.[29] Overall, only a few communities describe the villagers as hostile and aggressive to Jews prior to their displacement. A publication by Sasa describes Sa'sa' as a "center of rioting militants activity" in 1948, while Kabri describes al-Kabri as "a rioting militants' village."[30]

Most of the villages on which Jewish communities were established were emptied after being targeted by the Palmach or the Israeli army. Most of the kibbutzim and moshavim publications acknowledge the conquest of the village by Israel or the flight of its residents, but most make no reference to the actions that led them to flee. Writings surveyed from kibbutz Nachsholim, on the Mediterranean coast, make no reference to the expulsion of the villagers of al-Tantura and the claims that dozens of villagers were massacred.[31] The kibbutz website mentions the conquest of the village but nothing more. Moshav Tzipori ignores the aerial bombing of the village of Saffuriyya and the expulsion of the remaining villagers, and so on and so forth. Only five communities describe the attacks that had led to the depopulation of the village, including a newsletter of kibbutz Yir'on that mentions murder and looting perpetrated by an IDF unit on the villagers of Saliha and a publication by Kabri describing an act of collective punishment that included the destruction of the village and the expulsion of its residents.[32]

Appropriation of the Palestinian Village by the Jewish Community

According to Ghazi Falah, the Israelis tended to see the remains of the Palestinian cultural landscape—remains of cities, villages, and orchards—"in terms of its present utility, rather than its past function."[33] Ronnie Kochavi-Nehab found that after the establishment of the state, the missing Arab neighbors were scarcely mentioned, or simply entirely ignored, in the kibbutzim anniversary books. When they were mentioned, it was usually in the context of their land being transferred to kibbutz ownership.[34] Nearly all the communities covered here mention the physical characteristics of the Palestinian village in the context of their usefulness to the Jewish community. In some cases, this is the only context in which the village is mentioned.

Many publications mention the use to which the community put the remaining Palestinian homes upon its establishment. The reference to the homes in this context is a practical one, concerned with their new utility role in the Jewish community, while refraining from treating them as homes inhabited by others until recent times. The homes are frequently described as "abandoned," without an elaboration on who abandoned them and why. The first newsletter of kibbutz Sasa refers to the homes that "we inherited from the Arabs."[35]

The residents of moshav HaBonim state on their website that they chose to build their community on the site of the depopulated Palestinian village of Kafr Lam, among other optional sites, since it had empty homes which they could settle into: "A site some 25 kilometers south of Haifa: A gravel hill on top of which stand the remains of an abandoned Arab village—Kafr Lam. Moshe recommended the latter, for several reasons. The land was fertile, suitable homes were already there—that only needed to be refurbished, the place was lovely."[36]

The web page goes on to describe the way in which kibbutz members used the Palestinian structures once they moved in: "At first, they lived in the abandoned Arab homes, without electricity, running water or toilets. The kibbutz members bathed in the sea, until two Arab structures were refurbished as public showers."

Kibbutz Yir'on states in its first newsletter that "the Arab stone homes are serving us faithfully,"[37] and goes on to say in the second newsletter: "We have refurbished 17 residential rooms, and some 10 service structures. All of those—in the buildings of the village of Saliha, which we refurbished for their temporary usage and named Yir'on."[38]

Residents of moshav Rinatya describe the establishment of the local school: "At first the educational institution resided in a few rooms in the abandoned village of Rantiya, meager structures that could hardly be called classes."[39]

Moshav Kerem Ben Zimra, as well, mentions the use to which the Palestinian homes of al-Ras al-Ahmar were put by the moshav founders: "Most of the ancient stone houses were blown up by the authorities . . . leaving only a few homes. Of these, houses were used as a school, a dining room, a synagogue, a dairy and a bakery. They stand in the moshav to this day."[40]

In some cases, references are made to specific buildings of the Palestinian village, whose use was significant to the Jewish community in its early years. These houses were dubbed with nicknames based on their perceived roles in the village, like "the Mukhtar's house" or "the Sheikh's house," or sometimes simply "the Arab house." Sometimes the names were retained, becoming a term commonly used by members and a part of their folklore. The "Arab house" of kibbutz Karmia, for instance, which previously had served as the school of the village of Hiribya, is where the kibbutz members used to live immediately after the kibbutz was established, and where the kibbutz store was opened later. This house is referred to as "the Arab house" in the literature of the kibbutz, and an aerial photo of it is prominently featured in the collection published on the thirty-fifth anniversary of the kibbutz.[41] The members of kibbutz Megiddo, as well, appropriated "the Arab house," a remainder of the village of al-Lajjun, as a significant part of their own history: "When we came here in February 1949 / . . . we looked at you, house / to find a spark of hope and a glimmer of light. . . . you, the one and only / whom we call—the Arab house. / For without you, we would be lost / and as the homeless. . . ."[42]

In an encyclopedia of local terms published by moshav HaBonim on its thirty-fifth anniversary, there is an entry on a Palestinian building of Kafr Lam, which stresses its importance for the moshav:

"The Mukhtar's house": . . . the lot to the north of the building was a central courtyard—with Arab homes all around it. We have used them for many

A house in 'Ein Hod, originally Palestinian Ayn Hawd, April 25, 2007. Courtesy of Noga Kadman.

קור,
' אור.
קירותיך.
,

הבית הערבי

רי המגורים,

"The Arab House," kibbutz Megiddo newsletter, June 1985, p. 23. Courtesy of Kibbutz Megiddo, Yad Ya'ari Archive.

things—laundry, showers, carpentry, general storeroom, generator room, dining hall, kitchen, and more. . . . The Mukhtar's house has changed roles over the years. The general kitchen became the volunteers kitchen. The carpentry workshop—a club, the storeroom—a sewing workshop. . . . And the house has remained the nerve center of the moshav.[43]

A lexicon published by kibbutz Kabri on its fiftieth anniversary references the "Sheikh house," which indicates the house is a part of kibbutz mythology and folklore. Unlike other "Sheikh," "Mukhtar," and "Arab" houses in communities' writings, the sheikh in Kabri is not anonymous and his name is noted in the text. The house stood in the depopulated village of al-Nahr, where the members of Kabri took residence before founding the kibbutz on the hill above the nearby depopulated village of al-Kabri:

> The Sheikh's house—1. The first two-storied house that served as the first clothing storeroom—(the house of Sheikh 'Afifi), dining room (on first floor) and the temporary children's home (second floor). In one of the wings of the first floor the first livestock pen of the kibbutz was installed, housing a minuscule flock of sheep. . . . After moving to Kabri hill, the house was used by our first citrus growers. Later on, following heavy rains in one of the winters, the house collapsed.[44]

Some publications feature photographs of the Palestinian buildings inside the Jewish communities, with captions describing their role in the Palestinian village: moshav HaBonim published in its own encyclopedia a photograph from its early days in Kafr Lam, captioned "A view from the Mukhtar house." A newsletter released on the twentieth anniversary of kibbutz Beit Guvrin showed photographs of Palestinian structures with captions denoting their roles in the Palestinian village of Bayt Jibrin, as well as their use by the kibbutz: "District court house—the first children's home and today a junior high school"; "once a school, today a storeroom, a discotheque and an electrician's workshop."[45]

Some of the kibbutzim recount the use of stones of the Palestinian homes for building new structures in the community. For instance, in Kabri: "We loaded building stones to build our first generator shed at the entrance to the kibbutz, building stones for our first culture hall that served us for many years and was our pride at the time, [and] we also used building stones as the foundations of several sheds."[46]

This kibbutz's lexicon, too, describes usage of the remains of the Palestinian village, in an entry titled "abandoned property": "When we broke an access road to the community through the village and needed to clear the ruins, we found many iron beams that we used to construct our haylofts and for other needs."[47]

Kibbutz Har'el also notes the use of the stones from the adjacent depopulated village of Bayt Jiz: "the construction of the cowshed had begun. . . . We will not pave the floor with concrete, but with stones brought from Bayt Jiz."[48] The members of Sasa, who settled in the stone homes of Saʿsaʿ, also decided to build their new homes out of stone. At first they used "stones from the ruins of the Arab village," and after these were depleted, "stones from nearby demolished and abandoned villages." The residents of Sasa stress that they did not use stone from Kafr Birʿim, to which—unlike the other villages, so it seems—they "hoped that the original residents would return some day."[49]

Around the Jewish communities established on Palestinian villages stood fruit orchards, on which most of the livelihood of the Palestinian villagers had depended. The communities' writings describe the pleasures derived by the new inhabitants from the orchard fruits. In the Kabri lexicon, the entry "orchards in Kabri" pictorially describes the fruits, without mentioning the residents of al-Kabri who grew them: "When we mounted the hill of Kabri in 1949, we found not just stones and rocks. At the foot of the hill, between irrigation channels, we found orchards of pomegranates of a unique kind, large and juicy . . . also yielding were trees of white apricot . . . among all those stood fig trees with fruits of delicious taste."[50]

The text from moshav Rinatya focuses on the orchard fruits that became available to the Jewish inhabitants after the war. It does not deal with the dispossession of the people of Rantiya, who had cultivated the orchards until they were forced to leave them behind. The text seems to imply that their departure was voluntary: "When the Arabs abandoned the country after the war, the Jewish residents were left nearly without fruit supply. The available fruits were the Sabras [prickly pears], the grapes and the pomegranates from the abandoned orchards."[51]

The "botanical overview," within the general overview published by Kerem Ben Zimra, includes references to the plantations of al-Ras al-Ahmar and acknowledges the care rendered by the Palestinians to the trees, as well as their use by the moshav residents: "Kerem Ben Zimra . . . was in the distant past rich with orchards cultivated by the Arabs who lived where figs, grapes, pomegranates, mulberries, pecans, walnuts and plentiful olive groves grew. These trees still grow everywhere about the moshav, though not as nourished and cultivated as in the past. But still, in the summer weeks the residents enjoy the fruits and trees."[52]

When the new communities were established, their residents tried to cultivate the Palestinian orchards. In their writings, they took for granted their right to cultivate and profit from orchards that had been fostered by others, and from which these others had been uprooted. Kibbutz Kabri spoke of the olives as "inheritance" from the Arabs, which was meant to later become an integral part of the kibbutz: "As for the olive groves 'inherited' to us by the Arabs—much embarrassment. We have to learn. A few years will pass . . .—and the olive tree will be an equal-rights citizen."[53]

A structure and an olive tree, remains of depopulated Bayt Jibrin, within kibbutz Beit Guvrin, April 13, 2007. Courtesy of Noga Kadman.

An illustration accompanying the story titled "Building from Stone," in Sasa, *Sasa Stories*, p. 14. Courtesy of Hagar Noi-Kosta.

Kibbutz Netzer Sereni, which does not even mention the village of Bir Salim next to which it was established, describes the village groves as if the settlers have won them by sheer luck: "The main reserves within our borders were abandoned citrus orchards and olive groves."[54] The kibbutz sought to evaluate its potential profit from the cultivation of the groves. It did not specify who had profited from them before the war, using the popular term "abandoned" to explain the absence of the previous owners:

> When our first members settled the land we found here plots of olive trees spread across hundreds of acres, and an attempt was made, of course, to make these pre-existing groves a source of income for our young kibbutz. We do not know how profitable these had been in the days before the Liberation War. Even if they had been profitable enough, the period of neglect from their abandonment by their previous owners and the arrival of our comrades, the new owners, brought about a degeneration of the grove.[55]

The members of kibbutz Har'el, too, saw the groves of Bayt Jiz as a source of crops and income. The village name is used only as a nickname for the grove, which is perceived as "ours": "The Bayt Jiz grove—. . . it looks lovely. The olive bloom is gradually turning into fruit. It seems a large crop is forthcoming. . . . Our groves are the most beautiful in the area. . . . We expect serious income from this grove."[56] A similar approach was expressed by the kibbutz members regarding the village's grape vines: "We will harvest the grapes of Bayt Jiz this week."[57]

Similar plans were made on kibbutz Beit Guvrin for the citrus orchard of the village of Bayt Jibrin, described as an "Arab" orchard that had not been cultivated for some years for an unspecified reason: "There are many fruit orchards about, of plums and apricots, figs, mulberries, pomegranates, almonds, olives, and citrus. . . . As for the citrus orchard itself, it was decided to cultivate it. True enough, this is a thick, Arab orchard that has not been cultivated for some years. But with minimal work, pruning, whitewashing, . . . there are prospects for a hefty harvest."[58]

The publications of kibbutz Beit Ha'Emek hardly mention the village of Kuwaykat, on which the kibbutz was built, with some remaining structures still being used by the kibbutz members. However, the ancient olive trees of the village, many of which still grow today on the kibbutz lawns, are referenced a number of times. In a newsletter from 1994 the trees are poetically described as permanent fixtures that stay even as people come and go. The Palestinian residents of the village, who had harvested the trees before the kibbutz was founded, are not mentioned: "Many olive trees grow here in Beit Haemek. They were here before us and will probably stay after us. If the trees could speak, they could tell us many stories, of different people and many harvests, much of which has not changed."[59]

The memory of the village is silenced in the kibbutz writings, but its trees that remain support a different kind of memory: over the years, a new tradition evolved by which the youths of the kibbutz harvest Kuwaykat's olive trees within the kibbutz, sell the produce, and use the revenues to sponsor their "roots trips" to Poland, where they visit sites of uprooted and destroyed Jewish communities as well as ghettos and former labor and extermination camps. A kibbutz resolution from October 23, 2006, states it plainly: "The olives are the property of the kibbutz entrusted to the youths to sponsor the Poland project."[60]

In some cases, the Jews inhabiting the Palestinian village site found furniture, household items, and other property that the villagers had to leave behind. In their writings, the inhabitants describe how they used this property. The residents of Kerem Maharal recall how "we began baking bread in an oven left by its previous owners."[61] The use of Palestinian property was so widespread in the early days of kibbutz Kabri that its lexicon holds a separate entry of "abandoned property," describing it as "a kind of a first [economic] 'branch'" of the kibbutz. In the entry, the kibbutz members make it clear that they formalized the appropriation of the refugee property vis-à-vis the authorities, in a process which very much seems like an official whitewash of the looting:

> In the early days, those who stayed up on the hill to keep guard would go down at the end of their work into the village, for patrols and "scouting." Anything movable was moved up the hill, distributed between the tents for the members' use and between the different [economic] branches. Our clothes storeroom adorned itself with quite a few "mahogany" wardrobes from among the abandoned property. With time, we approached the authorities in charge and received permission and tenure over the village, so all our actions were legal and approved.[62]

A member of the kibbutz who authored a book on the community's early days wrote his own memories of the looting of Palestinian property by Kabri and described how it was institutionalized on the kibbutz:

> Here and there we saw stools and different household items lying about. We did not hesitate at all, and took them for our use in our tents and shacks, which were bare. . . . So, little by little, we equipped ourselves with the minimal conveniences. Some went beyond that, went on a roll, as they say, and began deliberately scavenging for real bargains, but most of us were content at this stage with minimal items. Later on, when we all went up, a systematic search for items began, and members were even arranged by turns to take out wardrobes, tables and chairs to be used in the clothing storerooms and for other needs.[63]

The author goes on to describe competition for the loot among various local Jewish settlers. The official permit that made Kabri the "legal" owners of the

Ancient olive trees of depopulated Kuwaykat within kibbutz Beit Ha'Emek, March 5, 2007. Courtesy of Noga Kadman.

Jewish immigrants from Morocco in moshav Rinatya, established in the houses of depopulated Rantiya, November 1, 1949. Courtesy of Zoltan Kluger, Government Press Office, Israel.

property of al-Kabri helped the kibbutz win the race with the residents of a neighboring camp for newly arrived immigrants:

> Very soon we found that we had business partners. The people of the Kurdish immigrant camp, located a little to the east of the village, also discovered the same possibilities of additional income and began working extra hours at night. . . . At first we looked the other way, since there was enough also for them, but when one day all the iron we collected and prepared for loading the next day had vanished, we realized there was no choice but to put a stop to that. We took a tractor and a wagon, traveled down to the camp and went from house to house. We found everything pretty fast. . . . We loaded it on the wagon, showed them the permit by the custodian of the absentee property, and that was that.[64]

Judaizing the Village, Changing the Landscape, and "Making the Desert Bloom"

> Here and there we see ruined houses, the place is desolate. . . . Here we shall build our house and create something out of nothing!
>
> —Kibbutz Beit Guvrin (previously Bayt Jibrin), March 30, 1951

A number of references in community publications express the enthusiasm felt by the new residents upon turning the Palestinian village where they settled into a Jewish place. This is, in a way, an expression of on-the-ground realization of the Zionist ideology of Judaizing the land. A poem written in Hungarian by one of the first Jewish inhabitants of moshav Mizra' Har, built atop the village of al-Muzayri'a, also known as Umm-Zara', expresses this idea poetically and with great pathos. The poem was described in a book by the Moshavim Movement as "most instructive": "This land was ours, and so it will be, / the furrow, the earth clod—are Jewish again / 'Umm Zara'' will no longer be host to the owl, we will build here a future with sweat on our brow. / We'll demolish clay houses, abandoned remains, / and build new dwellings in their place."[65]

Some publications describe the ancient period when the location of their community was Jewish, stressing its return to Jewish hands. One of Sasa's publications reads: "Far, far back in its glorious history, this village was inhabited by Jews, and then for several centuries it was held by Arabs. Now it is destined to be Jewish again for years, decades and centuries to come."[66]

Moshav Tzipori provides a detailed description of the thousands of years of history of the site, beginning in the Bronze Age. The text speaks in first person plural only about periods in which an ancient Jewish settlement existed there: "Some 2,400 years ago . . . we came back here as part of the Return to Zion. . . . We had experienced true independence in Tzipori for just 40 years, prior to the occupation of the country by Roman military leader Pompieus, in 63 b.c. . . . But we have awaited full independence for 2,011 years, until 1948."[67] The establishment of the moshav in 1949, next to the ruins of ancient Tzipori and the remains of the Palestinian village of Saffuriyya, is described as the "re-establishment of Tzipori." A similar trend was noted by Ronnie Kochavi-Nehab in kibbutz anniversary books, in which "the emphasis in the site's story is placed on the connection to very distant periods of independence of the Jewish people in their land," accompanied by quotes linking the ancient history with the contemporary era of Zionist settlement.[68]

In some cases it transpires that living in an Arab place was tainted with negative stigmas for the Jewish settler. A publication by Kfar Chabad uses the adjective "Arab" as a negative one when it describes the changes in the village of al-Safiriyya with the establishment of a Jewish community there: "The village turned from an Arab village, abandoned and neglected, to a pearl of beauty."[69] A moshav member writes in 1957 that settling people in depopulated Arab homes by the Moshavim Movement was a mistake, not only because these houses do not fit modern planning standards but also because of the negative associations evoked by Arabness among Israelis. He reiterates that many moshavim dwindled because of the compulsion to "live like Arabs."[70]

As part of her research, Shlomit Benjamin interviewed residents of the Kfar Gvirol neighborhood of Reḥovot, built atop the depopulated village of al-Qubayba. She quotes a Yemen-born Jewish resident: "Qubayba. An Arab village. Very negative, for years. It was shameful to say Qubayba. . . . It's a disadvantage that you live in an Arab village. It means you live in a weak place, not nice, your standard is low and your status is low."[71]

Benjamin writes that alongside the Judaization of the space through the demolition of the village of al-Qubayba and its repopulation with Jews, the new Yemenite Jewish residents were also "cleansed" of their Arabness. She notes, however, that the presence of "the Arab Jewish immigrants who arrived to Qubayba . . . prevented the eradication of the Palestinian memory space and even induced it with new ethnic meanings."[72] This concerns the eradication of Arab identity among Jews from Arab countries who arrived in Israel, a matter not discussed in the present work.

Ronnie Kochavi-Nehab found that in the kibbutz anniversary books she examined, the place prior to its settlement had always been "empty," "desolate," or abandoned, and its settlement served as a means of "conquering" the wasteland and making it "bloom." She says that the establishment of the kibbutz is presented "as an act of creation, in which something is made out of nothing." Kochavi-Nehab believes this perception is rooted in the myth that "prior to Zionist settlement the land was desolate, unpopulated, uncultivated and infested with malaria."[73]

The Zionist myths of "redeeming the land" and "making the desert bloom" are often present in the writings of the kibbutzim and moshavim that were built over depopulated villages, whose members often see themselves as materializing these myths. In their writings, the inhabitants describe the sites they arrived at as desolate, expressing their desire to make them lively and blooming, and going on to detail how they managed to accomplish it. Members of kibbutz Barkai, established on the site of the village of Wadi 'Ara, describe the desolation they encountered—in which they include a Palestinian building—and announce their intention to make it bloom: "there was nothing there! . . . in this desolation, upon the Effendi's [notable] house, between the flags of the nation and the class—our motto: 'Through building and creating we will make the wasteland fertile!'"[74]

The desolation and neglect encountered by the settlers were described while completely ignoring the life that had existed there before they arrived, and the reasons why this life had stopped. The founders of moshav Rinatya describe the desolation they found in the village of Rantiya, but it goes unexplained and is presented instead only as a challenge demanding intensive work: "When the men reached the site, no paradise was awaiting them—quite the opposite. They found an abandoned Arab village, homes without doors or windows, great neglect around them, the houses were surrounded with thorns, prickly pear cacti and abundance of mites. The 17 men . . . worked at weeding, cleaning the buildings and preparing them for the family dwellings."[75]

The anthem of kibbutz Erez, written on the fifth anniversary of the kibbutz, describes its establishment on the depopulated village of Dimra as an act of settlement in a desolate area: "By the sands and the desolate hills near the border / Erez rose and shaded by abandoned fruit trees / tents were pitched."[76] The title pages of a book published by Rinatya on its fiftieth anniversary display a poem that reads: "A small moshav rose from the ruins."[77] It ignores the causes of ruin and the fate of the village's original residents. The Kerem Maharal book quotes a seven-year-old girl born in the moshav: "The village, in which only ruins were once seen—is now blooming and thriving."[78] The Palestinian village is perceived here as if it had always been in ruin, a perception found also among the residents of 'Ein Hod, who thought of the houses of 'Ayn Hawd as having been "ruins" throughout all the centuries in which they were inhabited by Arabs—while the period in which the houses were "ruins" was in fact the years 1948–1954. Susan Slyomovics says that perceiving the Palestinian houses as ruins can negate the fact that an Arab-Palestinian village had existed there in the not-too-distant past.[79]

The community publications stress how lush and green the sites have become following their efforts and insinuate that the arid landscape was the result of the period in which Arabs inhabited the place: "No one knows the nature of the soil at Dimra, which has not been touched by a Jewish hand since the destruction [of

Jewish residents in moshav Kerem Maharal, established in the houses of depopulated Ijzim, October 3, 1949. Courtesy of Zoltan Kluger, Government Press Office, Israel.

Immigrants from the United States arriving at the depopulated village of Sa'sa', where they established kibbutz Sasa, January 1, 1949. Courtesy of unknown photographer, Government Press Office, Israel.

"WHY DID YOU COME HERE?"

n January 1st, 1943, in a crowded room at the hachshara farm in New Jersey, U.S.A., a group of about 90 youth at the age of 18 and 19, representing over 150 of their comrades in the U.S. and Canada,

The beginning of kibbutz Sasa's publication: *The Launching—Sasa's First Year*, 1949, p. 1. Courtesy of Jonas, Keren Hayesod, Central Zionist Archive.

the Temple]. . . . I am sure our group can do wonders in this deserted valley, and turn it into magnificently blooming fields and vineyards."[80]

Having described the difficulties of settling in Rantiya, the residents of Rinatya go on writing in their anniversary book: "After we have overcome all hardship . . . [we] have managed to make the desolate and abandoned place which we arrived at bloom."[81] The members of kibbutz Barkai write: "It's been a year since we came on the land. It was a wasteland. Thorns growing to a man's height, and destruction all around. Outside the Arab buildings—only sky and rock. . . . And see, from day to day, the place is shifting shape and acquiring the character of a kibbutz . . . the wasteland has become a living settlement!"[82]

A newsletter issued by kibbutz Megiddo goes further and links the act of planting trees on the kibbutz—set up on part of the village of al-Lajjun—to the acquisition of ownership over the site and the entire country:

> In a few years' time our entire spot will bathe in shadow and green—removing the shameful stain of desolation, which burdens also this part of our country. In olden days, when the land was populated by our ancestors, it too was green and cultivated. . . . Cultivating trees and ornamental gardening is also

a testimony to striking root and to feeling at home. Under foreign rule of our land, most of its trees have been destroyed. We are now commanded to restore ancient glory, to beautify our settlement spot by fulfilling it with trees, in order to become its owners.[83]

By contrast, kibbutz Sasa members acknowledged that their site of settlement was not empty. They expressed their wish that that would be the case and complained about having had to settle in a Palestinian village instead: "Once we dreamt about settling in a new place; arriving at once in a desolate, abandoned territory, and building our community from the foundations, according to our taste and background . . . we are mired in the ruins of an Arab village, that even before its destruction we had to run around in it among fleas and dirt, seeking and guarding property—despite our ideological reactions, so much so that the first days were about deconstruction rather than construction."[84]

Publications by communities founded on depopulated village sites tend to refer to the landscape around the site where they have settled. This usually comes alongside expressions of an explicit desire to change the landscape's Arab character and descriptions of the efforts to that end. A publication by kibbutz Nachsholim stresses the urgency ascribed by the members to changing the landscape of al-Tantura, and amplifies the contrast between the village landscape that they see and the environment in which the kibbutz members would like to raise their children:

> Have we considered the shape and character of our children's home? What a pity it is that their first steps have to be made among the ruins of the miserable, dirty village. When we sometimes see them on a walk—a glowing group of tanned, golden-haired [children], one thinks almost involuntarily how out of place they seem with this bleak, gray backdrop, this village that has nothing rural about it, no grass, no tree and no flower! How important it is for us to hurry up, to leave the village before it becomes embedded in the children's memory. [85]

The reference to the bright hair of the children juxtaposed with the grayness of the village brings to mind a yearning for a Western, European environment—something expressed also in kibbutz Beit Guvrin's desire to add lawns and gardening in order to alter the Arab character of the landscape: "Our community has existed for over two years, and except for [the land] by the sheds, the dining hall and the culture room, where you can find clumps of grass and gardens, the landscape remains unaltered, no boulevard, no central lawn, no tree has been planted until now. Deeds that could have changed the Arab landscape which surrounds us a great deal."[86]

Upon its establishment, kibbutz Yir'on set itself a goal to destroy all the Palestinian village houses and reshape the place: "It was clear to us that we must immediately get rid of all those village houses, leaning on each other and made of mud and straw."[87]

Kfar Daniel was established on the site of the depopulated village of Daniyal; in a book released by the moshav on its fiftieth anniversary, the replacement of the old houses by new ones was described as an improvement to the landscape: "In recent years, the appearance of the village has changed completely. The handsome stone houses replacing the Arab ones are without a doubt the most outstanding change for the better we have had."[88]

Other communities, however, seem to be admiring the village landscape, stressing its abundance of vegetation, as does a member of kibbutz Karmia: "On one of our walks, we've reached what used to be the village of 'Hiribya.' The area was then covered in orchards, vineyards and citrus groves, and seemed like heaven on earth."[89] The same writer expresses remorse over the damage to this landscape done by the establishment of the kibbutz: "In the first days, a Jewish National Fund tractor was at work, ripping out orchards and citrus groves to create a terrain for the building of the kibbutz. . . . The heart ached for every tree that was needed to be uprooted, and the misgivings were great: What should be uprooted? What should be preserved?"[90]

Kibbutz Erez also describes its establishment as a blow to the local landscape of the village of Dimra, defined as "natural," in a text stressing the aesthetic damage it sustained: "Orchards that surrounded the villagers' homes, with sycamores, mulberry, apricots, plums and almonds, figs, and with old grapevines stringing along the sycamores here and there. The family boundaries were marked with prickly pear hedges around the plots. A natural landscape that we broke into in order to set up our community, and obviously—disfigured its appearance with roads and structures."[91]

Some communities decided to preserve parts of the "Arab" landscape within their territory. For instance, members of Karmia wrote: "We have kept the olive grove in the middle of the kibbutz," and kibbutz Beit Ha'Emek, according to its writings, "was built partly within an olive grove, while trying to preserve it without uprooting trees."[92] The artists of 'Ein Hod, which has preserved the Palestinian village more or less intact, praise on their website in great detail the beauty and uniqueness of the village, its agricultural and built-up landscape, without mentioning that it is a Palestinian village:

> Ein Hod is characterized by the special setting of a village sitting on a hillside, surrounded by olive groves, . . . the village has managed to preserve its original, historic nature and the romantic and simple charm of Israel in its first years of independence. . . . One can still discern in the old structures the many textures and architectural forms of earlier occupants—from the Christian Crusades to the Turkish Empire. The roads and byways, a mixture of ancient and modern, all add to a very special atmosphere. . . . natural Mediterranean

gardens of olive, pomegranate almond and carob trees, grape vines and figs. Ein Hod has remained a nature reserve, preserving the biblical flora of ancient Israel—a perfect environment for the creative muse.[93]

Slyomovics noticed that the residents of 'Ein Hod tend to see the remains of the Palestinian village as part of nature. She says they see the Palestinian ruins as "both primitive and ancient features of the landscape," "pictures of purely natural existence," and an "element of the landscape." She even found that 'Ein Hod artists laud the "ruined beauty" of the Palestinian ruins and perceive them as a "piece of art" they have managed to salvage from Israeli bulldozers. Other objects found in the village from the Palestinian past, such as household items, are defined by the 'Ein Hod residents as aesthetic works of art, rather than archaeological or scientific findings.[94]

Part of the vision professed by the Jewish communities established on sites of depopulated Palestinian villages was the establishment of a modern, well-planned community, replacing the Palestinian village that they perceived as backward. This aspiration is manifest in kibbutz Yir'on newsletters from different times: "Our basic premise is that we want and do our best to turn our community as quickly as possible from a partially demolished Arab village into a handsome, planned Hebrew village."[95]

On kibbutz Nachsholim, the village's backwardness is blamed for the difficulties encountered by the community in its early years. The dispossession of the original residents is not mentioned in the text, which emphasizes the frustration caused by the stalling of the urge to build and create: "The rough conditions in the village nearly made us despair. . . . The dilapidated houses and the landscape of the backward village overshadowed everything we've created so far. The village stalled all pursuit of our plans, and had caused many members to depart."[96]

Harming the Arab landscape, even if not always seen by the settlers as desirable, was perceived as necessary for the sake of progress. Kibbutz Karmia, which had earlier expressed misgivings about the uprooting of the village orchards, went on to say: "At last, the recognition of the need for creating modern, mechanized agriculture became predominant, and for that end it was necessary to uproot the old and begin everything anew."[97]

The first newsletter of kibbutz Yir'on compares the uprooting of the villagers of Saliha and the settling of kibbutz members in their stead to the processes described in John Steinbeck's *The Grapes of Wrath*. According to the newsletter, "because of the mechanization by which also we build our homes, thousands of peasants were driven off their ancestral lands."[98] The author describes the modernization and mechanization brought by the kibbutz as an advantage over the earlier residents:

An ordinary Arab village stood here. . . . Only a year ago, simple, primitive people lived here, working their land with oxen and donkeys and ploughs, drinking from rainwater cisterns. . . . And now we have come, young, enthusiastic and inexperienced men and women. In their homes we settled and their fields we are about to work. And all our hopes for the revival of that land lie on the multitude of agricultural machines, on possibilities of intensive cultivation and carrying water through pipes.[99]

Over the years, the Jewish communities were expressing the satisfaction they found with their work to transform their place of settlement from backward or desolate, to modern. So asks a kibbutz Sasa publication: "What has changed? Then we arrived at an abandoned village. Today, we are developing a modern, flourishing settlement. Then we lived in abandoned houses. . . . Today we live with children in a spacious apartment."[100]

And a newsletter of kibbutz Lehavot Ḥaviva says: "The same exposed, barren hill which bore the miserable shacks upon it as the only testimony to human life is acquiring a cultural character and is slowly becoming a modern agricultural settlement."[101] The Palestinian village of al-Jalama, on the land of which the kibbutz was established, is not explicitly mentioned here and is portrayed as the antithesis of culture and modernity.

References to the Original Palestinian Villagers

In some cases, Jewish community members described encounters with the villagers, which occurred near the beginning of the Jewish settlement on the sites. A member of kibbutz Yir'on describes an encounter with residents of Saliha who remained in the village after it was mostly depopulated and before the kibbutz was built on its site. The recollection is informative, not displaying much emotional baggage one way or another: "When we wandered along the narrow paths, we came upon an old couple. They told me they are among the residents of the village and that everyone else fled across the border for fear of the Jews. . . . When we came to the village with a truck and all the gear to plant the kibbutz, we did not find the old couple from the village here anymore."[102]

In Sasa, however, a publication describes a meeting with refugees of Sa'sa', along with the embarrassment felt by the kibbutz member: "One day we were in Budia' and saw peasants working on the other side of the border. . . . [They] spoke to us in Hebrew. It turned out they were residents of Sa'sa' who ran away in 1948 after the occupation of the village. [They] asked me what there is in Sa'sa' today. It was an interesting conversation but a little embarrassing, and obviously—I did not have a pleasant feeling."[103]

For residents of Kerem Maharal, a few Circassian families remaining in the village of Ijzim after its occupation were seen as a delaying factor for the establishment of the moshav there. The moshav's book states: "After a meeting with the effendi, these were evicted, and the road to our settling there was wide open."[104]

In the Jewish communities' writings, most of the references to meetings with the displaced villagers after settling on their land appear in the context of the refugees' attempts to return to the country and to their former villages, in the early years of the state. A member of moshav Ge'alia describes the residents of the village on which the moshav was built, coming back to retrieve the belongings they had left behind: "[In] those days there were many infiltration incidents, mainly by former residents of the village. For when we came to the village, we found it as the Arabs left it during their flight. The beds were upset and there were food remains on the tables. The Arabs, who had surely hidden foodstuff and valuables around the village, would come at night to dig in their hideaways."[105]

The author goes on to add that while they were at it, the refugees were also stealing from the new residents. "The infiltrators, as they came to look in their hiding places did not refuse themselves, by the way, reaching out for our property."[106] In the overview of moshav Kerem Ben Zimra, the word "thievery" is even used to describe the refugees' attempt to harvest their own crops, which were confiscated from them. "Infiltration," the moshav said, was carried out "to steal grapes and olives from the groves around the village."[107]

In some cases the movement of refugees around the settlements established on their villages was perceived as threatening and frightening: "The previous residents used to pass through the area, taking into the [Gaza] Strip some crops and harvests from the abandoned fields and orchards, construction materials, doors, windows and furniture from the abandoned homes. The movement was large and threatening. The movement to the village of 'Hiribya' . . . was well-felt."[108]

Another member of a moshav recounts: "I could not close an eye the entire night. With a half-cocked rifle I was lying on my bed, imagining the people of that village, who had fled in fear and are probably not too far away, awaiting the first chance to return to their village, to their homes . . . what shall we do if some of the younger ones mustered the courage to come here in the night, exact vengeance and escape."[109]

In some communities, members came across former residents of their villages and treated them according to policy dictated by the Israeli army. The members of kibbutz Karmia were employed by the army in catching the refugees for pay. They even call this, in their writings, "the first 'economic branch' of the kibbutz." As they write about this practice, they refer to the uprooted villagers as "infiltrators" and "thieves," not mentioning they were refugees from the same area: "There were many infiltrators . . . they would come to steal citrus fruit at night and return to Gaza loaded with loot . . . We guarded the area of the kibbutz from them . . . taking captives and bringing them to the kibbutz, and the army would collect them in the morning and pay us . . . there was a sort of a "jailhouse" on the kibbutz—a small tin shack . . . we would hold the captives there until the army would take them away."[110]

The publication adds that in some cases these attempts at arresting the "infiltrators" would end with shooting at and even killing them: "Nearly every night, we would go out on ambushes by the sea shore, to stop smugglers and thieves. . . . You come out with your weapon and you shoot, if you did not shoot they would, and more than once some smugglers were killed and the entire business was not that pleasant."[111]

This occurred in other communities as well, like moshav Ge'alia: "Sometimes while on guard we would come across those Arabs and there would even be fire exchanges between us. . . . We once killed an infiltrator who was over two meters tall."[112]

These references reflect the common Israeli discourse and practice regarding the Palestinian refugees who tried to return to their lands in the years following their uprooting but were pushed back by armed force.[113]

Both early and late publications by the communities rarely refer to what the refugees had endured since being forced to flee. Similarly, according to Ronnie Kochavi-Nehab, kibbutz anniversary books only rarely mention the fate of the Arab residents after they were displaced.[114] I found a few exceptions, in which the kibbutzim quote the village refugees, with whom they made contact decades after the displacement. Kibbutz Erez describes meetings it initiated with the refugees of Dimra, who were displaced to the Gaza Strip, after the strip was occupied by Israel in 1967, and the feelings these meetings stirred in members of the kibbutz: "The first meetings with the previous residents were not pleasant. Suddenly, an invasion of strangers into our home. Yesterday's enemies are peeking in every direction and finger-pointing at every corner and every tree as their assets. It invokes in some of us feelings of guilt and responsibility towards them. But it also invokes an urge to push them away."[115]

Questions provoked by the meeting among the kibbutz members, who wanted to learn more about the village and its residents, are also described. For example: "What was here in the village before / how did they live in Dimra and in nearby villages / what was their relationship with the Jewish communities / how did the trade links work / what characterized each village? . . . when the dominant question is—why did they abandon the village in the War of Liberation? . . . how do they live today in the refugee camps? . . . and what are their expectations of the future?"[116]

The book includes verbatim records of conversations with the son of the Mukhtar of Dimra and another resident of the village, who visited the kibbutz and answered questions of kibbutz members, recalling the life in the village of the past, explaining the events of 1948 in it and describing their life since their uprooting.

A kibbutz Megiddo newsletter from 2000 describes the documentary *Rain of 1949*, directed in 1994 by kibbutz native Ilan Yagoda. The film presents the Palestinian refugees of al-Lajjun, displaced to nearby villages within Israel and to the West Bank, along the Holocaust survivors who came to build a new home on the site of the former village. The newsletter quotes responses from descendants of the village refugees, speaking of their pain due to the displacement and the establishment of the kibbutz on their site, wondering what kind of a connection exists between the new settlers and their own fathers' lands and orchards. The newsletter also quotes responses of veteran kibbutz members, mentioning battles that took place in the area, claiming that the villagers were not deported but just moved a few miles away, and saying that the place was empty when they came to settle it.[117]

Most communities do not speak of the present-day location of the village's refugees since its depopulation. A twentieth-anniversary newsletter of kibbutz Beit Guvrin, for example, states: "The Arabs of the area felt the approaching end, packed up their belongings and ran as fast as they could."[118] Where did they go? The newsletter does not say. Of the few publications that do mention the refugees' whereabouts, most do so only by casual reference, stressing not so much their plight as, for instance, the bothersome "infiltrations." A newsletter of kibbutz Yir'on notes: "No infiltrations. The refugees were moved into Lebanon."[119] The exceptions are moshav Ya'ad and kibbutz Erez, which detail the histories of Mi'ar and Dimra, including oral testimonies from the villages' refugees, and note their whereabouts since displacement.

Ambivalence and Misgivings on Living in a Depopulated Village

Ronnie Kochavi-Nehab finds that kibbutz jubilee books "nearly never express moral qualms subversive to the accepted Zionist narrative." She explains this by the gap "between the stated ideology of the kibbutzim on equality, brotherhood of nations, and democratic humanism on the one hand, and the reality forced upon the kibbutz as part of the Israeli society on the other." She also believes that the issue is silenced in the jubilee books because it is controversial and therefore inappropriate for such a celebratory occasion.[120] The publications I reviewed include personal texts expressing deep misgivings and ambivalence on settling into homes of refugees, alongside texts that ignore the entire matter.

In this context there is a considerable difference between the writings of the kibbutzim and the moshavim: writings by some of the kibbutzim discuss moral dilemmas about living in a depopulated village, while such dilemmas are absent from the writings of the moshavim. The kibbutzim constituted ideologically motivated communities of socialist convictions, and their members often discussed questions of values, justice, equality, and morality among themselves. By contrast, the moshavim, as a rule, were not characterized by social or political ideologies and members did not engage as a group in broad social questions. The kibbutzim also used to discuss such questions in depth in writing, and in general have produced more literature than the moshavim.

Publications produced by moshavim built on depopulated villages express no reservations about living in homes quite recently inhabited by other people, or moral questions about living in a village whose residents were dispossessed and turned into refugees. However, in books published by the Moshavim Movement, some moshav members express uneasiness about living in such homes. An immigrant couple from Yugoslavia, who lived in "a spacious home of stone" allocated to them in a moshav set up in a depopulated village, complain: "We cannot live in this home. Night after night we feel like the previous owner is standing behind the window. We want our own home, built with our own hands, even if it's just a shack."[121]

Another moshav member argues: "The settler feeling toward the abandoned village was the same as the feeling towards a used garment, which is never loved by any self-respecting person, no matter how fine the cloth may be."[122]

A Moshavim Movement activist reports on a visit to the home of an Eastern European immigrant living in an "abandoned village" in the western Galilee:

> I asked him how he feels in this spacious Arab house made available to him in this village. He replied: You touched upon a painful problem. This is actually what burdens me here. The flat here may be spacious, but what can I do, I do not feel in it as if it was my own. I would rather live in a more humble place but one that I've built with my own hands. You see, this house is foreign to me. I will always feel in it like an unwanted guest.[123]

In none of these cases, however, is the uncomfortable feeling explicitly attributed to guilt or moral misgivings. Writings of kibbutz members, on the other hand, reveal emotional difficulties in view of the destruction and depopulation of the village on which they settled. A member of Yir'on writes in a newsletter issued by the kibbutz on the jubilee of its founding: "When we reached the place where Yir'on was to be established . . .—the Arab village induced a gloomy mood in me. It was a place that one could see had been abandoned not so long ago, and many houses displayed signs of looting."[124]

A member of kibbutz Kabri recalls a trip to the Galilee on the eve of the War of 1948, in which stones were thrown at her family near the village of al-Kabri. Two years later, she settled on the kibbutz established by the village site. In a kibbutz newsletter fifty years later she recalls: "I found myself in the exact same place . . . in the village of Kabri. Exactly the same place, but without a living soul. The village looked as if it had just been abandoned. It was a hard feeling . . . but we were promised we'll be settled in a beautiful place upon a hill with a view to the sea. You cannot see any sea from the village."[125]

In a book about the first years of kibbutz Kabri, one of its members expressed feelings of sorrow and empathy with the demolition of al-Kabri and the displacement of its villagers:

> When you see what happened to the Arab village of Kabri, which stood where it did for hundreds of years, and was a home to people and children, and here it stands devastated and desolate and all its residents scattered all over, your heart aches and you feel how nakedly tragic this is. . . . Destroyed houses, with slanting roofs, here and there pieces of furniture that somehow were saved from being crushed. You feel a sort of pang in the heart.[126]

Before setting up Kabri, its members lived on kibbutz Beit Ha'Arava, established in 1939 just north of the Dead Sea. The kibbutz was evacuated in 1948, following the invasion of the area by Jordanian army units, and its members were acknowledged as refugees by UNRWA—just like the Palestinian refugees. In their newsletters the Kabri members often speak of their displacement from their original kibbutz and the pain and distress it caused them. However, the kibbutz members rarely draw a comparison with the plight of the villagers of al-Kabri; an implicit comparison can be found in a book on the founding of the kibbutz: "pangs in the heart, when you came across a toy or simple women's jewelry, and felt that here human dreams had been demolished, and recalled what you yourself had left behind."[127] The author acknowledges the loss of the villagers of al-Kabri and expresses his sorrow over it, without linking it to the establishment of the kibbutz on a part of the village site or expressing qualms or a moral dilemma.

In some kibbutzim, members took note of the contradiction between their universal ideology and the act of settling on property taken from refugees. This moral dilemma is expressed only by founding members of the kibbutz. It appears in writings of the time, reflecting questions that concerned members then, or in later writings, as recollections by veterans about the early days. Almost nothing is said on that matter by the second and third generations of the kibbutzim, neither in response to the story of the veterans nor as expressions of their own feelings and thoughts about the depopulated village in which they live.

In a collection of memoirs published by kibbutz Karmia on its thirty-fifth anniversary, one of the members writes that among the kibbutz members there were "pretty harsh arguments" about the members arresting "infiltrators" for the army—an activity that involved shooting at the refugees and sometimes even killing them. "This did not always sit well with our political outlook at the time," he says.[128] However, in the same publication some members recall their feelings about settling on the depopulated village of Hiribya, and all but one voice complete acceptance of the situation. Only in one case does a member express some emotional difficulty: "Emotionally, there were not problems at first about the Arabs. Later, when we went out to guard, infiltrators who had been villagers entered, and we had a problem about it—we basically dispossessed them."[129]

The members of kibbutz Yir'on maintained a universal socialist ideology that they often discussed in their newsletters. In the opening page of their very first issue, they speak of themselves as "breathing mountain air, carrying forth freedom and justice for man and working our land."[130] In an article titled "Death in Saliha—Life in Yir'on," published in the second issue of the kibbutz newsletter in late 1949, one member brings up the clash between that ideology and the brutal act of the depopulation of Saliha:

> The facts are that men, women, old people and babies were murdered, villages were destroyed and burned, without justification. . . . There will only be atonement when those guilty of murder will be judged and when the houses and the lands of the people of Saliha will be returned to them . . . but who but us, sitting upon skulls and ruins and eating from the "abandoned land," who but us knows that none of this will ever come to pass? And how can Yir'on be a memorial to *all* its dead, who fought each other and died by each other's hand? What a clash! What a horrific contradiction! Can Yir'on be much of a comfort to man and world when hundreds of its residents are in exile? . . . We, who "uphold brotherhood of nations and faith in man," will we be silent and will try to find atonement for that great crime, in ourselves? As if a community can atone for its crime by building a palace on the land of Naboth the Jezreelite! Is this what we call rising above all national, racial and religious barriers?[131]

This is a lonely voice confronting the issue in the kibbutz writings, and no further debate followed in later issues of the newsletter.

Unlike all other communities covered in this research, the members of Sasa have spent considerable time in their writings on the moral questions arising from building their kibbutz on the depopulated village of Sa'sa'. They have discussed it and have expressed their feelings and opinions on the matter on several occasions. In some cases—in early as well as late publications—they bring up what they see as a fundamental contradiction between their ideology of building a new and just society and its implementation on the site of a depopulated village: "I am thinking of the deserted village of Sasa, which we entered so proudly and energetically this morning, and the lives of the Arabs, who lived here. I wandered through some of the hovels, looked at the overturned jugs, grain, books, baby shoes, and smelt the smell of destruction. . . . Are we also destroying, pillaging, being cruel . . . , with our ideals and our refusals to stoop to the world's rottenness?"[132]

And elsewhere:

> Living in an Arab village, in homes of people who had left in an awful hurry, a short time before we arrived. . . . Here we were, American Jewish pioneers, come to help build a new homeland and create a new society. . . . We were bred

on American fair play, and Hashomer Hatsa'ir belief in bi-nationalism, living in harmony with our Arab brothers. It was bad enough living in the village where you could almost feel their presence, where part of their possessions were left behind, with their store rooms filled with last season's crop. . . . If all this was not enough to burst our ideological bubble, there was a problem of what to do with the mosque."[133]

Further elaboration on the mosque dilemma indicates the misgivings that split the members of the kibbutz:

The issue divided us into two camps. A basic view of one side . . . was "everything of value we acquired that was found in the village, should be sold. Everything we kept should be paid for and all the money should be sent to some Arab refugee fund." This view, I felt, was in contradiction of us being here. Another expression in the same direction came from another person, . . . [who] stated he would post himself in the mosque, preventing it from being destroyed. . . . For me the choice was between leaving Sasa or remaining. . . . It was nothing new to us we had been living in what was previously an Arab village, so why the hesitation now? People forget about the practiced and get carried with ideological trends.[134]

In a Passover Haggadah prepared in Sasa, the kibbutz dedicates the section on the bitter herbs, traditionally dedicated to the pain endured by the Israelites as slaves in Egypt, to the pain of displacement endured by the residents of Palestinian Sa'sa', and to Sasa's moral qualms:

Our herb is a very bitter one and even if we should succeed in removing all other physical traces of it, its taste will linger. Once there was an Arab village here. . . . The fields we tend today were tended by others—one year ago. . . . And when we came the desolation of their lives cried to us through the ruins they left behind. . . . What gives us the right to reap the fruits of trees we have not planted, to take shelter in houses we have not built, to till the soil preserved by the sweat of foreign hands? On what moral grounds shall we stand when we take ourselves to court?[135]

Justifying the Settlement of Depopulated Villages

The internal discussion among kibbutzim members over moral aspects of their settlement on a depopulated village notwithstanding, even the critics remain on the kibbutz. Their publications list a variety of justifications for this choice. One argument raised by kibbutz Sasa in favor of staying at Sa'sa' draws on the lessons learned by the members from the Holocaust: "those who died in camps and battles bequeath to us our life here."[136]

In general, new communities comprising Holocaust survivors write in great detail about the catastrophe they had endured in Europe and the new life they were determined to create in Israel. Members of kibbutz Megiddo, established in part on the site of the village of al-Lajjun by partisans and Holocaust survivors from Poland and Hungary, write: "We, the remaining survivors of ghettos and concentration camps, fighters for the dignity of nation and man, forest fighters and partisans, we stand here today building a home."[137]

The foundation scroll of kibbutz Netzer Sereni, founded near the site of the village of Bir Salim by survivors of the Auschwitz and Buchenwald extermination camps, was written in June 1950 and reads: "In this place we begin building a permanent spot for our group. A kibbutz of the remainder of the destroyed European Jewry is striking root in the homeland, a sapling of the cut down trunk has been planted. . . . Great is the suffering that we suffered, and our aspiration was to find rest and inheritance on our forefathers' land."[138]

In these cases and others, the Holocaust is not referenced in the context of settling in the Palestinian village. However, the words seem to imply that those people, who had survived the Nazis and lost everything not too long ago, were entirely preoccupied with overcoming the horror of the past by belonging to a group of pioneers building a new home and a new homeland, and had no ability to open their hearts to those who lost their home and land as a result.

Another sort of argument sought to justify the depopulation of the Palestinian villages and their settlement by Jews, based on events of the 1948 war: several members of kibbutz Karmia justify their settling on the site of Hiribya by evoking the choice the Palestinians had allegedly made to escape from the village and to abandon it:

> I did not feel like I was stealing from others, I did not feel any guilt at all . . . those who had lived in the kibbutz area had abandoned their homes and fled, there was hardly anything left here—maybe shacks and huts but no belongings left at all.
> . . . There were homes here, Arab huts actually. It did not bother me, they fled and it was their fault, they had listened to the Mufti [a Palestinian leader] and I do not pity them.
> . . . They told us that the Arabs who were here were asked whether they wanted to stay, and they preferred to leave . . . this is what we were told. It was in the 1950s.
> . . . I did not feel like I took something that belonged to the Arabs. They ran away, and they fought us . . . we felt at peace with our location and with the kibbutz, but we knew we were living on an Arab village.[139]

The airborne bombing and machine-gunning of the village of Hiribya are not mentioned in the Karmia residents' version of what took place in their area in 1948.[140]

One of Megiddo's founders justifies his clear conscience regarding the displacement of the residents of al-Lajjun and the establishment of the kibbutz on the same site, while avoiding any reference to the attack on the village and the demolition of twenty-seven of its homes by the Haganah:[141] "No one expelled the residents here . . . the residents of Lajjun were looking for a quieter place and moved over only six kilometers from here, to Umm al-Fahm. . . . When we came here there was not a single living soul here. The Jewish National Fund bought the lands, which were in a dire state."[142]

At times, the justification for the depopulation of the villages is presented with empathy toward their plight. Hence, after presenting what he calls the "tragedy" of the depopulation of al-Kabri, the same Kabri member justifies what had happened by invoking the violence used by some of the villagers in 1948, and concludes that the situation was the inevitable result of war:

> In most wars everyone pays the price, with both life and property. It has always been the case. We have paid the price of the War of Liberation, like everyone else, with both. . . . In fact the village was abandoned by its residents after a murderous assault by the locals on the convoy trying to break through the siege on kibbutz Yeḥiʻam, a siege laid by the villagers to the road from Nahariya. Maybe some of the villagers did not support the action or did not take an active part in it, but "when the fire begins to burn it burns everything, damp and dry."[143]

Having described the loss suffered by the villagers of Saʻsaʻ and the moral questions it raises for the kibbutz, the members of Sasa conclude that they had to choose whether to stay in Sasa or leave. They decided to stay. One member of Sasa writes: "We have moved into Sasa; it is ours; we are responsible for our acts. . . . But do we have an alternative, can we step aside, refuse to be morally sullied by Sasa and demand some other section of our homeland on which to build our homes? I do not think so.[144]

The members of Sasa go on and explain their decision to stay: "We are not responsible for this cruel and forced contradiction; we would prefer to disown it if we could; we bear no hatred towards the Arab workers and peasants. But we have been forced into a position where we must fight for our lives and the lives of our people, and today life is largely determined by frontiers, and frontiers must be defended no matter the price. We do not have the right to shunt this physical and moral and political responsibility off on others."[145]

The controversy in Sasa over the fate of the Saʻsaʻ mosque notwithstanding, eventually the mosque was demolished by the IDF. Sasa members retroactively justify both this act and their decision to remain: "The blowing [up] of the mosque has had its effect on us. . . . Most of us agree now that it had to be done. . . . It would have been a useless gesture to preserve this symbol of a population which showed itself to be, when one views the thing factually and unsentimentally, our hardened enemies whom we have no intention of permitting to return."[146]

The Passover Haggadah, too, provides several justifications for the decision to remain in Sasa, based on the community's faith in the Zionist way:

> Because we have taken upon ourselves the task of pioneering . . . , [which] is more than the romantic notion of coming to a clean untouched land and planting one's own clean fresh seeds. Because building a homeland requires more than physical sacrifice . . .—it requires a spiritual struggle and a spiritual sacrifice. Because we must learn to translate our final ideology into the reality of a nation's fight for existence, and if that reality should require the accomplishment of such tasks, which are painful to us, all the more will it strengthen us. And only we can camp on borders. Because once a Jewish community stood here and a Jewish community will again arise. . . . Because we, American Jewish youth must learn to feel ties to this land—Israel—and to our ancestors, and in defending and building on this same soil, Sasa, we will find those ties.[147]

The dominant Zionist ideology, which sees Judaizing the land as an incontrovertible goal and rejects any alternative—such as the binational arrangement espoused by the political movement to which the kibbutz was affiliated—was taken up wholesale by the members of Sasa and overruled all their doubts and qualms. When talking of a "sacrifice," members of the kibbutz spoke of the moral sacrifice they themselves were being called to make, ignoring in this context the heavy price the Palestinians were forced to pay for a cause that was not their own.

Susan Slyomovics lists other justifications—which she calls typical justifications employed to support Zionism—brought up by the residents of 'Ein Hod for settling in a depopulated Palestinian village: casting contemporary Jews as descendants of historical, biblical Jews; claims that the country had been empty or abandoned or neglected by the Arabs who lived in it, awaiting its repopulation; and alluding to the shared fate of Jews and Palestinians—the Jews being refugees from Europe and the Arab world. She also finds that the 'Ein Hod residents use "rewritings of history" to mistakenly conclude that the Arabs were as newly arrived as the Israeli Jews, and no more authentic or local than the latter. The Jewish residents of 'Ein Hod also stress their right to live in the village by presenting the Arabs of 'Ayn Hawd as descendants of biblical Jews converted to Islam, as descendants of Crusaders, or as recent immigrants from other parts of the Arab world.[148]

Along with their presentation of the decision to stay in Sasa and their justifications for that, the members of the kibbutz also offer some ways to cope with the moral dilemma this decision entailed. A poem in the kibbutz Haggadah advises to close one's eyes to the pain and concentrate on the daily life and the making of the community:

> Not bitter but rank / is our once hallowed ground / And blood too stains our hands. / . . . Babies shoes need no explaining / A civilization gone in one

blow / And we unknowingly dream. / To dream perhaps will heal the wounds / that now lie gaping open. / But vivid ever the pain of war / and painful ever the sight of death / and so we shame seeing nought / a painless dope for our daily lives— / and we go on building.[149]

One of the authors suggests covering the ruins with trees: "The whole appearance of the village has undergone a transformation. It's now a mass of ruins, and yet most of us agree it's better this way. . . . Bring now the bulldozers and let's plant trees!"[150]

The Haggadah calls for idealist universal activity against evil: "Oh my brothers, of all the strains and shades of mankind . . . , we cry out to all of you: this is our pain, this is our burden—our hands are unclean. . . . Let us join together and tear away our shame, let us build a new world where ruined villages will not stand in mute protest against the sky!"[151]

Another writer expresses the universal ideology, stressing that it also applies to the Arab residents of the land: "The kibbutz that we build at Sasa will be dedicated not only to the renaissance of our own people but to mankind and the future of mankind. . . . This includes our Arab neighbors."[152]

Another exceptional—and more recent—case of a Jewish community demonstrating active empathy with the Palestinian refugees of the village on the lands on which it has settled, voicing reservations against the demolition of its remains and willingness to discuss alternatives, is that of moshav Ya'ad. The founders of Ya'ad had built it in 1974 on lands of the village of Mi'ar in the Lower Galilee, near the village remains. In 2002, a plan was approved to expand the community by building a new neighborhood on the location of the remains of Mi'ar and its cemetery. In July 2003, several members of the moshav submitted their objections to the plan to the District Planning and Construction Committee, alongside objections by the village refugees, who live in other villages nearby, and by Zochrot—an Israeli association devoted to educating the Israeli public about the Palestinian Nakba.

In their objection, Ya'ad members state, among other things, that "building on the ruins of the village and next to its cemetery, as a unilateral act, is a hardhearted act that ignores the pain of the other, the catastrophe he experienced and his need for remembrance." The JNF, too, filed an objection to the plan, because of a public forest way running through the area where the new neighborhood was to be built.[153]

In February 2004, the committee decided to partly accept the objections and reduce the construction in the area near the village cemetery. As a result of negotiations with the exiled villagers, the Ya'ad residents gave up several more houses, in exchange for the villagers withdrawing their appeal against the committee decision, a process that would have delayed new construction in Ya'ad for years.

As part of this process, a relationship was established between some Ya'ad residents and villagers of Mi'ar. The joint group fenced the cemetery of the village in order to protect it but failed to persuade the majority of Ya'ad members to place an explanatory sign there.

* * *

The moral dilemmas of the founders of kibbutz Sasa in 1949 and the early 1950s, in the face of the dispossession and displacement of the villagers of Sa'sa', and the sensitivity of residents of Ya'ad to potential damages to the ruins of Mi'ar more recently, are both exceptions to the rule in the attitudes of Jewish communities regarding the Palestinian villages on the lands and sites on which they had been established.

By and large, based on their writings, the members of these communities voice acceptance of and live in peace with the act of settlement in a village whose residents were dispossessed and turned into refugees. Usually they see the villages simply as abandoned, ruined places they need to restore and rebuild, using the remains left in place. The Jewish residents tend to ignore the reasons for the destruction of the village and the absence of its original inhabitants, as well as the latter's subsequent fate. The few who acknowledge the fact of dispossession see it at best as an undesirable, yet inevitable result of a national conflict and war. When speaking of the villages, it seems that members of all kibbutzim and moshavim—even those belonging to political movements that upheld the idea of binationalism and the return of refugees—have internalized the hegemonic Israeli narrative, which lays the blame for the war and its results, including the refugee problem, on the Palestinians themselves, while refusing to allow their return to their homes. This narrative does not see any alternative but the establishment of a Jewish state in the place of the former inhabitants of the land, on top of their property, while denying any responsibility for them and for their fate.

Most of the early Jewish settlers on Palestinian village sites were themselves refugees or exiles who tried to cope with the loss of the world they had left behind. Their settlement in the new place was fraught with difficulties and struggles for survival. The spirit of revolutionary Zionism that swept many of them, especially members of the kibbutzim, drove them even more decisively to concentrate on the new world they were building. We may assume all this did not leave much space to consider or even notice others who had lost their homes and their world. It is probably not coincidental that deliberation on moral dilemmas took place mainly among members of a kibbutz like Sasa, who had come to Israel out of Zionist conviction, from a developed country such as the United States, having experienced no bereavement or persecution before coming to Israel.

Nevertheless, coping with the displacement of the villagers is almost exclusively confined to the writings of the first generation of the settlers, who suffered from the difficulties and distress of striking root in a new environment. Their successors, whose lives are much more comfortable, do not address the issue, according to the writings that have been surveyed. Unlike the founders, the following generations did not usually need to confront the issue in their daily lives: they did not have to decide the fate of physical remains of the Palestinian village, as in the case of Kibbutz Sasa and the Sa'sa' mosque. They also did not have to cope with attempts by refugees to return to their villages. The fact of living in a space that was once a Palestinian village is self-evident and well known to them, a part of events that happened long ago. They do not deny it, but neither do they struggle with it nor engage with it in their writings.

As in Sasa, the second exceptional case—that of Ya'ad—might also be explained by looking at the different background of its residents: unlike other rural settlements mentioned here, which were established shortly after the 1948 war, mostly by refugees from Europe or from Arab countries, Ya'ad was established in 1974 by graduates of the computer science and engineering faculty at the Technion, the Israeli Institute of Technology. This different background of the residents of Ya'ad might explain the exceptional sensitivity some of them showed in the face of a plan that would possibly have hurt Mi'ar's refugees, even at the expense of future expansion of their Jewish community.

4 Naming and Mapping the Depopulated Village Sites

What is the name of this place? A few years ago there was a place and it had a name. The place is lost and the name is lost. What is left? At first, a name torn out of a place. Soon, that, too, is erased. Neither place nor name....

—S. Yizhar, "The Silence of the Villages," *Stories of a Plain*

NAMING A PLACE and presenting it on a map is an acknowledgment of its presence in the landscape, its historical importance, and its cultural significance. Most of the sites of depopulated Palestinian villages were never granted an official name in Israel, even though the traces of many still remain in the landscape, and despite the Israeli pretension of naming any geographical object in sight, including ruins. Even where names were given to village sites, in most cases the Arab name was not recognized: if the Arab name preserved a biblical name, that earlier name was restored as the official name; in other cases, village sites were given Hebraized names, which usually ignored the content of the Arab names and the cultural world that they reflect. Sometimes the new names were even devoid of any meaning in Hebrew.

The majority of the depopulated village sites appear on official Israeli maps but generally in a diminished fashion—as anonymous, nameless locales, as sites with Hebrew or Hebraized names that blur their Arab identity, or as meaningless ruins, with no reference to the date of their demolition. Most of the villages that retain visible remains on the terrain have been ignored by mapmakers, in contrast to the latter's manifested policy of mapping every possible object in the landscape.

In most cases when depopulated villages were named and marked on the map, this was thanks to having dwelt on more ancient sites that Israel found it important to emphasize because of the historical periods they represented. The villages themselves were not perceived as historical sites because of their own history, even if they had existed for hundreds of years, and therefore were not seen as worthy of receiving a name and of being shown on the map.

As with other national movements, the Zionist project used mapping and naming as mechanisms for attaining national goals. These acts were a political statement of ownership over places and amounted to the erasure of their previous owners. The struggle over names of sites in the country and their mapping constitutes yet another arena of the Israeli-Palestinian conflict. Renaming places and the Hebraization of the map reflect the profound demographic, political, and cultural transformation Zionism brought about in Palestine/the Land of Israel, and are part of this process.

Naming and Mapping in Israel

> In America they retained vestiges of important Indian tribes or tribes that are still dwelling. This is not the case here. We have nothing to do with the name of a minuscule Bedouin tribe, and we can assign a Hebrew name here.
>
> —Yitzhak Ben Zvi
> At the Negev Committee meeting, September 29, 1949, ISA, GL-22171/6.

In the nineteenth century, British explorers collected some nine thousand Arabic place names in the Land of Israel, which had come into being during a period of over 1,400 years, beginning with the Arab conquest. The names referred to physical and topographic characteristics of the sites, to names of plants and animals, and to the names of leaders or religious figures. About 10 percent of these names had more ancient Greek or Hebrew-Aramaic origins. Many of those were Hebrew names that survived from biblical times and continued to be used by the Arabs, sometimes with slight modifications.[1]

In 1948, on the eve of the establishment of the State of Israel, maps of Palestine printed by the British Mandate showed thousands of Arabic names for communities and geographical sites. Only 5 percent of the names on the map were Hebrew—traditional Hebrew names retained from the distant past and names of the Jewish Zionist communities established up to that point.[2] The latter were selected by the JNF Names Committee, formed in 1925 to bestow Hebrew names on new Jewish communities established by Zionist organizations. By May 1948, the committee had assigned some two hundred community names. In the following three years, up to March 1951—a period characterized by intense settlement activity—it produced two hundred more.[3]

When the state was established, the names of thousands of geographical locations across the country—mountains, hills, springs, and valleys—were still Arabic. The Arabic names were seen by Israel as foreign and negative and as a nuisance that needed to be removed, and it threw itself into work:

> The Negev, half our country, was terrifying with the foreignness of its names, mostly Arabic, and even these [were] mangled and castrated, some meaningless and some of negative, indecent or humiliating content. A foreign aura pervades these names. With the conquest of the Negev and the raising of the Israeli flag in Eilat, the urgent need arose . . . to assign Hebrew names,

to cancel out the foreign sounds and to enrich the Negev map with original names, names close to the heart and the ear of the Hebrew defender and settler of the Negev.[4]

David Ben-Gurion stressed the political meaning he attributed to Hebraizing the names: "We must remove the Arabic names due to political considerations: just as we do not recognize the political ownership of Arabs over the land, we do not recognize their spiritual ownership and their names."[5]

The Negev Committee, formed of cartographers, archaeologists, geographers, and historians, was established in July 1949 and tasked with replacing the Arabic names of geographical sites in the Negev with Hebrew names. Upon accomplishing its role, the committee was also authorized to assign geographical names in the rest of the country. By the time it concluded its work in March 1951, the Negev Committee had assigned 533 new Hebrew names to geographical sites previously known by Arabic names. According to the committee's own records, more than half of the new names were based on the Arabic ones, whether through translation (175 names), choice of a phonetically similar name (150 names), or retention of the Arabic name (8 names). The other names were historical (120 names), alluded to biblical characters (50 names), or were completely new (30 names).[6]

The Hebraization of names of Negev sites was seen as complementary to the military conquest of the area, as Ben-Gurion himself observed: "By granting Hebrew names to all areas of the Negev . . . you have removed the infamy of alienage and foreign tongues from half the State of Israel, and completed the action begun by the Israel Defense Forces: liberating the Negev from a foreign rule. . . . I hope you will continue your work until you redeem the entire land of Israel from the rule of foreign tongues."[7]

As names were being changed from Arabic to Hebrew, Israel began presenting the new names on its maps. The founding of the state saw the formation of the Survey Department—later renamed as Survey of Israel (soi)—as the authority charged with preparing official maps of Israel.[8] The book *50 Years of Mapping Israel*, published in the half-centenary year of both soi and the State of Israel, states that upon its establishment in 1948 the department was tasked with "converting the maps to the Hebrew language." It describes that after the War of 1948 its work was based on "remapping as part of the drive of reconstruction after the war and the demands for accelerated development, which came up in all their weightiness thanks to the absorption of the immigration waves, the preparation of new regions for settlement and the establishment of new communities."[9]

The new Hebrew names produced by the Negev Committee were publicized in the government annual for 1950–1951, together with a Hebrew transliteration of the old Arabic names they replaced. The list was accompanied by a map bearing the Hebrew names. That map was described later on as "a first fruit . . . a Hebrew map of the Negev, cleansed of foreign names, in which every place is called by a Hebrew name."[10] At the same time, the Survey Department produced another map of the Negev, bearing the new Hebrew names and alongside them, in brackets, "the old names, no longer in use"—the Arabic names of the same places.[11] This map was the only one of all official Israeli maps deliberately listing the Arabic names alongside the Hebrew ones that replaced them.

The Government Names Committee (hereafter the Names Committee) was appointed in April 1951 as a merger of the two earlier names committees—the JNF Names Committee and the Negev Committee. The members of the committee, which is active to this day, are JNF officials, members of the Knesset, Interior Ministry officials, historians, archaeologists, geographers, lecturers in the field of "knowing the land," and experts in Arabic. The task of the committee, carried out through three subcommittees, is to determine names for communities, historical sites, and geographical sites—including ruins—across the country. Names already in use prior to the establishment of the committee required its confirmation in order to become official. Naming within cities is outside the committee's purview and is decided by the respective municipalities.

The names confirmed by the committee are recognized as official names in Israel: they appear on governmental publications and are included in official maps produced by the SOI. The SOI is required to include all the names confirmed by the committee in its maps on a scale of 1:50,000 and a selection of them in smaller-scale maps.[12] Early on there were voices on the committee calling to retain the Arabic names on the maps, if only temporarily: at the committee's first session, in April 1951, Yossef Weitz suggested an interim period of printing bilingual maps, until all places on the map were assigned Hebrew names.[13] His proposition was never implemented.

Like the two committees that preceded it, the Names Committee adopted the basic principle of giving priority to "the revival of historical Hebrew names," that is, determining official place names based on the names of historical sites that had existed in the past in the same place, mostly Jewish sites from the biblical or the Mishnaic era. The revival of ancient names was used to prove the connection between the Jewish people and the land and amounted to a statement on the right of the Jewish people to resettle its ancient homeland: "The historical Hebrew names of the places in the Land of Israel are the most faithful testimony that these places belonged to our forefathers since time immemorial, and our rights and claims on these places and the land are ancient, historical ones."[14]

Beyond that, the stress put on historical Jewish and biblical names was used to connect the new Jewish immigrants to the new land, which was foreign to them, by introducing them to the names they recalled from religious practices, from traditions, and from their collective memory.[15]

In a description of an atlas it published later, the Names Committee defined the purpose of the book—and, indirectly, of the committee itself—as the formation of a bond between the space and the history on one side, and the Zionist endeavor on the other: "[The atlas] tangibly expresses that strong bond between the Jewish people and its land . . . [it is] meant to be a fundamental layer . . . in the weaving of the threads that tie the past of our people to the present and future in our renewing state."[16]

In many cases, ancient names were given to places even though the location of the alleged ancient site was controversial. One example is the site of 'Ein 'Evrona, in the south of Israel, named after one of the camping sites of the Israelites following their exodus from Egypt. In other cases, new communities were given the names of ancient ones, although the Names Committee was fully aware that the former were not on the site of the latter. One such example is kibbutz Yotvata, a biblical name of another Israelite camping site in the desert.[17]

The policy determined by the Names Committee (and the Negev Committee before it) regarding Arabic names was to first try to find ancient Jewish names concealed in the Arabic names, and, if they were found, to revive these ancient names and recognize them as official names. "Unidentified Arabic names"— meaning Arabic names not identified as preserving ancient names—were "to be translated if they have reasonable content, or be Judaized by bringing the Arabic sound closer to the Hebrew sound."[18] This policy was based on the assumption that perhaps the Arabic names were mangled versions of ancient Hebrew names after all; however, the policy was also applied to Arabic names that alluded to Arab leaders who bore no relation to Jewish history. Thus, Tall Abu Hurayra, named after one of the prophet Muhammad's companions, was changed to Tel Haror. This new name has no meaning in Hebrew, as is often the case in Hebrew names based on phonetic similarity to the Arabic ones.[19]

Arab communities that remained populated by Arabs after 1948 were largely spared the policy of Judaizing Arabic names. Regarding these, the committee stated that it would not act as a tyrannical state forcing its own language on the local population but would retain the Arabic name as the official name of each community.[20] That decision notwithstanding, communities where a certifiable link to an ancient Jewish settlement could be established were still given Hebrew official names, with the Arabic names following in brackets: Gush Halav (Jish), Shfar'am (Shefa-'Amr), and Peki'in (al-Buqei'a).

New communities established on locations not identified with particular historical sites were given biblical names, names alluding to the War of Independence, and "symbolic names hinting at redemption and resurrection, the ingathering of exiles, striking roots,"[21] as well as "the names of the nation's great figures and leaders, heroes of Israel, pioneers, lovers of the land and its benefactors."[22] An idea of the desired content of a the new names can be gleaned from an appeal issued by the committee to intellectuals, early on in its work, requesting them to provide "a list of suggestions of names for communities that would reflect the stupendous enterprises of our generation—our war for independence, the establishment of the State, the ingathering of exiles, making the desert bloom and acclimatizing into the land."[23]

In an introduction to the settlement atlas it produced in 1999, the Names Committee goes through the source of nearly 1,300 names it had coined in its then 50 years of operation and the messages the names are meant to convey:

> The names of the communities depicted in this atlas express the love of the land of Israel, the history of the land of Israel and the changes that occurred throughout its landscapes and among its dwellers. . . . Among them are historical names originating from Jewish sources, idioms, the flora and fauna, names linked to the values of security and defense, names bound to the history of Zionism and the building of the country, and local names given a Hebrew sound, form or meaning.[24]

Thus, beyond changing the language of the names from Arabic to Hebrew, the new names convey, through their content, ideas and values championed by the national narrative and portrayed vividly the Jewish-Zionist cultural world. The same is also noticeable in street names in cities. Thus, after its conquest in 1948, some of the Arabic street names in Haifa were changed to Hebrew names conveying the Zionist national narrative: Independence Street, Ingathering of Exiles Street, Return of Zion Street, and so on. Maoz Azaryahu observes that "the vanquished did not only lose their homes, but also the right to tell their national story by way of street signs."[25]

Giving Official Names to Depopulated Palestinian Villages

> This is our task—to Judaize the names, and this is what we do.
>
> —Avraham Biran, chairman of the Names Committee, May 1952

Among the thousands of places carrying Arabic names up to 1948 were the hundreds of Palestinian villages that were depopulated and demolished during and after the war. The members of the Names Committee held lengthy discussions on whether these villages should be named at all, and if so, how. As early as late 1948, Yeshayahu Press, then a member of the JNF Settlements Names Committee, wrote to the interior minister of the time: "Many villages within the boundaries of the State of Israel fell into our hands and Jews were settled in their place—and the commonly accepted names must be exchanged for new ones . . . we are obliged to begin 'Judaizing' the map of our country from its foundation."[26]

Most of these villages, however, remained empty, and for some years no policy was determined regarding their names. Some of the different views espoused on this matter by members of the Negev Committee came to light during a discussion in December 1950 concerning the naming of al-Jammama, a destroyed Palestinian village in the northern Negev. Some of the members called for abolishing all names of all depopulated villages and erasing them from the map; Shmuel Yevin supported naming the ruins of a village "only if it is on an ancient settlement which interests us. Then the name should be preserved and Judaized." David Amiran suggested marking the ruins with a name so they could be used as a landmark, and Avraham Biran argued that "Jammama was, and is no more. It should be erased from the map." Eventually, it was decided to give that ruin a meaningless Hebrew name—Ḥurbat Gmama (Gmama ruin)—based on the sound of the Arabic name, but no overall policy on naming depopulated villages was decided.[27]

The members of the later Government Names Committee also wondered what should be done about the names of the depopulated Palestinian village sites, and in 1951 they sought the advice of the then–foreign minister, Moshe Shertok (later Sharet).[28] In response, Ben-Gurion instructed the committee not to include the names of demolished villages on the map: "No name of a place that had been is to be published on the new map. When we establish a new community in the ruined place, we shall assign it a name and publish it on the maps."[29]

Some of the committee members were not happy with that principle. Michael Avi Yona complained: "in some cases the omission of the abandoned names will interfere with the studies of the history of the War of Liberation." Yeshayahu Press argued that "the omission [of the names] will interfere with the exploration of the Land of Israel."[30] Yossef Weitz proposed the creation of a limited-edition transitional map, which would present "the abandoned villages, the ruins, and other places that were not given Hebrew names." The committee endorsed his proposal, but failed to implement it.[31] Eventually, the committee came to the position of Hebraizing the names of ruined villages identified as "historical" and presenting these names on maps. It decided to appeal to the prime minister for that change of policy.[32]

No further decision was made for some months, which delayed the Names Committee's work.[33] In early 1952, Ben-Gurion qualified his earlier decision and "agreed to the assignment of Hebrew names to those ruins of abandoned villages whose inclusion in the map is essential."[34] We might assume that Ben-Gurion referred to village sites with ancient history. Yeshayahu Press opposed the erasure of Arab names, and in a discussion in May 1952 he complained that "the previous, Arabic names are unrecognizable in the new Hebrew names of the ruins."[35] In a memorandum submitted to the committee the following day, he argued that "the Arabic names of the ruined villages should be preserved for reasons of historical and geographical identification" and for practical needs of orientation.[36] His position was not accepted, and the policy that was eventually announced was one of Hebraization of the names of depopulated villages that were to be assigned official names.

In its meetings that year and in the years that followed, the committee discussed from time to time specific depopulated villages and the possibility of assigning them official names. When the members of the committee concluded that a site had an ancient history, they decided to officially assign it its ancient name, which was often preserved within the Arabic name of the corresponding village. Thus the committee created a sense of continuity between the names of the places in biblical times and their present names, mediated by the names of the Arab villages. For example, the committee decreed: "The Arab village of Bayt Nabala is ruined. . . . We will assign this place, which shall serve as a landmark on the geographical map of the land, the historical name of the place, Nevalat, with the additional word Ḥurba [ruin]."[37] In another case, the committee concluded that the depopulated village of al-Bassa had resided on the ancient site of Betzet, and decided that "the abandoned village should bear the name Betzet."[38]

The Hebrew names revived by the committee were in many cases older than the Arabic ones that were lost.[39] However, the importance of preserving historical names was reserved exclusively for Jewish history. When the committee members believed a particular ruined village did not sit on top of an ancient site, they decided not to assign an official name to it or, alternatively, to Hebraize its name. Thus, for example, the committee ignored hundreds of years of Arab history when it declared that "no historical identification was confirmed" for the village of Dayr-al-Dubban, and declined to give it an official name.[40] On the village of al-Dawayima, the committee declared: "The source of the name Dawayima (the name of the abandoned-demolished Arab village) has no base in the Hebrew history perspective. . . . The name should be Judaized . . . and given a Hebrew form."[41]

The committee decided to name the site 'Iyei [ruins of] Beit Admona, and if it came to host a new Jewish settlement—which indeed occurred some years later—to name it Amatzia, after a biblical king of Judea. The committee attached the prefix 'Iyei, meaning "ruins of," to the new names of an additional eleven depopulated villages in the southern half of the country. Thus, for example, the site of the village of 'Iraq Suwaydan became 'Iyei Sidim; Kudna became 'Iyei Kidon; and Dayr Nakhkhas became 'Iyei Naḥash.[42]

The committee tried to keep abreast of changes and developments on the ground, through tours of village sites across the country. At a meeting on August 16, 1959, following one such tour, the committee decided to abolish the official names it had already assigned to dozens of ruins of depopulated villages: "We have found that no traces are left of abandoned villages. Since the objects no longer exist on the ground—the names of the objects to which the committee had attached [the word] "Iyim' [ruins] are also abolished."[43]

An official, detailed list of official names assigned to sites of depopulated Palestinian villages does not exist. The records of names confirmed by the committee list the villages under four different categories: ruin; 'Iyim, ruins, and abandoned villages; historical name; and historical site.[44] The "ruin" category lists different kinds of ruins, from different times, including recently demolished Palestinian villages. In *Toponomasticon,* Naftali Kadmon lists all the names confirmed by the Names Committee since its establishment, according to different categories.[45] The "ruins" category includes 835 names, with no distinction between ruins of Palestinian villages, renamed shortly after their depopulation, and other ruins from older times. The archive material produced by the Names Committee does not include a comprehensive list of all the names assigned by the committee to depopulated villages.

For lack of an official list, part of my research involved creating such a list based on Kadmon's work and comparing it with the full list of depopulated villages, other sources such as official registries and archive materials from the Names Committee, and the work of other scholars.[46] The full list can be found in appendix B. It does not include the names of Israeli communities established atop depopulated villages, which will be discussed separately later.

The list suggests that the majority (302) of Palestinian depopulated villages were never assigned an official name in Israel. Of the 116 village sites that were named, only 69 names were given based on the category of "ruins"—meaning that the names were given to the remains of the Palestinian village itself. In the rest of the cases, the names were assigned to ancient sites underneath or beside the village (24 cases, such as the name Tzipori for the depopulated village of Saffuriyya), or to a mountain, hill, well, or another site at the location of the village (23 cases; for instance, Honen wells, given to the wells of the village of Bayyarat Hannun).

Of the 116 official names given to sites of depopulated villages, only 13 are the original Arabic names of the villages, mostly given to signify the village itself. In half of those cases the Arabic name also has a Hebrew meaning or sound, and was therefore confirmed as an official name; for example, 'Iyei [ruins] Zeita for the village of Zayta, Hurbat [ruin] Beit Natif for the village of Bayt Nattif. The other names given to depopulated villages are Hebraized names based on the Arab ones through phonetic resemblance (55 names) or translation (7 names), or names of ancient sites lying under the villages (41 names).

All in all, 98 demolished villages built atop ancient sites were named, constituting a clear majority of the 116 villages named by the committee.[47] For comparison, of the 302 villages that were not named, only 143—less than half—were on ancient sites. We can conclude that the location of a village on an ancient site increased its chances of being assigned an official name in Israel.

Most of the 41 ancient names given to sites of depopulated villages are Hebrew names, including 34 names preserved in the later Arabic name of the village.

The ancient name of Korazim, for instance, was preserved in Khirbat Karraza, Beit Guvrin in Bayt Jibrin, and so forth.

Fifty-seven additional villages that were given official names are located on ancient sites whose original names are unknown, and they are named by phonetic resemblance to the Arabic name of the village: Abu Shusha became Tel Shush, for instance, and al-Muzayri'a became Ḥurbat [ruin] Mazor. Seventeen of the Hebraized names assigned based on phonetic resemblance to the Arabic names have no meaning in Hebrew. This is the case of Ḥurbat Burgin (Khirbat Umm Burj), Ḥurbat Kipoz (Khirbat Qumbaza), and Ḥurbat Gmama (al-Jammama).

Of the 195 depopulated villages in which some remnants of structures remained,[48] only 55—less than a third—carry official names today. We can conclude that in the case of depopulated Palestinian villages, not each site on the ground was named.

Naming Jewish Communities Established on or Near the Sites of Depopulated Villages

> If the Arabic name of a place does not give reason to believe that its source is historically Hebrew, the Names Committee does not take into account the Arabic name, but rather chooses a memorial or symbolical name for the new community.
>
> —JNF Names Committee, July 1949

Many of the Jewish communities in Israel were established after 1948 atop or very near depopulated Palestinian villages. When naming these new communities, the JNF Names Committee and later the Government Names Committee followed the same principle—trying to restore the ancient Hebrew name occasionally preserved in the Arabic one. The JNF Names Committee determined the following:

> If the Settlements Names Committee is convinced that the new community lies near a place—and especially on a place—that had hosted a Jewish community in one of the eras of the People of Israel in the Land of Israel and that community has been forgotten over time, or has been preserved in a different form in the mouths of the different occupiers until coming down to us in its current form, embodied as a name of nearby Arab community, the remains of a "ruin," of a "tell" [mound] and so on, the Settlements Names Committee shall assign the community the historical-Hebrew settlement name in its original Hebrew form.[49]

For example, the ancient names of Parod, Kisalon, and Sifsufa were given to modern Jewish communities established near the ruins of the Palestinian villages of al-Farradiyya, Kasla, and Safsaf, accordingly. An ancient name was sometimes given to a new Jewish community even when the site identification in the nearby Palestinian village was mistaken or disputed. For instance, the moshav established in the Galilee on top of the demolished village of Dayr al-Qasi was named Elkosh, to mark the birthplace of the biblical prophet Nahum of Elkosh, although the committee recognized that most experts believed already then that biblical Elkosh was actually in the Judean plain, in Syria, or in Lebanon.[50]

Scores of Jewish communities received new names based on the Arabic names of the depopulated villages near which, or on top of which, they had been founded, amended slightly to sound Hebrew. Ghazi Falah lists fifty-six such names.[51] The immigrant camp set up in the depopulated Palestinian village of al-Masmiyya was named Mashmia' Shalom ("Sounder of Peace"), a biblical Hebrew phrase that sounds reminiscent of the Arabic name.[52] The new Jewish residents of the depopulated village of 'Ayn Hawd ("Spring of Trough") offered to "change one letter only" in the name and make it into 'Ein Hod ("Spring of Splendor"), so that "the name suits the place and the place [suits] the name."[53] In some cases, Jewish communities were assigned the translated names of nearby depopulated Palestinian villages. One example is the name of the Alona Regional Council, derived from the Hebrew word for "oak" (Alon), a translation of the name of the earlier Palestinian village, al-Sindiyana (the Arabic name for "oak.")[54]

The settlement atlas produced by the Names Committee details all the names given over the years to Israeli communities, sorted according to their origins.[55] The list of communities whose names, according to the committee, are based on "a Hebrew sound, form and meaning for local names," contains ninety-one communities (7 percent of all the names assigned by the committee). A review of the list finds that twenty-six of the names were given based on a similar sound or a translation of the name of a depopulated Palestinian village. Regarding none of them does the committee mention that the name had belonged to a village demolished by the state.

The records of scores of other names of Israeli communities, also based on the names of depopulated Palestinian villages, do not attribute the origin of the name to the Arabic names of these villages, but rather to other sources, seemingly unrelated to the village name beyond the phonetic level: moshav Zekharia, established on the depopulated village of Zakariyya, is listed as named after a biblical figure; moshav Kfar Daniel, set up on the ruins of the village of Daniyal, is listed as "named to commemorate Daniel Frisch, the president of the Zionist Organization of America"; moshav 'Agur, by the village of 'Ajjur, is said to be named "after a common bird mentioned in the Bible" ("agur" is the Hebrew name for "crane"); and moshav Ora, near the village of al-Jura, was "named symbolically after a quote from the book of Esther."[56] In these cases and many others, the authors of the atlas ignore the Arabic names that served as sources for the new Jewish ones.

Depopulated Palestinian villages that lacked any link to past Jewishness were declared by the Names Committee as "lacking any historical identification,"

Remains of 'Aqqur, under the trees of JNF's Martyrs Forest, March 27, 2007. Courtesy of Noga Kadman.

however old they were, and their names were not used for the Jewish communities established on the village site or lands. For instance, in a letter addressed to the committee of moshav Kerem Maharal, founded in the houses of the depopulated village of Ijzim, the Names Committee argued: "There is no doubt that the name 'Igzim' has no bearing on, from the Hebrew history perspective, and no connection to the history of the people of Israel in the country."[57] The moshav was therefore named after the famous Rabbi of Prague, known as the Maharal, without any reference to the name of the village.

Other communities were assigned purely symbolic names, like Ḥosen ("strength"), near the site of the village of Suhmata; names from the agricultural and natural world, like Mataʻ ("orchard") near ʻAllar; names of Israeli and Zionist leaders, like moshav Yad Natan, founded by Bayt ʻAffa and named after one of the presidents of the Zionist Federation of Hungary; and names commemorating battles and commanders of the IDF and the Palmach, such as moshav Ben ʻAmi, set up on the site of Umm al-Faraj and named after Ben ʻAmi Fechter, commander of the Yeḥiaʻm convoy of the Haganah, whose members were killed by Arabs near the village of al-Kabri.

Public Advocacy for the Renaming of Sites

> The mission of Judaizing our country's map does not stop at giving names. Everyone concerned should constantly work to instill the Hebrew names and cancel out the foreign ones.
>
> —The Names Committee, November 1951

Already at their first meeting, in April 1951, the members of the newly founded Names Committee took heed of the importance of printing and distributing maps for instilling the new names among the public.[58] The committee members also understood that assigning new names and writing them on the map were insufficient to introduce them into daily use by the Israelis. The committee, therefore, busied itself over many years—alongside the actual naming process—with advocacy and educational activity, designed to put an end to the persisting usage of Arabic names and to instill the new names among the Israeli public.

The committee fought against the habit of some immigrant transit camps and newly erected Jewish communities to pick up the original Arabic name of the village on or near which they stood. The members of the committee found it urgent to assign Hebrew names to such places, which would replace the Arabic ones. They complained: "In the meantime, the transit camps have gained Arabic names that are taking root and distorting the Hebrew face of our State (Kurdani, Ras al 'Ayn, Saqiya, 'Ajjur . . .)."[59]

The committee urged the settlement authorities to inform it in advance of any plans to build new communities, so that it would have enough notice to come up with a Hebrew name and prevent the usage of the previous Arabic name of the place. In January 1952 the committee wrote to the Jewish Agency:

> The press is advertising you have begun the construction of a new moshav in the abandoned Arab village of Dayr Muhaysin. . . . The effort to determine a Hebrew name for the place cannot be delayed. And it is not dictated from the heavens that first the name of Dayr Muhaysin takes root, and then energy will need to be spent to uproot it. . . . In the future, do not wait . . . , approach us at once.[60]

In some cases, new Jewish communities insisted on keeping the Arabic name of a depopulated village as their own. The Names Committee fought bitterly against the trend, but sometimes it gave up. It spent some years trying to persuade kibbutz Kabri, which was built in 1949 near the depopulated Palestinian village of al-Kabri and retained its name, to Judaize its name. The committee's demands to the kibbutz and the United Kibbutz Movement failed to produce results,[61] and in 1953 the committee agreed to confirm the name Kabri as the official name of the kibbutz.[62] The members of the kibbutz established near the depopulated village of al-Hamidiyya also insisted on retaining the name. The committee was displeased, arguing that the Arabic name "commemorates a Turkish despot"—Sultan Abdul Hamid. According to a compromise that was reached, the name's pronunciation was changed somewhat, and the kibbutz was assigned the Hebrew name Ḥamadia.[63]

The Names Committee would also approach municipalities whose jurisdiction swelled to incorporate depopulated Palestinian villages, urging them to assign these locations Hebrew names. After several unsuccessful attempts, the committee launched yet another complaint with the Tel Aviv Municipality, beseeching it to assign Hebrew names to the neighborhoods built on the ruins of al-Shaykh Muwannis, al-Jammasin al-Gharbi, and Salama: "The neighborhoods that had Arabic names have remained in their Arabness, . . . and [there has been] enough shame and outrage in the lack of a Hebrew name for a neighborhood. We have received many complaints against this state of things, and the complaints are just. Please, instruct the names committee attached to the municipality to assign Hebrew names to neighborhoods whose names are in Arabic."[64]

The Jerusalem Municipality was also on the receiving end of recurrent reminders to find Hebrew names for the Palestinian villages and neighborhoods within the city. The committee sent similar requests to the Ra'anana Municipality, advising it to find a Hebrew name for the village of Khirbat 'Azzun (Tabsur) within its borders, and to the Petaḥ Tikva Municipality, regarding the village of Fajja.[65] The committee also called on the IDF to produce Hebrew names for its camps: "It does nothing for the Jewish and Hebrew education of the soldier when he uses an Arabic nickname for the military camp: Wadi Sarar, Qastina, Tantura and so forth."[66]

The committee reprimanded institutions that were still using Arabic names for various settlements instead of the newly minted Hebrew ones. In a letter sent to the Jewish Agency in January 1954, the Subcommittee on Settlement Names writes: "On an issue of your monthly magazine, a story was published under the title Safariyya—a moshav of Chabad Ḥasidim. We are obliged to point out: "Safariyya" was the name of the Arab village. The name of the Chabad moshav is Shafrir. . . . You must therefore use only the name Shafrir to refer to the aforementioned moshav."[67]

The committee would also contact the communities directly, urging them to use their Hebrew names rather than the Arabic ones. An example can be found in a letter from November 1952 to moshav Beit El'azari, built on top of the depopulated village of 'Aqir and informally referred to by its residents as "New 'Aqir": "Please exterminate the Arabic name definitively and use your Hebrew name alone. Accustom your fellow residents and your children to it, and likewise all public institutions and organizations that come in contact with you. Please advertise this in the press and also inform all nearby communities."[68]

The committee approached regional councils and municipalities with requests to ensure the usage of Hebrew names. Thus, it reminded the municipality of Jerusalem: "The Arab settlement of 'Ayn Karim is gone, and with it the name in its Arabic sound. The name of the Hebrew settlement was determined: 'Ein Kerem. Under your authority, kindly inform the many people working in your field of this correction: representatives and supervisors, school teachers and their pupils, clerks and subordinates."[69]

The committee's archives hold numerous requests sent to educational institutions, such as the education departments in municipalities, officials at the Education Ministry, school principals, daycare supervisors, training institutions, tour guides, "knowing the land" institutions, university departments, and teachers' seminars; to media groups, such as the Voice of Israel, the Israel Broadcasting Authority, the Government Press Office, newspapers, and magazines; and to cultural institutions, publishing houses, agricultural institutions, and organizations such as the Public Works Department, the JNF, and the Ministry of Tourism. All these were asked to work "vigorously" to "instill the chosen Hebrew names and replace the Arabic names with Hebrew ones" among the public with whom they work, and other organizations with which they come into contact.[70] Thus, for example, the committee urged the Culture and Public Diplomacy [Hasbara] Center: "Please inform us at once about vigorous advocacy activity on your part towards institutions and individuals, to your lecturers and to your guides, to schools and teachers, in a bid to exterminate the Arabic names once and for all and use the Hebrew names alone."[71]

The committee asked the children's magazine of the Davar newspaper: "Your newspaper is commanded to fulfill also the following mission: in addition to the love of the homeland, plant in the hearts of the children the knowledge of the language of the homeland, Hebrew names instead of Arabic ones. You do not always insist on that, and the Arabic names appear on more than one occasion."[72]

Egged, the national bus company, was reprimanded for writing Castel and Dayr 'Amr on its signs, instead of Ma'oz Zion and Eitanim—names of Israeli communities established in the depopulated Palestinian villages of al-Qastal and Dayr 'Amr: "Your insistence on the Arabic names is neither commendable nor legal: you are failing the public and misleading it with names that have been completely and decisively abolished, and you are interfering . . . with the instilling of the Hebrew names."[73]

Gradually, the Hebrew names took root in the public consciousness, and the Arabic ones were forgotten. Still, in a number of places Israelis maintain the usage of the Arabic names to this day: residents of the moshavim 'Agur and Zekharia still name their communities by the Arabic pronunciation of the original name of the Palestinian village: 'Ajjur and Zakariyya; other village names are commonly used to denote junctions and intersections (Masmiyya, Qastina, Julis), military camps (Julis, Jalama), and resorts (Tantura). In Jerusalem, residents still use the Arabic names of neighborhoods and villages depopulated in 1948—Baqʻa, Talbiyeh, Qatamon, Maliha, and Abu Tor, and rarely use the Hebrew names produced for them—Geʾulim, Komemiut, Gonen, Manaḥat, and Givʻat Ḥanania, respectively. Yehuda Ziv notes that Dayr Yasin is "the only Arabic name Jerusalemites are reluctant to use to this day, unlike other Arabic names in the city"—in all likelihood owing to the infamous massacre that took place there—and they call the neighborhood built on it by the Hebrew name of Givʻat Shaʾul.[74]

Mapping the Depopulated Villages

The Survey Department produced its first series of maps, on a scale of 1:100,000, in the second half of the 1950s. The series was based on maps produced by the British Mandate Survey Department in 1947, in Latin transcription, with Hebrew added in purple superscript to account for the political and geographical changes that took places since then, such as cease-fire lines, new settlements, and new roads. Two hundred ninety villages that had appeared on the Mandate maps were labeled "ruined" on the updated Israeli maps.[75] Meron Benvenisti describes the updated map as one that "immortalizes the earthquake that took place in 1948, the erasure of the old world and the construction of a new world upon its ruins."[76]

At the same time, the IDF was printing military maps, also drawn over British maps. The depopulated Palestinian villages were erased from these maps, but the access roads leading to them remained, as did other traces left by the villages in the landscape: ruins, caves, tombs, and wells. Some of the sites where ancient findings had been discovered were marked "ancient ruins" and gradually, as the Names Committee progressed with its work, these were given Hebrew names.[77]

The Survey Department held back its first printing of original maps of the entire country until the Names Committee finished Hebraizing all the site names in Israel. From time to time, the department would urge the committee to come up with Hebrew names for various sites, usually ruins, so that "the maps would appear flawlessly Hebrew."[78]

In the early 1960s the Survey Department printed new maps for the entire country, bearing the Hebrew names affirmed by the Names Committee. Thus, Israel enshrined on its maps the changing of place names from Arabic to Hebrew. Many demolished villages were altogether erased from these maps. The Survey Department stressed that "a ruin where no visible traces remain will not be listed, since we are aiming at a contemporary map, not a historical one."[79] Still, many villages with remaining visible traces were not mapped either, despite the claim of the Survey Department director of the time, Yossef Alster: "We take care not to omit any object from the map, because all objects are invaluable for orientation."[80]

The changing of the country's place names from Arabic to Hebrew, the concealment of the names of most depopulated Palestinian villages and the Hebraizing of the rest, and the intensive efforts to advocate instilling the new names and the Judaization of the country's map—all took place in the 1950s and 1960s. In order to check how the villages and their names appear on maps today, I reviewed official and up-to-date maps in common use by Israelis.

The most popular official hiking and walking series of maps currently in use in Israel is known as the "trail marking maps." They are published by the Israel Trails Committee (ITC), part of the Society for the Protection of Nature in Israel (SPNI), which plans, constructs, signposts, and maintains some six thousand miles of walking trails across the country. The committee comprises delegates from the SPNI, the INPA, the JNF, the SOI, the Antiquities Authority, and other organizations.[81] The trail maps represent objects on the ground in great detail, on a scale of 1:50,000. The cartographic data on which they are based comes from the SOI, which places on maps the names confirmed by the Names Committee. The ITC updates the map with information gathered through landscape surveys and adds to them places of interest to travelers, including archaeological sites and landscape sites. The SOI authorizes the changes and additions before each map goes to print. The full series of trail maps is printed only in Hebrew, and we can assume its target audience is Israeli-Jewish. A handful of the maps have also been printed in English, for the use of foreign tourists. None of them appear in Arabic.

The ITC does not have a specific policy on mapping the ruins of Palestinian villages.[82] Nevertheless, the widespread use of its maps makes these a useful indicator of how depopulated villages appear to Israelis walking across their country and looking at a map. In order to check how many depopulated Palestinian villages are marked in those maps, and in what way, I have examined contemporary trail maps, which cover all the areas in which Palestinian villages once stood.[83]

Most of the depopulated village sites—256 of them—appear on the maps in some way or another. The rest—162 villages—do not. More than half of the villages (229) are marked with at least one standardized symbol, usually—in 169 cases—the symbol for "ruins." Of the latter villages, 70 are also marked with other symbols, denoting historical sites, demolished houses, or religious sites. The same "ruins" mark appears on many other sites besides depopulated villages: archaeological sites, communities that had ceased to exist in different eras, and branches of Arab villages (khirbot). Thus, there is no way of distinguishing among the different types of ruins on the maps and locating the villages depopulated in 1948 specifically.

Over a quarter of the depopulated villages still have visible remains on the ground—structures or freestanding walls—but are not marked as ruins. One example is the village of al-Kunayyisa, of which some twenty dilapidated houses are still standing, a few kilometers west of the city of Modi'in.

Thirty village sites are marked with one of the standard markings for religious sites. These include three mosques, seven churches, and twenty sacred tombs. A comparison of this number to Ghazi Falah's finding of sixty-eight religious sites surviving in depopulated villages leads to the conclusion that over half of the remaining religious sites were not marked on the map. Cemeteries are even more sweepingly ignored: of the forty village cemeteries still visible according to Meron Benvenisti, only ten are marked on the map.[84] The cemetery of the village of Kuwaykat, for example, whose remains are now within kibbutz Beit Ha'Emek, does not appear on the map at all.

Seventy villages are marked with the sign for historical sites. In all cases but two, these villages had stood on sites of earlier settlement, from biblical times to the Crusader era. The village of al-Zib, for instance, had been built on the ancient settlement of Achziv, which dates back to the Canaanite era. The historical site symbol does not refer to the village, but to the older site beneath it. Palestinian villages that had not stood on historical sites were not marked in this fashion, even though many of them had been hundreds of years old. The site of the village of Umm al-Zinat on Mt. Carmel, for example, is not marked as a historical site on the map even though it was founded in the fifteenth century.[85] In most cases, villages that are both marked as historical sites and carry a name on the map are represented by the Hebrew names of the village site.

Nearly two-thirds of the villages (269) do not appear on the maps under their names or do not appear at all. Most of the villages are not mentioned on the map by their names because most of the villages had never been assigned official names. Moreover, about one-fifth of the official names assigned by the Names Committee (24) were omitted from the map, despite the rule that obliges official mapmakers to present every name given by this committee.

The maps carry the names of 149 village sites—over half of the mapped villages, over one-third of all villages in total. Still, in most cases these are Hebrew names—the ancient Hebrew name of the site or the new Hebraized name assigned to it—rather than the Arabic name of the Palestinian village.

Of the names of the mapped village sites, 92 are official names confirmed for the depopulated Palestinian villages by the Names Committee. This amounts to one-fifth of the 418 depopulated villages, so this is the ratio of all villages appearing on the map under official names. Sixty-two additional names that appear on the maps, of almost half of the villages whose names are mapped, are unofficial names: 11 are in Hebrew, like Giv'at Merar marking the site of the village of al-Maghar, north of Gedera; and 51 are the original Arabic names of the villages, which appear on the maps despite not being officially recognized by the Names Committee.[86] Some of these names are popularly used, sometimes despite the existence of official Hebrew alternatives. For example, the village of Lifta, at the western entrance to Jerusalem, appears on maps and is commonly referred to by its original name, rather than its official one of Mei Nefto'aḥ. Some of these names survive as the official names of national parks, including Castel National Park on the site of the village of al-Qastal, or Sidna 'Ali National Park, which includes the site of the village of al-Haram (Sayyiduna 'Ali). The informal Arabic names were put on the map by the editors of the trail maps, who regularly mark on the map informal names of village ruins (and other objects) that are in common use by the public; that is the practice regarding sites that do not have a formal name to go by, or when the formal name is not commonly used.[87]

Of the 229 villages appearing on the maps under any kind of sign, almost half (107) appear without a name. Of the 169 villages marked as ruins, only half (81) appear on the map also with a name, and only less than a third (50) appear under official names. It follows that not every village included in a map has also been recognized by name. In about a quarter (38) of the village sites whose names appear on the map, there is no indication that the name belongs to a settlement that had been destroyed and no longer exists. In the other cases, this is implied either through the prefixes of "Ḥurba" or "'Iyim" (both Hebrew words for "ruins"), or thanks to the "ruins" mark appearing by the name.

A map search of the 195 depopulated villages where traces of structures still remain visible on the ground yields that most (119) do not appear on the map under any name, and over a third (72) do not appear at all. It follows that in the case of over half of the 162 villages not mentioned on the map, the map editors ignore villages whose remains are still visible on the ground, in contrast to SOI's own statements. One example is the village of 'Aqqur in the Jerusalem hills, which does not appear on the maps, although its remains still stand in the forest planted over the site.

By contrast, most of the totally demolished villages do appear on the map: of the 233 villages that retain only piles of stones, if that, 133 appear on the maps. One explanation is the lack of ongoing map updates relative to the changing situation on the ground. Sometimes details such as ruins, springs, wells, and orchards continue to appear on the map even when they have vanished from the ground, covered up by newly paved roads or newly constructed buildings.[88] Other possible explanations for villages being mapped despite leaving no remains, while others that have left traces on the ground are ignored, include the tendency to map ancient sites even if no visible traces remain, and the tendency to avoid mapping villages supplanted by Israeli settlements, even if Arab buildings are still standing on the sites.

Three-quarters of the villages that had stood on ancient sites (177 of 238) appear on the map. Less than half of the villages that had not stood on such sites are mapped (79 of 180). Most of the villages marked on the map as historical sites are also named (56 of 68), a much higher percentage than for all villages named on the map (82 percent versus 36 percent). In these cases, the depopulated village was named and mapped thanks to the ancient site on which it had stood. Without it, it would probably have been left unnamed.

In half the cases of mapping villages that had stood on ancient sites, villages with no visible remains have been mapped. In addition, of the 133 villages that have been mapped although nothing remains of them, two-thirds had stood on an ancient site.

We can conclude that the location of a village on an ancient site does more for the likelihood of its appearance on the map than does the existence of its remains on the ground. Some villages where distinct remains still exist were never mapped, perhaps because they do not preserve any ancient remains of interest to the map makers. Another possible reason is that 53 of the 72 unmapped villages that still have some visible remains are situated today within Israeli urban or rural communities. Those villages appear much less frequently on the map than villages outside existing communities: almost two-thirds of the villages within contemporary communities have not been mapped (67 out of 108), while more than two-thirds of the villages outside contemporary communities have been mapped (215 of 310).

Villages on which Jewish communities were built are scarcely mentioned on the maps, in spite of the fact that these villages retain the highest proportion of their old buildings, which often continue to be used by the Jews. Thus, villages like 'Ayn Hawd or Ijzim on the western slopes of Mt. Carmel, in which many houses have been renovated and populated by Jews in the communities that supplanted them ('Ein Hod and Kerem Maharal), do not appear on the map. The Jewish residents have replaced the Palestinian residents in their homes, and the names of the new Jewish communities have replaced the Arabic ones on the maps. This is not always the case, however: The name of the village of al-Shaykh Muwannis, for example, is mentioned on the map, despite the fact that the village site itself, including some of the remaining houses, is within a built-up area of Tel Aviv University.

In ninety-nine cases the maps carry names based on the name of a depopulated village, in reference to some object that was once a part of it—such as a spring, a well, a fort, or a tomb—or to a nearby geographical feature such as a hill, a stream, or a mountain. In three-quarters of such cases, the names are Hebrew. In most cases (sixty-five), the Arabic name of the landscape feature is echoed in the Hebraized name, even if the village itself is left unmarked and unmentioned. Examples include Tel Grisa by Jarisha village in Tel Aviv's HaYarkon Park; Tsemach Beach, near which the village of Samakh used to stand; the Hadas Stream passing by Biyar 'Adas village in Hod HaSharon; the Nurit Spring once serving the village of Nuris on the Gilbo'a ridge, and the Naḥash Well by the village of Dayr Nakhkhas. Ronnie Kokhavi-Nehab calls this phenomenon "present-absence," pointing out its recurrence in the names of places within kibbutzim, "such as the name of the stream flowing by the kibbutz, or a ruin remaining within its boundaries, or a grove still bearing fruit, or the name of land plots in the field."[89]

*   *   *

The failure to name places is tantamount to a deliberate act of disregard, which sentences these places to oblivion. Places without names do not latch onto the consciousness of people living nearby, traveling through them, or passing by them. Israel has chosen to refrain from giving names to most of the sites of depopulated Palestinian villages and has replaced the original names of the rest of them with Hebrew names, whose content is mostly unrelated to that of the original Arabic names. By doing so, Israel has ignored the existence of the villages as communities in recent history, as landscape features, and as sites of communal and cultural heritage.

The erasure of the villages' names and their marginal representation on the map symbolize the erasure of the actual villages on the ground and the exclusion of their former inhabitants. The Arab character that the country used to have, and that had been expressed, among other ways, in the existence of hundreds of Palestinian villages and thousands of Arabic place names, has been largely wiped off the ground and off the map by Israeli rule.

The main mechanisms for carrying out this erasure are the Names Committee and the Survey of Israel. A comparison of the results of the practice of mapping depopulated villages to that of naming them shows that the villages received more attention in the mapping process than in the naming process. The number of villages indicated in some way on official maps is more than double the number of those that were officially named, and 14 percent of the villages still carry their Arabic names on Israeli maps. In contrast, the Arabic name was upheld in only 3 percent of the villages as the official name. One possible explanation for this is that the Names Committee, as its records confirm, is more ideologically motivated than the soi, which operates in a more "scientific" field. The popular perception of maps as "scientific" and "objective" enhances their success in conveying the message of Judaization. Their common usage by Israelis in everyday activities such as travel allows them to instill the message implicitly.

5 Depopulated Villages in Tourist and Recreational Sites

NEARLY ALL THE depopulated Palestinian villages were demolished in order to erase them from the landscape. However, most of the village sites are located today in open areas, and in many some remains of the village can be seen.[1] Over the years, in many of these areas forests were planted, parks were established, national parks and nature reserves were declared, and hiking paths were paved. Today, the previously built-up area of almost half of the depopulated Palestinian villages (182 out of 418) is included within tourist and recreational sites, such as JNF forests and parks, nature reserves, or national parks run by the Israel Nature and Parks Authority (INPA), marked hiking trails signposted by the SPNI, and privately operated tourist sites. A full list of the villages and the recreation sites that came to include them can be found in appendix A, along with a map showing their locations across the country.

Many of the village sites have thus become accessible to the Israeli public, and therefore many encounters between Israelis and the villages take place during hiking and sightseeing. Unlike the symbolic encounter through reading a name or a map, these encounters are a tangible, physical experience. For most Israelis, who were born after the villages had been demolished, the first and only physical encounter with the villages occurs when they come across their remains. This encounter is mediated by the authorities who maintain the nature and recreation sites.

Using both observations from my own visits to such sites and official publications, I will consider in this chapter the ways in which the authorities concerned present the depopulated villages to the visiting public, if at all, and by extension, whether Israelis who roam the crumbling ruins and enjoy the almond blossoms have a way of knowing that these are the remains of Palestinian villages, and whether such visits can teach them anything about the identity of the villages and their fates.

Most of the depopulated villages whose built-up area is now part of Israeli nature and recreation sites are included in sites managed by the JNF or INPA.

This applies to 149 villages, over a third of all depopulated villages. The built-up areas of these villages are included in 46 JNF forests or parks, 41 national parks, and 25 nature reserves. They include 63 villages whose built-up areas are now part of INPA sites, 62 villages on JNF sites, and 24 village on sites jointly managed by the two organizations, or sites officially managed by INPA but with some JNF involvement, including signage, production of information brochures, and forestation.

Some of the parks and reserves are small and include only one village. Other spread far and wide, covering the areas of several villages. Forests of pines, cypresses, and eucalyptuses were planted by JNF in what was the built-up area of forty-five villages—over half of the villages on JNF sites. Parts of JNF parks also serve as grazing areas, on a territory that covers more than one-quarter of the depopulated village sites now within JNF parks.

The JNF publishes and distributes informational brochures on most forests and parks under its charge. The leaflets include descriptions of the park's natural environment, its history, and its geography, as well as a map. Web pages of almost the exact same content, with added suggestions for walks and hikes around the area, also appear on the JNF website. In its "Green Guide," the JNF compiles information, maps, and walking routes in dozens of parks.[2] These publications refer to twenty-eight JNF sites that contain sixty-seven depopulated Palestinian villages.

The INPA hands out informational brochures at all parks where it charges for entry, and it has produced brochures for several nature reserves. The INPA also publishes information regarding most of its sites on its website. Nowadays, forty-three depopulated villages are within twenty-four national parks and eight nature reserves, about which the INPA has produced printed brochures or web pages. Unlike the JNF, the INPA publishes different texts about the same places on these two channels.

Descriptive and informative signs are placed, among other places, at twenty-three JNF parks that include the remains of fifty-two depopulated villages. In about half of the cases, the signs are placed on the demolished village site itself. All the JNF signs are in Hebrew, and a minority also include text in English. No signage in Arabic exists in JNF parks. INPA sites that carry signage include eighteen national parks and five nature reserves, which contain altogether the remains of twenty-three depopulated villages. In the first decade of the twenty-first century, the INPA has placed trilingual signs on all of its sites, in Hebrew, English, and Arabic. Prior to that move, very few signs in Arabic could be found at its sites. The overwhelming majority of brochures by both organizations are published in Hebrew only.

I examined the information on depopulated villages that appears—or not— on contemporary Hebrew INPA and JNF signs and publications regarding the depopulated Palestinian villages. Among the publications, particular attention was given to texts in brochures that are distributed to visitors at the sites themselves. If no relevant information was found there, website texts, a more remote channel of information, were reviewed as well. Although both organizations provide on their websites information in both Hebrew and English, I examined the Hebrew texts—and refer to them—as a better indication of the information they convey to Israelis. When the content in both languages is identical, I refer to the English web page.

Before looking at the JNF and INPA texts, one can already say that both organizations ignore many villages on their sites, regarding which they have not produced any information at all—neither publications (19 villages on JNF sites, 44 on INPA sites) nor signage (34 villages on JNF sites, 64 on INPA sites). Overall, of the 418 depopulated villages, only 25 are mentioned on INPA or JNF signs, and only 46 are mentioned in publications by either organization—the main bodies concerned with signposting and distributing information on tourism and recreation sites in Israel.

I found that JNF publications ignore forty out of the sixty-seven villages (60 percent) in parks about which publications were produced. Signs fare worse, even though they are physically located on or near the village ruins: signs do not mention thirty-nine of the fifty-two villages (75 percent) located in signposted parks. Moreover, 86 percent of the village names are missing from signs directing visitors to different parts of the park, and 80 percent of the village names do not appear on the park maps attached to JNF publications and posted in the park itself. In total, thirty-five depopulated villages are mentioned in some way by the JNF—whether in print, signage, or both.

INPA signs and texts ignore over half the depopulated Palestinian villages in its territories. Texts, both printed and electronic, ignore twenty-four of forty-three villages (56 percent), and signs ignore eleven of twenty-three villages (48 percent). Directions signs in national parks and nature reserves fail to mention 85 percent of the village names. The villages are even more determinately ignored on the Internet: INPA brochures handed out at the sites that include villages mention most of them (seventeen out of twenty-three, or 74 percent), while web pages ignore most of the villages on sites they describe (twenty-seven out of thirty-nine, or 69 percent). Of all the villages within its sites, the INPA refers to twenty in total—whether in publications or in signs.

Only rarely are the remains of the Palestinian village mentioned in the general description of the area. This description can usually be found at the top of JNF and INPA information leaflets, and it gives an overview of the park's different sites. An example can be found in the information leaflet of Ramot Menashe park: "The main characteristic of the area is a mix of planted forests and natural forest of Valonia oak, open space, fields and groves, springs and streams. The gentle slopes and the rural character of the communities impart a feeling of tranquility. Archeological findings that were uncovered here are kept in collections in the kibbutzim, and they join sites of heritage and early [Zionist] settlement, like Jo'ara and the Palmach Cave."[3]

The sites of the seven depopulated Palestinian villages within the boundaries of the park—Abu Shusha, al-Butaymat, Khubbayza, al-Rihaniyya, Daliyat al-Rawha', Abu Zurayq, and al-Kafrayn—are not mentioned in this overview. Even in the detailed brochure, only one of them is mentioned (see the discussion that follows).

Even when JNF and INPA texts do mention villages, they usually do it partly and sporadically, thus themselves expressing forgetfulness and neglect. The texts offer little information to visitors in parks, forests, and reserves regarding Palestinian villages that once stood on the site and their inhabitants. Many villages are not presented as Arab—and never as Palestinian—and at times even their names are not mentioned. Information is rarely provided regarding the date of establishment of the villages, their population, their income sources, and other details about their residents' lives.

The texts tend to present the Palestinian villages in passing, ignoring their histories and focusing on earlier, usually Jewish sites that had existed in the same place. The texts also tend to stress Zionist history, while describing only sites of Jewish settlements that resided there, never Arab ones, whether depopulated or currently existing. The Palestinian villages are not presented as historical sites or as modern settlements. Thus, the texts express the common trend in Zionist collective memory, which stresses the periods during which there existed a Jewish community in the land. This collective memory presents the land as if had been empty until the Zionists arrived to settle it in the modern era, and it ignores a long period of Arab settlement in the land between the ancient and modern eras.

Many villages are mentioned as hostile elements or as targets of conquest, in the context of the "combat legacy" ("*moreshet krav*") of the War of 1948, but the circumstances of their depopulation are nearly always silenced. The texts ignore acts of attack, massacre, and expulsion committed against the villages and their residents. They do not specify explicitly the severance of the village's existence. The texts also ignore the fate of the residents made into refugees and omit the policy of village demolition. This approach matches the Israeli narrative that eschews responsibility for the refugee problem and tries to keep the issue off the agenda.

Another type of reference to the village ruins is as part of nature—as nonhistorical elements of the landscape, such as streams and springs, or as landmarks on a hiking trail. War and displacement, which have severed the existence of these villages, are not mentioned in this context. As a rule, reference to specific structures and orchards is more common than reference to the entire village and its people; at times, references to structures and orchards are made without mentioning those who have used and cultivated them.

Information on the Villages and Their Inhabitants

In the minority of cases when JNF and INPA texts do mention Palestinian depopulated villages, they offer very little information to visitors of their parks, forests, and reserves about the Palestinian village that once stood there, and about its former inhabitants.

Eight out of the nineteen INPA publications that do mention the villages fail to mention that the villages and their inhabitants were Arab: in four cases, the identity of the residents goes unmentioned, and in the others it is merely implied, whether by describing the residents as "Maronite Christians" (Kafr Bir'im), as originating in "Egypt and Sudan" (al-Mirr), by referring to the village mosque (Dayr al-Shaykh), or by mentioning "Arab gangs" that were present there (Saffuriyya). Of the twelve villages mentioned in information signs put up by the INPA, only five are described as Arab villages. The residents of two additional villages are described as Bedouin, and the residents of a third village—Qisarya—are correctly described as Muslims from Bosnia, which is mentioned both in the information leaflet and in signage at the site. Four other villages are not assigned any ethnic identity, although one is described as having been used as "a base for the Arab forces."

Nine villages out of thirteen mentioned in JNF signs are described as Arab. By contrast, publications referring to nearly half of the villages mentioned in JNF publications (twelve out of twenty-seven) fail to mention their Arab identity. The depopulated village of Kudna, for instance, now in British Park, is described as follows: "'Iyei Kidon—a picturesque ruin spread across a prominent hill. Among the building remains, orchard trees grow, as well as tamarisk trees and prickly pear cacti. The hill and its surroundings contain numerous water cisterns and different caves."[4] The description lacks the Arabic name of the village, the Arab identity of its inhabitants, or any other information about them.

In most cases, INPA signs and publications that mention Palestinian depopulated villages specify their names. In three cases, however, signs posted by INPA refer to the village without specifying its name. Al-Zib, for instance, is referred to simply as "the village" in the signage of Achziv National Park. In two other cases the name of the village goes unmentioned in the signs but can still be inferred from the name of the park—Castel and Caesarea. JNF signs referring to villages all mention their names, and the same is true for JNF publications, with two exceptions in which the Hebrew name assigned to the village site is used, rather than the Arabic name of the village itself: 'Iyei Kidon for Kudna, Ḥurvot 'Agur for 'Ajjur [Kidon ruins and 'Agur ruins, respectively).

None of the JNF signs that refer to villages specify the date of their establishment. The JNF publications, mentioning twenty-seven villages in total, specify the date of establishment for only three villages: al-Mazar, Nuris, and Zir'in. According to the publications, these villages were built in the eighteenth and nineteenth centuries;[5] Walid Khalidi, however, relies on Ottoman tax records to show that Nuris and Zir'in had already existed in the sixteenth century.[6] INPA publications note the establishment date for only four out of the nineteen villages they mention. The same is true for four of the twelve villages mentioned in INPA signage. The establishment dates provided in INPA texts match the ones provided by Khalidi.

Nearly no INPA or JNF text or publication mentions the number of inhabitants who had lived in each of the depopulated villages. The exceptions to this are a JNF publication on the village of Bayt 'Itab and an INPA sign in Tzipori National Park (Saffuriyya).[7]

None of the JNF signs or publications mentions the villagers' source of livelihood, nor do INPA publications. INPA signs on the sites of only three villages provide this information, telling visitors that the villagers of Kawkab al-Hawa were peasants, those of Qisarya worked as fishermen, and that the inhabitants of Bayt 'Itab worked in agriculture and raised sheep and goats.

Only in a few cases do JNF and INPA texts elaborate on the lives of the villagers. When they do so, the tone is somewhat anthropological. One example is a JNF text on the village of al-Nabi Yusha':

> We will arrive at the remains of the Shi'ite village of Nabi Yusha', and to the tomb of the Sheikh. The structure of the tomb of Nabi Yusha', where Shi'ite religious scholars used to study, has been left almost intact. . . . In the past, many believers made pilgrimage here for rituals of dissolution of vows and celebratory meals, and the encircling of the tomb was considered by the villagers as a warrantor of good health.[8]

Other examples are a description of how the villagers of Hunin used masonry from the nearby Crusader castle for building their houses, and a reference to the sanctity attributed by the villagers of Suba to the ancient trees that grew by their cemetery.[9] In these cases and others, the villagers' customs are described without any clear statement of the fact that their villages ceased to exist after 1948. Furthermore, the violent circumstances through which this occurred are completely absent from the texts. Similarly, an INPA leaflet describes a holy tree in al-Qubayba, in which a demon used to live, according to the belief of the children of the village:

> "The demon tree"—the plum tree is the only tree remaining on the hill, probably due to its sanctity to the residents of Qubayba, an Arab village that stood

by the hill until 1948. . . . According to the legend, the villagers of Qubayba would send their children to bring water from the well, and to make sure they came back quickly, would tell them a demon lived on the plum tree, guarding the water. Bringing water from the well thus became the "test of courage" for the village children.[10]

This text does not tell us why the village stood by the hill only until 1948, and what happened after that year to the villagers who hallowed the plum tree.

Publications and signs of INPA refer in most cases to the physical elements that have remained on the site, such as structures, cemeteries, flour mills, orchards, and springs. As a rule, JNF publications tend to mention structures and other physical remains of the village (twenty out of twenty-seven) more often than they mention people who lived in the village (nine out of twenty-seven). Sometimes the only mention of a village and its residents is in the context of a still-standing structure, such as the room where the women of Sataf washed their clothes, and a school that served the children of Bayt Jiz.[11]

JNF signs refer to structures remains in five villages, but not in five others, despite the structures standing quite visibly just near the signs. Thus, for example, a sign posted by the JNF on the site of the village of Bashshit ignores a clearly visible surviving structure on the top of the hill, the very center of the village site. Some changes have taken place over time, and a number of Palestinian buildings that had been ignored for decades are now mentioned in new signage. For example, large churches that served the village of Ma'alul prior to its depopulation had stood for years in JNF's Kfar HaHoresh forest, without being mentioned in the signs around them. In the end of the first decade of the twenty-first century, new signs jointly sponsored by the INPA, the JNF, the Israeli Tourism Ministry, and others were put up, referring to the churches and to the village to which they belong: "Remains of churches. The Orthodox church and the Catholic church were part of the village of Ma'alul (Arab Muslim-Christian village) which was abandoned in July 1948. The churches and a number of tombs on the hill are the remains left of the village."[12]

On occasion, JNF and INPA texts describe an Arab structure with no mention of the village to which it had belonged, and without providing details on the people who had used it. Such is the case, for example, with a JNF brochure that describes a tour in Biria Forest: "The Fighters' Path continues and arrives at a big abandoned structure of two stories. In the southern part of the structure, under an arched dome, flows the spring of 'Ein Zeitim ('Ayn al-Zaytun). Orchard trees stand all around."[13] The text fails to mention the village whose name is the same as that of the spring, whose residents used the spring's water and built the structure above it.

A similar approach can be found in an INPA leaflet that mentions a mosque but ignores its village, al-Nabi Rubin: "About a kilometer from the Paratroopers Forest, up the stream, stand the remains of a large mosque built over the tomb of

Nabi Rubin. The estuary of the Sorek Stream was once called Wadi Rubin, hence the official name of the national park—Rubin Stream."[14]

The church of Kafr Bir'im is mentioned in an INPA description as a site along a hiking trail. The only information on the church is a folkloristic anecdote. The text ignores the fact that the church belongs to a Palestinian village, whose name is omitted. It also omits the fact that the villagers, who had been displaced, have become Israeli citizens and are still fighting to return to their village, as well as the fact of their ongoing use of the church: "We advise leaving the synagogue and walking up the nearby hill, topped with a Maronite church. Try identifying the animal on the lintel. Did you guess? It's the kangaroo, which carries its offspring in its pouch and protects them as the church protects its followers. We will then ascend the building in front of the church for a spectacular vista of the Meron Mountain Nature Reserve all around us."[15]

Mentioning Depopulated Villages in the Historical Sequence

As a rule, the JNF and INPA focus on ancient sites, mostly those with Jewish history, as well as sites of Zionist history. The history of the Palestinian villages located on their sites is marginalized and ignored, echoing the physical erasure of their structures.

Most of the national parks administered by the INPA are dedicated to ancient sites. The boundaries of seventeen sites of INPA correspond to single depopulated villages. In almost all of these cases, the village had been built on an ancient site, to which the national park is now dedicated, as in the cases of Achziv National Park on the site of the village of al-Zib, Qaqun Fortress National Park on the site of the village of Qaqun, and Castel National Park, on the site of the village of al-Qastal. Thus, depopulated villages that are located on ancient sites, whose historical values are considered by the INPA as justifying the declaration of a national park, have "found themselves" included in the parks and are hence frequented by travelers. Except for one case, no national park has been declared on the basis of the historical importance of the Arab village itself. The exception is Sidna 'Ali National Park, established on the site of the depopulated village of al-Haram (Sayyiduna 'Ali) around a religious Muslim site still frequented by pilgrims; this is the only national park declared on a site of a depopulated village without a pre-Arabic history.

Even though most publications and explanatory signs of the INPA refer to the ancient history of the site they describe, only less than half of them also mention the Palestinian village that had been located in the same place. Village sites that had been in the past the loci of ancient Jewish settlements are usually referenced in INPA texts, but these regard the remains of the Jewish settlement, while the Palestinian village is mentioned only incidentally. The village of Danna, for example, is mentioned as the dwelling of an ancient Jewish site, and not as a village in its own right, which had existed in the same place for hundreds of years: "Among the ruins of Danna village . . . architectonic items were found, which testify to the existence of a Jewish settlement on the site during the periods of the Mishna and the Talmud."[16]

The explanatory signs of Bar'am National Park refer only to the ancient Jewish history of the place, while completely ignoring Palestinian Kafr Bir'im, even though its remains—church, houses, and alleys—can be clearly seen within the park boundaries.[17] The choice to focus on the Jewish past on this site and others is a political one. In the words of Jonathan Boyarin, "the excavated synagogue . . . is not only a tourist attraction but a mark of the Jewish claim to this area and of the persistence of Jewish habitation in Palestine after the end of the second Jewish commonwealth." He adds: "The attempt to impose a sense of the place as uniquely and properly Jewish is effectively undercut by the remains of an Arab village."[18]

The JNF often develops ancient sites and presents them to the Israeli public, as a means of conveying a Zionist message of bonding with the ancient Jewish past of the land. Palestinian villages that had been "lucky" to be built on the remains of older settlements have "profited" from these circumstances, since they are usually mentioned in JNF texts along with the description of the ancient sites: in JNF texts that describe ancient sites, seventeen villages are mentioned, while eight others are ignored; in JNF texts that do not mention ancient sites, thirty-two villages are ignored, and only ten are mentioned.

Sites of depopulated Palestinian villages that are thought to have been inhabited during biblical times, and remains of villages that are perceived as representing biblical ways of life—such as flour mills, water installations, stone terraces, and fruit orchards—are often integrated into tourist sites in Israel. The most famous example is Sataf, a demolished Palestinian village near Jerusalem, which had been built on an ancient site. The JNF has preserved there a few structures, springs, and agricultural terraces—which it leases to Israelis—presenting them as the remains of ancient Jewish agriculture. In its park brochure, the JNF portrays the agricultural activities in the place—which were most recently carried out by Palestinian farmers about sixty years ago—as very ancient actions, carried out by Jews:

> In the heart of the Jerusalem Hills, . . . a green slope tumbles down to Sorek Stream, the two springs that emerge from it water agricultural terraces, a reminder of an almost vanished ancient Hebrew culture thousands of years old. Here, just like the ancient Israelites at the time, people tend irrigated vegetable gardens alongside orchards that require no irrigation. . . . This is Sataf, a hidden gem, as if it has stopped the time from passing.[19]

The focus on the ancient past of depopulated villages erases their Palestinian character and neutralizes their contemporary and political context. Tali Tamir found that the attribution of relatively recent remains to antiquity was also done in the depopulated village of Suba, where "[t]he signage that tells the archeological history of the place, attributes the village to ancient mythology and infuse the ruins with a romantic aura of cultural relics."[20]

A number of other JNF texts highlight the biblical and Jewish layers of certain sites and ignore or utterly marginalize periods when there were Arab villages in these places, just as they ignore or marginalize the physical remains of these villages.[21] The Palestinian village of al-Haditha, for instance, was built on the site of the ancient town of Ḥadid, which had existed in the Lydda area until the ninth century. The information sign posted on the site nowadays describes the village exclusively as an object that has preserved the name of the ancient town, rather than as an integral part of the history of the place. In another case, that of Tel Gimzo, the brochure's authors choose to focus on the ancient site of the place, overlooking the Palestinian village of Jimzu, which had stood on the same spot for centuries, until its 1,500 inhabitants became refugees in 1948: "East of moshav Gimzo established in 1950, there is an ancient settlement with carved graves. Some believe that this is the location of biblical Gimzo. Potsherds from the Roman and Hasmonean periods were found there."[22] The text describing Begin Park, and the ancient communities that it had comprised, completely ignores the depopulated villages of al-Qabu and Ras Abu 'Ammar, which had also existed on the site: "Entwined in this 'dramatic' topography are 3,000 years of intensive settlement. The park holds the archeological remains of a Jewish community from the First Temple Era, and from the time of the Mishnah."[23]

According to Meron Benvenisti, Crusader remains located within depopulated village sites are mentioned on maps and in guidebooks, but the prolonged Arab history of these structures, after the Crusader period and sometimes also before it, is ignored; he offers that "the identity of their builders and their renovators—local fellahin [peasants] and their leaders—is not considered worthy of mention in Israel guidebooks."[24]

The national parks run by the INPA include fourteen depopulated Palestinian villages with Crusader remains. Eight of these are signposted, and the signs in seven of them refer both to the village and to its Crusader past (Saffuriyya, al-Zib, Suba, Bayt 'Itab, Kawkab al-Hawa, Bayt Jibrin, and al-Qastal). The signs in the eighth village, Khirbat Jiddin, report the Crusader history and ignore the Arab one. The INPA offers nine publications about these sites, with seven mentioning both the Crusader history and the village and two covering Crusader history only (Khirbat Jiddin and Majdal Yaba).

Six depopulated Palestinian villages that include Crusader remains lie today within JNF parks. Three of those contain JNF signs on the village site itself: on one site the signs refer to the Crusader history and ignore the village history (Khirbat al-Tannur); on another site, they report the village history and ignore its

Crusader past (Suba); on yet another site, the signs do neither (al-Qastal). Of the four JNF publications dealing with the same sites, three mention both the Crusader history of the site and the village (Bayt 'Itab, Suba, Hunin), and one covers the Crusader history alone (Khirbat al-Tannur).

It would seem, therefore, that the existence of Crusader remains on depopulated village sites increases the odds of a village being mentioned in JNF and INPA texts. This is similar to the link found between the existence of older remains and the mentioning of villages in JNF publications.

In certain cases, JNF texts refer to "structures from the Ottoman period," without stating that these are structures of an Arab village that had existed in the Ottoman period and also beyond it, until 1948. The overview of Rabin Park, for example, does not clearly state that it contains the sites of five destroyed Palestinian villages (Bayt Jiz, Bayt Susin, 'Islin, Saris, and Bayt Mahsir), but rather hints at it through the mentioning of the Ottoman period: "The park includes . . . sites of historical and archeological interest that provide evidence of continual Jewish settlement since Biblical times. The remains of a Roman road, Byzantine and Ottoman ruins and the remnants of comparatively recent settlement—all these form part of the varied and interesting landscape the park has to offer."[25] The villages are not included in the category of "comparatively recent settlement," which, one can assume, refers to Jewish settlements only.

Another example is the westernmost watermill in the Seven Mills compound of HaYarkon Park in Tel Aviv, described on the JNF website as "one of the five mills built along the banks of the Yarkon river in the Ottoman period." The mill was used by villagers of Jarisha, which goes unmentioned.[26]

The use of the term "Ottoman," just like the emphasis on the Crusader period of village sites, fits well the tendency of presenting the historical periods between the Jewish exile to Babylon up to the establishment of the State of Israel as a sequence of foreign occupations, while ignoring the local Arab population that was living in the country at the same time.[27]

The text on Naftali Hills informs us about the historical eras the JNF sees fit to emphasize. In addition to ancient sites, the JNF also focuses on sites with Zionist history: "On the Naftali ridge, there are also impressive sites from past times. Tel Kadesh Naftali and the Hunin Fortress are outstanding remains of ancient times, while the Ko'aḥ Fortress, Tel Ḥai and Kfar Gil'adi are sites of settlement and battle from the modern era."[28] The depopulated villages of Qadas, Hunin, and al-Nabi Yusha', which had stood precisely on the sites listed in the preceding text, are neither included in the list of "outstanding remains of ancient times" in Naftali Hills Park, nor in the list of modern settlement sites.

Other JNF texts try to tie ancient sites to Zionist history. This is done, for example, in the general description of the Rabin Park: "In addition to sites of combat legacy, the park hosts historical and archaeological sites, agricultural terraces, and remains of ancient agriculture, that attest to the historic continuity of Jewish settlement in the place."[29] The five depopulated Palestinian villages within the park boundaries (Bayt Jiz, Bayt Susin, 'Islin, Saris, and Bayt Mahsir) are not part of the Jewish settlement continuum and do not appear in that description.

A brochure on Biria Forest also stresses the links between ancient Jewish settlements and Zionist settlements of the area: "In the center of the forest lies the Biria Fortress—a special site which symbolizes the struggle of the Jewish people to settle its land once again."[30]

The text provides an extensive description of the Biria Fortress, including its Jewish history in the Talmud era and the Middle Ages, and estimates that "Jews abandoned the site in the late 16th century."[31] Then it glosses over centuries of history to focus on the Zionist enterprise of acquiring lands and the attempts to settle Jews in the area. There is not a single word about the Arab settlement that existed on the site throughout these centuries, in the village of Biriyya.[32]

The village of 'Ayn al-Zaytun, where nearly a thousand people had lived prior to its depopulation in 1948, is also included today in JNF's Biria forest. The village is mentioned only in passing in the JNF brochure, in the context of its proximity

Israelis visiting the spring of depopulated Lifta, February 22, 2007. Courtesy of Noga Kadman.

A church of depopulated Ma'alul in JNF's Kfar HaḤoresh forest, December 16, 2006. Courtesy of Noga Kadman.

to a Jewish colony set up on the site: "The old 'Ein Zeitim—. . . the colony was founded near the Arab village of 'Ayn al-Zaytun."[33] The JNF website speaks of 'Ayn al-Zaytun, but fails to describe it as a Palestinian village: "The Ein Zeitim Recreation Area is an active leisure recreation area. . . . There was a village here named Ein Zeitun, which was inhabited by Jews from the Middle Ages until the early 18th century. Since then, four resettlement attempts were made, but they all failed."[34]

The JNF also refers to nonlocal Jewish history on its sites. In some thirty sites of depopulated villages, lying within JNF parks or forests—comprising over a third of the villages on JNF sites—memorial or dedication stones have been placed to commemorate lost Jewish communities or to pay tribute to Jewish donors from abroad.[35] In most places where such rocks can be found, any explanatory signs are absent, and when they exist, they do not refer to the Palestinian villages that had been there. One of such site, the Martyrs Forest, is dedicated to the memory of Holocaust victims: "The six million trees planted in 1951 are an enormous project of ever-green memorial candles, in memory of the six million of our people who perished in the Holocaust of the European Jews in the Second World War."³⁶ The villages of Dayr 'Amr, Khirbat al-'Umur, Kasla, Bayt Umm al-Mays, and 'Aqqur, the remains of which can be found between the trees of the Martyrs Forest, are not mentioned in the signs or brochures of the forest, and are not commemorated in any way. The JNF has never dedicated a single forest to the memory of depopulated villages, not even when the forests were planted directly on their ruins.

A detailed reference to the history of the Palestinian villages themselves is rare in JNF and in INPA texts, even when they do mention a village. In a few cases, the existence of a village—even if it lasted centuries—does not appear as part of the historical sequence presented to describe the place, and is mentioned only in a brief and casual way, as shown earlier regarding the villages of al-Haditha, Danna, and 'Ayn al-Zaytun. Another example is the brochure on Achziv National Park, in which the INPA does mention the Palestinian village of al-Zib that had stood there, but ignores it in the opening paragraph, which provides a general history of settlement in the place: "The historical and archeological sources point at settlements from the Canaanite, Israelite, Persian, Hellenistic, Roman, and Crusader periods."³⁷ The village of al-Zib, which had been established in the thirteenth century and continued to exist throughout the Mamluk, Ottoman, and British periods that followed, does not appear as part of the historical sequence of the site, even though the most visible remains there go back to these later periods.

By contrast with the INPA brochures, which tend to ignore the history of the Palestinian villages, approximately half of the signs posted on the INPA sites provide historical details about the villages, such as the source of the name of the village of Bayt Daras and its use as a postal stop between Egypt and Syria in the Mamluk period; the Bedouin settlement in Khirbat Karraza and Kawkab al-Hawa in the seventeenth and nineteenth centuries, respectively; and the conquest of Tzipori by the Mamluks in the thirteenth century, when it "turns into a small and miserable village" by the name of Saffuriyya, which developed only in the late nineteenth century.³⁸

The JNF offers a relatively detailed historical description only in the case of the village of Bayt 'Itab: the brochure describing the USA Independence Park, which includes the village site, tells of the family that ruled the village and its struggle with a neighboring village and quotes the impressions of foreigners who visited the village in the nineteenth century.³⁹

The Villages as a Part of Nature

Several authors have observed the references to village ruins on hiking sites as mere parts of nature: Ilan Pappé describes a text about Biria Forest on the JNF website, which refrains from mentioning the depopulated villages within the forest and presents their remains as "a wonderful and organic part of the nature and its secrets."[40] Tali Tamir finds a similar reference in a JNF sign by the ruins of Suba: "in which the location of 'Mount Suba' is marked as 'nature,' and the ruins within it are a part of the natural landscape, as the rocks and the forests."[41]

In the texts analyzed for this book, the JNF and INPA tend to write about the parks and nature reserves they manage in a language that describes the atmosphere there as calm and idyllic, often using superlatives such as "magical" and "picturesque." One such example is a hiking suggestion in the Carmel Coast Forest, posted on the JNF website:

> The Carmel Coast Forest is one of the most magical places in the country. It is big, wide and has many spots of grace and beauty that can be visited. The forest has hiding places from the noise and tumult of the big city, mountainous, evergreen landscape—all these create a magical atmosphere, like in a fairy tale. We invite you to walk with us along the green forest belt that wraps the communities of Kerem Maharal and 'Ofer. To visit magical forest trails. . . ."[42]

The depopulated villages of Jaba', 'Ayn Ghazal, and al-Sawamir, the sites of which are covered today by the Carmel Coast Forest, are not mentioned in the text.

Both JNF and INPA texts often refer also to the village sites themselves as parts of the tranquil nature and pastoral landscape. Such is the description of the village site of al-Kafrayn in the JNF's brochure regarding the Ramot Menashe Park (while ignoring six other depopulated villages included in the park boundaries): "Two springs flow in the valley and the ruined remains of a village can be seen, with prickly pear thickets and orchard trees among them. These are the ruins of 'Ein Kufrin. In respect for the peacefulness of the place, we will walk down towards it by foot. The larger spring serves the cattle herds of kibbutz 'Ein HaShofet."[43]

This pastoral description does not relate to the war that had violated the peacefulness of the place and brought about the destruction of the village, which is not even identified as Arab.[44] In other cases, the village remains themselves are described as part of the picturesque nature. Thus, the remains of 'Ayn Ghazal are described as "adorning the slope," the ruins of Danna as "adorned with prickly pear fences," and the site of the depopulated village of Kudna as a "picturesque ruin."[45] Similarly, Jonathan Boyarin notes that the depopulated village of Lifta, which attracts numerous Israeli visitors, is sometimes perceived as "a refined and picturesque remain of traditional dwellings."[46]

In the texts describing nature reserves or hiking trails, the INPA and JNF tend to portray villages as landmarks, along the rivers, hills, and springs, without any further elaboration. The remains of Dayr al-Shaykh are described in a hiking trail guide of the INPA as landscape details that hikers will encounter,

The only remaining structure of 'Ayn Ghazal, within JNF's Carmel Coast Forest, March 30, 2007. Courtesy of Noga Kadman.

The mosque of depopulated Dayr al-Shaykh, today within Sorek Stream Nature Reserve, February 21, 2007. Courtesy of Noga Kadman.

without providing information regarding the village or explanation on how the ruins came to be: "Further down the road, a big stone wall 'blocks' the trail. It is the wall of the compound of the mosque of the village of Dayr al-Shaykh. The trail bypasses the compound from the right. It's possible to enter the mosque yard through a stairway. The structure has remained almost intact. In the yard—a water hole. Terraces and abandoned orchards lie around the mosque."[47]

An INPA brochure describes a hiking trail that includes a visit to the Sufla spring, which had once served a village with the same name. The village is only mentioned in passing, in the context of the spring's name, and nothing is said about its history and its residents:

> At the end of the crevice, under a tree, is a tiny opening in the rock. Those who are brave, thin and equipped with a flashlight can squeeze in and crawl into this small, dark cave. Within the cave flows the spring of 'Ein-Sufla, whose waters accumulate into a subterranean pool. The spring takes its name from an Arab village that used to stand here—al-Sufla (the low)—named so because it stood on a topographic saddle between two hilltops. Warning: The cave visit is not advised for the claustrophobic. The mud—it is plentiful.[48]

A similar reference can be found in a JNF brochure that presents the remains of the village of Sataf as hiking sites, rather than as the remains of a destroyed community: "The trail goes along an ancient route, through olive groves and cultivated land plots, descending towards the 'Ofer corner, where an impressive vista opens up over the site and the houses of the abandoned village of Sataf, which the trail reaches next. . . . The trail leads to the central spring of the village, 'Ein Sataf."[49]

In several cases the name of the village is mentioned as a landmark on a hiking trail, without any further elaboration. For instance, the JNF instructs hikers: "We shall embark on a circular walk on the Yitle scenic trail to the remains of the village of Bayt Thul," or "We shall walk left up the hill, on a trail rising between the terraces and orchard trees to 'Agur Ruin."[50] In all these cases, the texts do not offer any indication of the hiking site being a depopulated Palestinian village.

JNF texts tend to refer to the depopulated villages' orchards, describing them as part of the natural landscape, while often ignoring the villages themselves, whose residents tended the orchard trees and made their living from them. The general description at the top of the Biria Forest JNF brochure lists the sites in the forest: "No wonder that in such a large forest one can find a variety of interesting and fascinating sites: woods, orchards, springs, an ancient synagogue, a lime pit, tombs of [Jewish] sages and rich vegetation, scenic roads and hiking trails, alongside picnic sites and observatories."[51] The text ignores the five ruined villages that lie in the same forest—Mughr al-Khayt, 'Ammuqa, 'Ayn al-Zaytun, Fir'im, and Qabba'a—but lists the orchards and springs these villages have left behind.

A sign directing hikers to Bayt Thul in JNF's Kfira Forest, February 23, 2007. Courtesy of Noga Kadman.

Remaining orchards of Dayr Aban within JNF's USA Independence Park, February 20, 2007. Courtesy of Noga Kadman.

Another text, describing a hiking trail in Biria forest, directs hikers to the site of the village of 'Ayn al-Zaytun and focuses on the orchard that survives in it: "Near the stream many orchard trees remain, which 'invite' us to spend time among them."[52] The village itself, whose residents tended the very same orchards, is only mentioned further down in the text, in passing, in the context of the establishment of the Jewish colony of 'Ein Zeitim. Nothing is mentioned of the depopulation of the village and the violence this involved (discussed below).

A JNF sign describes a hiking trail in the Carmel Coast Forest, which leaves the site of the village of 'Ayn Ghazal and ends at the site of al-Sawamir. The text does not mention the villages explicitly, but refers to their orchards: "JNF invites you to travel in this new marvelous trail, which leads from Shimri Stream to Shimri Ruin and to 'Ein 'Razala.' . . . On the way, we will encounter a diverse forest which has been undergoing renewal in the past few years. Remains of orchards, olives, pomegranates, figs, mulberries and almonds accompany the trail, imbuing it with color and taste in different seasons."

A hiking trail through Tzor'a Forest, which appears on the JNF website, describes the combination of the conifers planted by the JNF and the ancient orchards. The village of Sar'a, the owner of the orchards, is absent from the text: "The pine trees, planted in the forest in the 1950s, have grown very high today, and through their needle leaves shine beams of light. Among them, orchards of very old fig and olive trees bloom. It is worthwhile to look for the quiet intimate corners, hidden between the forest trees."[53]

The JNF webpage on Canada Park provides a short description of the depopulated village of Dayr Ayyub, ending by informing us that the JNF "maintains the groves in the village."[54] The village is not mentioned at all in the brochure distributed to travelers in the park.[55] As in the case of the irrigation installations in the village of Sataf, the JNF stresses here the preservation of agriculture, but not the preservation of the village itself.

Other texts present the orchards as a type of vegetation; the text that describes British Park goes as far as to define the "abandoned orchards" as a "flora unit" that is "extraordinary in its vitality and importance" and tends to grow beneath terraces.[56] The text lacks any reference to the villages of 'Ajjur, Dayr-al-Dubban, and Kudna, whose inhabitants cultivated the orchards and terraces in the past.

INPA publications also describe in some cases the orchards of depopulated villages while ignoring the villages themselves. For example, the brochure of Telem Springs National Park describes the orchards and terraces of Qalunya, with no references to the village and its residents: "Down the stream lie impressive remains of orchards and fruit trees, including olive, pear, almond and fig trees, and the remains of grapevines. The agricultural terraces here are well preserved, and demonstrate well the character of the mountainous agriculture, which uses steps built of stone to keep the slopes from soil erosion."[57]

Sometimes INPA publications that mention depopulated villages depict the orchards apart from the description of the village, as a separate site in the nature reserve or the national park. For example, following a description of the customs of the residents of al-Qubayba, a village that "stood near the hill until 1948," the text mentions another site on the national park: "The bustan [orchard]: an orchard with olive, almond, and prickly pear trees, rehabilitated by the INPA for the enjoyment of the visitors."[58] The orchard is presented here as a separate site located in the national park, as if it is not related to the village.

The 1948 War and the Depopulation of the Villages

On most signs and in about half of the JNF and INPA publications that refer to depopulated Palestinian villages, there is some kind of reference to the 1948 war as part of Israel's "combat legacy." Nevertheless, the battles, the conquest, the circumstances of depopulation, the uprooting of the residents, and the demolition of each village are portrayed in the texts only partially, if at all.

Yitzhak Laor finds that signs mention the ruins of depopulated villages only if a major battle between Zionist and Arab forces took place nearby, in which case the Arab aggression is emphasized.[59] The JNF describes the hostility or belligerency of Palestinian villages against Jews before and during the 1948 war, in texts on nearly half of the villages it mentions on its signs and over a quarter of the villages it mentions in its publications. This hostility is usually mentioned explicitly; for example: "In Lavi Forest lies the Arab village of Lubya . . . during the War of Independence the villagers never missed a chance to attack Jewish transport, and they terrorized all the [Jewish] communities of the lower Galilee."[60]

In other cases, the possibility of hostile intensions by the villagers or their involvement in actual hostilities against Jewish forces is implied by the JNF, even if such intentions or actions did not actually take place: two villages are described as controlling main roads (Dayr Ayyub, for instance, "controlled the road leading to Jerusalem," according to a Canada Park sign), and in two other cases, there are references to incidents in which Haganah and Palmach fighters were killed near a village.

Villages described as "hostile" in JNF's publications are all identified as Arab, except for one. By contrast, only eight out of the nineteen villages not presented as hostile are described as Arab. JNF signs do not display a similar trend; however, in three cases in which signs do not state the Arab identity of a village, they also do not describe it as aggressive toward Jews. Some of the JNF texts refer only to the aggression of the villages and their occupation in 1948, without ascribing a more civil and "innocent" side to them, one of an agricultural community with

JNF signs near al-Qastal, mentioning the occupation of the nearby villages Qalunya and Saris, February 23, 2007. Courtesy of Noga Kadman.

INPA sign near ruins of depopulated Kafr Bir'im, in Bar'am National Park, November 26, 2006. Courtesy of Noga Kadman.

daily routine and family life. The JNF thus creates an equation between Arab national identity and violent behavior, and between a violent opposition to Jewish dominance and the absence of normal civil rural life. Bashshit, for example, is described in a JNF sign as a base for attacks by Arabs, and as a target for Israeli occupation, nothing more: "The village of Bashshit, located between Kibbutz Yavne and the colony of Gedera, was an obstacle to our forces and a security link for the Arab transport between Masmiyya and Isdud. On May 11, 1948 the village was occupied by the 52nd and 54th battalions of the Giv'ati brigade. This operation paralyzed the Arab transportation in the area."[61]

Unlike the JNF texts, which often stress the hostility and belligerency of the villages, only a few INPA texts make similar references to the depopulated villages they describe. INPA signs only describe one village (al-Zib) as hostile to the Jewish community in the War of 1948, referring to it as "a base of the Arab forces." Two information signs insinuate the hostility of two villages, noting that sabotage activity against Jews was carried out near the village of Kawkab al-Hawa, and that the village of al-Qastal "controlled the road to Jerusalem." INPA brochures present two villages (Saffuriyya and al-Qastal) as hostile toward the Jewish community in the war. In neither case are any details offered about the villagers' lives.

In almost all cases, the signs and publications of the JNF and INPA keep silent regarding the circumstances that led to the depopulation of the Palestinian villages, or they relate to them only vaguely. According to Benny Morris, in 'Ayn al-Zaytun, units of the Palmach Jewish forces expelled women, elderly people, and children by shooting over their heads. Around seventy men from the village and other villages nearby were gunned down into a nearby creek, their hands tied, following instructions of a local battalion commander. Meanwhile, Palmach units blew up and burned houses in the village.[62] The JNF provides no information on these events and has placed a sign that merely defines the village as "a base for Arab fighters," which was overrun by a Palmach force.

According to Benny Morris, the military attacks against Jaba' and 'Ayn Ghazal included heavy bombardment of the villages by artillery and airplanes, followed by the expulsion of the residents.[63] These attacks, regarded as "unjustified" by the UN, are not described by the JNF, which only states that Israeli forces "acted" there, and that the villages "were abandoned and their residents escaped, without a battle."[64] In almost no other case do JNF texts mention artillery attacks by the Jewish forces or the Israeli army during the 1948 war against the villages, even though such events led to the depopulation of most of the villages mentioned in JNF texts.[65] Only two such attacks—against Lubya and Zir'in—are mentioned in the publications, and another one—against Suba—is listed on the signs.

In other cases, texts refer to a village but completely ignore the fact of its depopulation and the circumstances behind it. A JNF sign describes, for example, a "structure that had served up to 1948 as the school of the village Bayt Jiz," without explaining why the school ceased to operate that year and what happened then to its pupils and the rest of the village residents.

Eight out of the twelve villages mentioned in INPA signs were depopulated due to artillery attacks. Residents were deported from two other villages and fled from another one in fear of being attacked. The circumstances of the depopulation of another village remain unknown. Eleven of the villages mentioned in INPA publications have been depopulated due to military assault. Residents were expelled from two other villages, left another village as a result of psychological warfare, and fled from two more villages in fear of being attacked.[66] None of these events are cited in INPA texts, except for the evacuation of Kafr Bir'im (discussed shortly). The deadly attack committed by the Stern Gang in late January 1948 on a bus that had just left the village of Qisarya made all the residents of the village flee.[67] The attack is not mentioned in signs or publications about the place. The explanatory sign at the entrance to Caesarea National Park only says that the village that had stood there "did not last for long," without elaborating. The village is mentioned in the park brochure, but with no hint that it no longer exists.[68] Similarly, the sign that the INPA has posted in Gvar'am Nature Reserve is silent on the deportation of the villagers of Simsim, and only points out that the village "was abandoned in 1948."[69]

The only instance in which the INPA explicitly describes depopulation circumstances in its publications is Kafr Bir'im. According to a Bar'am National Park brochure, the residents of the village were "evacuated from it during the War of Independence." The INPA website adds that in 1948 the villagers "had to abandon their houses by IDF instructions, for security reasons."[70] It specifies that the village church functions today as the "spiritual centre of the community members," who are not described as "Arabs" but as "Maronite Christians." INPA texts disregard the fact that the former villagers of Kafr Bir'im are Israeli citizens, the ruling by the Israeli High Court of Justice calling on the government to return them to their houses, and their decades-long struggle to get the state to implement the court's decision. The texts are also silent regarding the political struggle conducted by the villagers for their return to their village of origin, which is part of their visits to the village and to its church, and ignore the role played by these visits in commemoration activities related to the depopulation of the village.[71]

The INPA does not explain the depopulation of the rest of the villages, even if the fact of depopulation is mentioned. According to the INPA, the residents of Khirbat Karraza "lived here until 1948"; al-Qubayba "stood near the hill until 1948"; and the village of Suba "existed on the mountain until the War of

One of the remaining structures of Kafr Bir'im, today within Bar'am National Park, April 27, 2007. Courtesy of Noga Kadman.

Independence." In all of these cases, no information is provided as to why the villages ceased to exist.[72]

All the depopulated Palestinian villages had been occupied by the Haganah or by the IDF, before or after their depopulation. Nevertheless, out of the nineteen villages mentioned in INPA publications, the occupation of only five is mentioned, and the same is true regarding six out of twelve villages mentioned in INPA signs.

JNF publications mention explicitly the occupation of only eight villages out of twenty-seven. In most of these cases, there is no reference either to the uprooting of villagers or to the fact that the villages ceased to exist following their occupation. The JNF text that mentions the village of Dayr al-Hawa, for example, acknowledges the fact of its occupation, but the fate of the village and its inhabitants later on remains unknown, as opposed to other details provided to the visitors: the meaning of the village's name, the related "combat legacy" from 1948, and expressions of enthusiasm over the landscape: "During the War of Independence, this was the location of the Arab village of Dayr al-Hawa, whose name (in Arabic: the dwelling of winds) was given to it due to the strong winds that blow here. In 1948 the village was occupied by the Palmach Har'el brigade, during Operation 'Mountain.' A visit to the mountain at sunset is astonishingly beautiful!"[73]

Things are different when it comes to JNF signs, all but three do refer to the occupation of the village. However, not a single one provides information on the fate and whereabouts of their residents. A map presented on signs on two of the village sites—Dayr al-Hawa and al-Qastel—details the progress of Operation "Mountain," conducted by the Haganah in April 1948. All the villages in the area are marked by the same symbol: both those that were overrun, depopulated, and demolished, and those that were occupied but were neither depopulated nor demolished, like the village of Abu Ghosh and nearby villages in the West Bank, across the green line.

In several cases INPA texts describe villages being abandoned by their residents; for example, Simsim "was abandoned in 1948," and Saffuriyya "was abandoned by its inhabitants" after its occupation.[74] In Kochav HaYarden National Park, over the site of depopulated Kawkab al-Hawa, a sign declares that "the local residents took flight during the War of Independence." In all of these cases, nothing is written regarding the reason for abandonment, and no occupations, military attacks, or deportations are mentioned. The fact that Saffuriyya residents, for instance, "abandoned" their village after it was bombed from the air is ignored, and so is the deportation that caused the "abandonment" of Simsim by its residents.[75] The IDF attack on Kawkab al-Hawa, which had led to the residents' flight, is not mentioned, and the same holds true for the eventual conquest of the village by the IDF.

Nine villages are regarded as abandoned in JNF publications. In most of these cases, the text labels villages as "having been abandoned" by their residents during or after the war, while another village is described simply as "abandoned." Another "abandoned" village appears on a JNF sign. The texts do not relate explicitly that all these villages—all presented as "Arab"—were conquered by Israeli forces, and they do not describe the attacks waged against them, which were the reason for their abandonment. Both the INPA and the JNF, therefore, imply that the responsibility for the depopulation of the "abandoned" villages lies with the villagers, who chose to "abandon" them, and ignore Israel's role in the events.

INPA and JNF texts provide almost no information regarding the fate and the whereabouts of the villagers after they "abandoned" their villages, or after their villages were occupied. In the only two cases in which the INPA mentions the location of the villagers after having left their village, these are Palestinians who have remained within the boundaries of Israel: the villagers of Saffuriyya, who "moved to the Nazareth area" after their village "ceased to exist" (sign in Tzipori National Park) and the villagers of Kafr Bir'im, whose ongoing visits to the village church that are mentioned imply that they still live in Israel.

Except for the nine "abandoned" villages, JNF publications do not state explicitly that all the other depopulated villages have ceased to exist as a result of the Israeli occupation. This fact can only be inferred from the texts regarding most of the villages: fourteen of them are called "ruins" or "remains"; one is mentioned in the past tense; and another village, it is told, has been supplanted by a Jewish moshav. Regarding 'Ayn al-Zaytun and al-Haditha, nothing hints that they no longer exist. Most of the JNF signs that mention depopulated Palestinian villages note that they were occupied by Israel, but they give no hint as to the fact that these villages ceased to exist afterward—which is made clear by looking at the space around the sign. Three signs do not state explicitly that the village has ceased to exist, but this is implied by referring to the village in the past tense (e.g., "the village of Bashshit . . . was an obstacle"), or by referring to the Jewish community that has supplanted it ("The Arab village of Saris [nowadays Shoresh]").

INPA brochures convey explicitly the fact that nine villages have ceased to exist by describing them as abandoned, demolished, evicted, or "having existed up until 1948." The fate of seven others can be inferred from the use of the past tense or the word "ruins" to describe them. The texts on Qisarya, Kawkab al-Hawa, and Dayr al-Shaykh, by contrast, provide no clear indication that the villages no longer exist. INPA signs imply that the villages no longer exist in only six cases: Saffuriyya has "ceased to exist," the people of Khirbat Karraza "lived here until 1948," the village of Qisarya "did not last for long," Bayt Jibrin existed "up until the War of Independence," the residents of Kawkab al-Hawa "took flight" in 1948, and the village of Simsim was "abandoned" in the same year. In the case of four other villages, one can infer that they have stopped to exist through the use

An INPA sign near remnants of depopulated Bayt Daras, today within Zmorot Pool Nature Reserve, April 24, 2007. Courtesy of Noga Kadman.

of words like "ruins" and "remains," or the use of the past tense. Regarding two villages—al-Zib and Suba—there is no indication that they have ceased to exist following their occupation, even though the empty structures and ruins attest to this.

Although the existence of "ruins" or "remains" is evident on the ground and is presented in JNF publications regarding most of the villages as well as in INPA publications regarding half of them, only rarely do the texts explain how a village has become ruins, why, and by whom. In the INPA brochure that describes the history of Achziv, for instance, the remains of the village of al-Zib are mentioned, but nothing is said about how they have turned into remains, and on what has happened to the villagers: "The Mamluk Sultan Baibars conquered Achziv in 1271. Since then, there had been a small village here by the name of al-Zib, which had kept the sound of the name of the more ancient settlement. . . . Most of the remains seen today on the ground, including the structure of a mosque, were left of the abandoned village al-Zib and the Crusader castle that stood here once."[76]

The only text that tells that a village was demolished by Jewish forces appears on the INPA webpage concerning al-Qastal, which describes the fighting that took place there and concludes: "the battle was unique in several aspects: . . . in the military aspect, this was the first nighttime battle and the first time an Arab village was occupied and demolished."[77]

The JNF explanatory signs do not mention ruins at all, even when ruins are clearly visible around the sign. Only one JNF sign refers to "remains" that have been left, of the village of Ma'alul. INPA signs refer only to Bayt 'Itab, Simsim, and Bayt Daras as "remains" or "ruins." They do not detail the circumstances of the demolition of these villages and do not discuss at all the demolition of the rest of the villages.

* * *

Zionist ideology rests on the formation of a bond to the land and ownership over it, both physical and emotional, stressing "knowing the land," excursions along its landscapes, and visits to Jewish historical sites. Such knowledge and values are instilled through numerous institutions, including the JNF, which deals with forestation and recreation, and the INPA, charged with the preservation of natural and historical sites in Israel.

The JNF is an organization with an unequivocally Zionist ideology and a stated commitment to work for the Jewish people. Its legacy is one of "redeeming the land"—transferring it from Arab to Jewish ownership—and it has been complicit in the actual erasure of the villages. The establishment of the INPA in the 1960s occurred in a different historical context, with the establishment of the state being no longer a question but a fact, and with confidence that the Palestinian refugees would not return. The differences between the two organizations affect their approaches to the depopulated Palestinian villages. The JNF has planted forests over most of the depopulated villages on its sites, specifically in order to conceal them. Hence, there is no surprise that most of the villages included in JNF parks and forests go unmentioned in its signage and publications. By contrast, the INPA mentions the depopulated villages in most of the brochures it distributes. Perhaps the fact that it is a professional, scientific organization makes it more committed to the facts and to a broader perspective on history. It may also be the case that the INPA is less encumbered than the JNF by the ideological baggage that demands relentless Judaization and erasure of the Arabness of the land. Nevertheless, on its website, the INPA ignores most of the depopulated villages within its sites—including ones mentioned in its own brochures—and INPA signs bear no reference to more than half of the signposted depopulated villages.

Beyond these and other differences, both the JNF and the INPA mediate between Israelis and their country in a way that is shaped by ideology. National values affect the manner in which they present the land, its history, and its characteristics. Both authorities have chosen to ignore most of the depopulated villages on natural and recreational sites within their responsibility, and to refer to the rest of them in a partial and selective manner, stressing Jewish and Zionist history, referring to the villages as battle sites, or describing them as part of nature. The manner in which these authorities refer to the villages is characteristic of some of the ideas at the very core of the Israeli-Zionist ideology and practice: Judaization of the land, marginalization or silencing of its Arab history, the shrugging off of responsibility for the refugee problem, and a one-sided view of the War of 1948.

Through their silence regarding the depopulation of the Palestinian villages, and by withholding most of the information on this process, the JNF and INPA have implicitly downplayed and belittled the scope of the tragedy experienced by the Palestinian people in 1948. They have failed to provide any contemporary political context for the depopulation of the villages and have obviously refrained from turning the sites of depopulated villages they manage into memorial sites for the ruined villages and for the uprooting and dispossession of the villagers. They have thereby avoided officially commemorating the Nakba, the Palestinian tragedy. By refraining from using the Arabic language in JNF and INPA brochures and in JNF signs that refer to the sites that include depopulated Palestinian villages, the authorities have also reinforced the message that these sites no longer belong to Arabs, and perhaps should not even be of interest to Arabs.

This ideological approach is communicated to visitors at national parks, natural reserves, forests and parks, and contributes to the shaping of their views and their national identity, as they engage in everyday activities like hiking or picnicking in nature.

Conclusion: The Remains of the Past, A Look toward the Future

THE LOWER GALILEE VILLAGE of Saffuriyya had over four thousand residents in 1948. In July of that year the village came under aerial bombardment and artillery attack by the IDF, which led most of its residents to flee, including the village's armed defenders. The following year the villagers who remained were expelled. Some of the village refugees today live in nearby villages, and others live beyond Israel's borders, mostly in Lebanon.[1] The houses of the village were razed to the ground, and only a few public buildings remain. In 1949 a moshav was established next to the village site, on its land, by Jewish immigrants from Turkey and Bulgaria. A forest was planted over part of the village site by the Jewish National Fund. The rest was declared a national park by the Nature and Parks Authority, with the aim of preserving the site's ancient history and the traces of the Jewish center that had existed there in the Roman period.

The official name given to the site where Saffuriyya stood was Tzipori—the ancient name of the place, preserved in the Arabic variant. The same name was also given to the Jewish moshav built nearby. The official Israeli map shows the village site with marks signifying a ruin and ruined houses, and a caption—Tzipori National Park. The signage at the JNF forest on the site mentions a convent that remains from the village, but not the village itself. The national park signs refer to the remains of the village and describe it as "small and miserable" for most of its days. The text is oblique as to the circumstances of the village's depopulation, stating curtly that the village was conquered and "ceased to exist," and that its residents "moved out." The information leaflet handed to the park's visitors speaks of the village only in the context of battles and conquest. It says that "gangs" inhabited the village, and that it was later conquered and "abandoned by its dwellers." A publication by moshav Tzipori describes its own establishment as a revival of the local Jewish community on the site, after temporarily providing a home to Muslims who brought about its decline. The Arabic name of the village is absent from the text, which states that the village was conquered after its residents "ran for their lives."

These representations of Saffuriyya are part of a pattern of marginalization of the depopulated, demolished Palestinian villages in Israel, across all of the fields examined in this book. Most of the village names have been erased, and most of the rest have been replaced with ancient Hebrew names or Hebraized variants of their Arabic names. Many villages were erased from the map, and the identity of those that remain on it has been blurred. The JNF and INPA ignore most of the villages that fall within their tourist sites and suppress the identity, history, and circumstances of depopulation of most of the villages that they do acknowledge. When they do refer to villages, it is often only in passing, while focusing on older communities that had existed on these sites and presenting the villages as part of the natural landscape, rather than as communities that existed until fairly recently. The JNF and INPA refer to the villages while focusing on their remains, rather than the people who lived in them, and stressing "combat legacy" and the villages' alleged aggressiveness. Jewish communities established on or near depopulated villages tend to accept the dispossession of the Palestinians while minimizing the engagement with their history, the circumstances of their depopulation, the fate of their refugees, and the moral questions of using their homes and property.

The village of Saffuriyya is relatively "lucky," compared to most of the depopulated Palestinian villages: the village site has been graced with an official name, presented on an official map, declared a national park, and mentioned by local signage and publications about the site. The village has "won" all of these thanks to its location on top of an older site with a prominent Jewish past, which Israel thought important to preserve and commemorate. Palestinian villages that did not exist atop ancient sites were not recognized as being of historical value to Israel, even if they had existed for centuries, and therefore, in most cases they do not carry an official name nowadays—not even a Hebraized one. They are marked on the map, if at all, as nameless locations; are not recognized as worthy of conservation; and are not mentioned on signs or in publications.

One example of such a village is al-Dawayima, a village that like Saffuriyya had also been home to some four thousand residents who were displaced to the West Bank in the War of 1948. The site of this village has never received an official name, it does not appear on the map, it is not signposted, and it is not mentioned or referred to by moshav Amatzia, which was established on some of its built-up area. The massacre that took place when the village was captured by the IDF, in which dozens of men, women, and children were murdered, remains unknown and untold in Israel.[2]

The Palestinian villages are remnants of periods in the history of the country in which Jewish presence was scant—periods that the Israeli collective memory prefers to marginalize and suppress. This collective memory emphasizes those ancient periods in which there was a sizable Jewish presence in the country, and the resettlement of the country with Jews in the modern era. It ignores a long period of Arab settlement in the country, or frames it as a passing, temporary, and negative episode, all traces of which need to be erased as soon as possible.

In addition to ignoring the villages as historical sites, Israel also suppresses their more recent history and the actual present-day reality of their refugees. Official discourse in Israel silences the circumstances of their displacement; ignores acts of aggression, massacre, and expulsion of the villagers; and remains indifferent to the fate of the villagers who have become refugees.[3] The cataclysm and shock experienced by the residents of the villages in the wake of the War of 1948, which still affects their lives and the lives of their descendants, is not a part of the dominant Israeli narrative, which ignores or belittles the Palestinian tragedy.

The marginalization of the villages is underpinned by the ideology of Judaization, which has guided the Zionist movement and the Israeli state. In order to create a Jewish space, Israel edged out the Palestinian residents and their heritage physically and symbolically. To preserve that space as such, Israel continues to marginalize its Palestinian citizens and to renounce the refugees outside its border.

A number of organizations and governmental institutions serve as mechanisms through which the marginalization of the villages is instilled in the Israeli public. The Government Names Committee, the Survey of Israel, the Jewish National Fund, and the Israel Nature and Parks Authority, as well as rural communities—each in its own field—mediate between Israelis and their country. These institutions are guided, to changing degrees, by Zionism and are affected by the basic tenets of its narrative, especially the Judaization of the land. Not only do they convey these ideas, they also ensure their continuity and in turn contribute to the formation and conservation of Israeli-Zionist national identity. They introduce national ideas into the daily lives of Israelis as the latter go about their everyday activities such as using place names, looking at maps, traveling in nature, or living in rural communities.

Among all the organizations and institutions that have been mentioned here, the JNF stands out as a nongovernmental organization with the stated mission of preserving and developing the land of the country for the benefit of the Jewish people, rather than for the sake of all Israeli citizens. Israel has vested the JNF with the authority to do so, thus regarding the JNF as a central instrument of Judaization. Indeed, the JNF took part in many of the erasure activities described in this book: demolition of villages, planting forests over their remains, establishing Jewish communities on refugee land, Judaizing place names, and marginalizing the villages in the information it provides about the sites that contain their remains today. The Names Committee, the Survey of Israel, and the Israel Nature and Parks Authority are public institutions officially committed to serving all citizens of the state equally, whether Jewish or non-Jewish. Nevertheless, by being part of the mechanism of the Jewish state, their actions are dictated by the goal of Judaization, at least to some degree.

Among Israelis who grew up in the aftermath of the expulsions and demolitions, the work of these organizations contributed to the poor awareness of the existence of the villages in their country in the not-too-distant past, and the human significance of the ruins scattered around on the ground. The ignorance with which I experienced the remains of Lifta in my own childhood, seeing the village remains as picturesque, ancient landscape features rather than the homes of Palestinians who had been dispossessed and who have remained refugees to this day, is one manifestation of that. The overall picture conveyed to Israelis is that of the dominant Zionist narrative: a Jewish land, with very little Arab legacy, history, or geography, whose Arab residents chose to abandon it—and ever since they did, they are no longer of any interest to us. Thus, the Judaization project has left its mark not only on the landscape and the demography of the country but also on Israeli consciousness.

Marginalizing and suppressing the villages and their history brings about an underestimation of their role in the conflict among Israelis, with evident contemporary political implications. Ignoring the circumstances in which the villages were depopulated, the crisis that struck their residents in 1948 and its implications for the fate of the refugees until this very day all serve to neutralize the human aspect of the Palestinian loss and omit it from the picture of the Palestinian-Israeli conflict as instilled to Israelis. This results in the flattening of the complexity of the conflict in the Israeli consciousness; the shifting of attention from the fundaments of the conflict—the loss of a homeland by most Palestinians and the enormous personal price paid—then as now—by the Palestinian refugees; and the increase of dehumanization of Palestinians in the eyes of Israelis.

Israel took an active part in turning most of the Palestinians into refugees and has been using the property they left behind. This defines the moral aspect of the attitudes toward the villages. Israel eschews its responsibility for the depopulation of the villages and the fate of their refugees and refrains from engaging with moral questions regarding its part in creating the refugee problem, perpetuating it, and exploiting what the Palestinians have lost. The depopulated villages from which Palestinians were exiled and of which they were dispossessed, may raise such questions—and so their memory is being suppressed.[4]

Israelis do not suppress the memory of the villages out of personal instinct; the suppression is collective, and it is shaped through direct manipulation by the state, which prefers to keep Israeli awareness of the issue dormant and distorted. The marginalization of the depopulated Palestinian villages in Israel has a political rationale that goes hand in hand with the ideology of Judaization and Israel's ethnocratic structure, and it is motivated by the desire to cement Jewish domination of the land. For Israel, the greatest possible threat to this aspiration is the return of the Palestinian refugees to their communities of origin within Israel. The depopulated villages are seen in Israel as a permanent reminder of that threat, and their marginalization is meant to reject the bond that exists to this day between the refugees and their villages, silence any open discussion of the refugee problem and their return to their villages and towns, and keep the entire subject off the agenda.[5] The refugee issue is used by Israel as a threatening concept—but one that is devoid of specific content, as it is not substantiated by the imparting of knowledge and awareness of the historical and geographical moves that had created it in the past, or of the present-day state of the refugees and their families.

Conservation of the villages, and even their mere mention, continue to be a highly charged and threatening topic for Israel, not least because the refugee problem has yet to be resolved. Conversely, there is no controversy in Israel around the conservation and restoration of buildings belonging to the German Templer sect, for example, despite their occupants' pro-Nazi leaning, because the Templers have been recompensed for their homes and have no intention of returning to Israel.[6] According to historian Anita Shapira, "it is far easier to contend with remembrance of a past that has become inoperative—that is, having no immediate implications for the present, than with a past that still challenges the present," like the past of the villages and the refugees.[7]

A collective, just like an individual, might find coping with past events and overcoming suppressed memories a traumatic experience, involving opening old tombs and old wounds. Still, in the long term, this experience might also be liberating.[8] The dispossession and depopulation of Palestinian villages in 1948, as well as the erasure of hundreds of years of their history, are key elements in the Palestinian narrative and collective memory, inextricably bound to the experience of loss and injustice visited on them by Israel. An Israeli recognition of the implications of its triumph for the other, the other's loss and the legitimacy of the other's narrative and collective memory, the understanding of what caused their creation, and breaking free from collective convictions that justified actions against the other side—can all go a long way toward a more nuanced, multidimensional, and humanistic understanding of the conflict. Such an understanding will be essential if a true, comprehensive, and long-term solution for the conflict is to be reached—a solution involving true reconciliation, not just technical arrangements.[9]

It follows that the Israeli discourse regarding the depopulated villages can serve as an indicator of Israel's ability to recognize the Palestinian narrative and its readiness to move toward reconciliation and true resolution of the conflict. Edward Said observed that "most Israelis refuse to concede that Israel is built on the ruins of Palestinian society" and went on to conclude that " there can be no hope of peace unless the stronger community, the Israeli Jews, acknowledges the most powerful memory for Palestinians, namely the dispossession of an entire people."[10] The overall picture emerging from the present book, however, is that of suppression and marginalization of the depopulated Palestinian villages—which does not leave room for much hope for peace in Said's terms.

Stanley Cohen notes that "historical skeletons are put in cupboards because of the political need to be innocent of a troubling recognition; they remain hidden because of the political absence of an inquiring mind."[11] The "historical skeletons" represented by the depopulated villages are very much in the cupboard. Still, a handful of voices, few and unofficial, driven by political insight and an inquiring mind, have appeared in Israel in recent years, emanating from a number of nongovernmental organizations and professionals, working to bring the Palestinian villages into the public consciousness. Some are also engaging in dialogue with official institutions, urging them to change their approach to the villages. In some cases, they have managed to produce change.

The most notable activity in this realm is by Zochrot, a nonprofit set up in 2001, whose goal is "to promote Israeli Jewish society's acknowledgment of and accountability for the ongoing injustices of the Nakba and the reconceptualization of Return as the imperative redress of the Nakba."[12] Among other things, the organization holds tours of the depopulated villages, signposts the sites, runs a center for distributing information on the villages, and engages in public, educational, and even artistic activity around the Nakba, the Palestinian loss of 1948. The journal Sedek (crack), published by the group since 2007, is dedicated entirely to various aspects of the Nakba and to engagement with it among the Israeli public. One of its volumes is a comprehensive guidebook to depopulated Palestinian villages and towns, published in both Hebrew and Arabic.[13]

According to Zochrot, signposting the villages is an act of recognition of the suffering caused by their displacement, indication of the perpetrators of the injustice and their victims, and an expression of desire for reconciliation. According to the organization, the signposting is intended to "serve as an expression of humanity" within the Jewish public, "encourages a more ethical discourse," and assists in the "attempt to mold a peace-seeking Jewish-Israeli consciousness."[14] Ronit Lentin suggests that by signposting the villages, Zochrot includes the Palestinian existence in the Israeli memory landscape, challenging the hegemonic Israeli landscape and the power dynamic that it reflects.[15]

In addition to independent signposting activities, the organization is lobbying the authorities to place signs commemorating the depopulated villages. Following a Zochrot appeal to JNF and a petition to the Supreme Court, JNF erected signs in its Canada Park in 2006, mentioning the villages of 'Imwas and Yalu, which stood there until 1967, when their residents were expelled and the houses were demolished. The park was built over the villages' lands and ruins, and prior to the Zochrot campaign the signage included a wealth of information on the history of the site throughout the millennia—except the last several hundred years of Arab settlement.[16] Following another request by Zochrot, JNF expressed in 2008 its tentative readiness to mention depopulated villages within those of its parks in which there are already signs explaining local history. This intention, which could have resulted in signage for some thirty villages, is yet to be implemented.[17]

Zochrot is also urging the authorities to recognize the Palestinian-built heritage by submitting objections to construction plans that eradicate it. Among other cases, the organization filed objections to the expansion of moshav Ya'ad over the site of the village of Mi'ar (mentioned earlier), while engaging moshav residents and Mi'ar refugees.[18] At the end of the process, the moshav members agreed to partially relinquish the expansion plan, which would have caused further damage to the village remains. The Ya'ad-Mi'ar case is an exception to institutional planning activity in Israel, which normally implements Zionist ideology across the geographical space and ignores "the sense of belonging and memory of the Palestinian Israelis," according to Toby Fenster. Fenster argues that this exceptional case is a part of a new trend among the Jewish-Israeli majority—however "initial and limited"—of "acknowledging the Palestinian memory and its spatialization."[19] Zochrot's activities are a part of that trend, and they instigate its spreading to other circles as well.

Another association, Bimkom, offers the Israeli public a planning perspective that links planning and human rights and prompts the planning establishment in Israel to follow suit. The association has submitted an objection to the plan to construct an upscale neighborhood on the site of the village of Lifta and has called for developing the site while integrating "elements of Palestinian memory, culture and heritage, in the same vein as [the development of] settlement sites of the Zionist movement." According to Bimkom, this type of conservation can be a focal point of reconciliation between Jews and Arabs in Israel, instead of symbolizing conflict. Most of the Lifta construction plan has remained intact, but following the approval of some of the motions submitted against the plan, a subplan to turn the village cemetery into a natural reserve has been canceled, and a decision was made to produce a plan for the conservation of the village mosque.[20]

Various authors have begun speaking out on how they believe the village sites should be treated in order to preserve their memory, both on the ground and in the Israeli popular consciousness. Architect Kobi Peled has proposed the preservation of the ruins of Lifta in their current state, in order to commemorate the village and the Arab lives destroyed in the War of 1948, and create the possibility of a deep understanding of that time. "In its crumbling and death, the place honors its own history and the Palestinian and Jewish attachments to it," he writes.[21] Architect Shmuel Groag suggests we should see the 418 demolished villages as memorial sites and sites of cultural heritage worthy of conservation. He believes this can contribute to a change in the Israeli narrative and collective memory, toward respecting all historical periods that passed on the land, the Palestinian narrative of the Nakba and the Palestinian built-up heritage.[22] Meron Benvenisti has called for the depopulated villages (along with other relics of Palestinian culture) to be made present and visible through signage, tourist information, and conservation. He suggests mentioning the Palestinian villages in guidebooks, with extensive information about their history and their social and economic characteristics. He also calls for defining historical Arab sites that are not linked to earlier landmarks as archaeological sites under the protection of the state.[23]

The comprehensive *Mapa Encyclopedia* presents information on "any place that has a name—a community or any kind of site—that has traces on the ground," and includes in this definition the depopulated Palestinian villages. The editor of the encyclopedia writes in the introduction that "it would be wrong to erase or conceal the Arab-Palestinian past of the country, as has been done in many books, and to a great extent also in official maps published by the State." He goes on to add that a browsing of the encyclopedia "would therefore raise thousands of Arabic names that have 'disappeared' over time, but whose existence is beyond any doubt. The history of this country would not be whole without them." And the encyclopedia does, indeed, mention some 80 percent of the depopulated villages, while 25 percent of the villages get their own entries.[24]

All of these indicate the beginning of a new discourse in Israel, one of dialogue among political activists, academics, planners, officials, and parts of the general public, concerning the importance of the memory of the depopulated Palestinian villages.

The villages are a reminder of events that took place over sixty-five years ago. Numerous developments have taken place since then within the realm of the Israeli-Palestinian conflict. I engaged with the topics of this research for the first time in 2000, in an atmosphere of cautious hope, of gradual steps toward improvement and dialogue; at that time, a hesitant casting about by Israel and its willingness to compromise and reach agreements, a budding outlook on the past that could be more brave and fair, and the lending of an ear to the position of the other side began to emerge. The steady escalation of hostilities later that year and in the following years shuffled the deck. A daily reality mired in violence and bloodshed has pushed each side to close ranks, dwell on its own victims and distress, entrench itself in its own narrative, and refuse to acknowledge that of the other. It seems that approaching a process of reconciliation, often seen as the end phase of conflict resolution, is nowhere in sight.

Focusing on the memory of villages and their remains may seem anachronistic and irrelevant, with the present being so violent and bloody. Nevertheless, even in the face of the most urgent issues of the present, it is essential to deeply know and understand the past—not in order to return to it, fixate on it, sanctify it, or engage in commemoration for the sake of commemoration—but in order to deal in a full, responsible, and tangible manner with the present, which is the product and continuation of the past; in order to know, understand, and comprehend the roots, the loss, the absence; to see the events since then as a single historical sequence; to acknowledge the dispossession and the injustice, to assume responsibility, to bring about a value-based discussion. From there, one could try to go on, on a path that would allow for a different future, a future with more well-being, growth, equality, and partnership.

There is no single answer for the question of what this path would be or what it might look like. Be that as it may, this path must incorporate an honest engagement with the events of the past, a true recognition of the heavy price paid by the Palestinians in 1948 to this day, and sustainable solutions to the human hardships that were produced then and have been created since then.

Instilling the depopulated villages in the Israeli public's awareness and bringing these villages back into the history and geography of the land are a step in this direction. Stressing the presence of what remains of the past can shed light on the roots of the present-day conflict, and help blaze the trail to a future of reconciliation.

Appendix A: Maps and Lists of the Depopulated Palestinian Villages

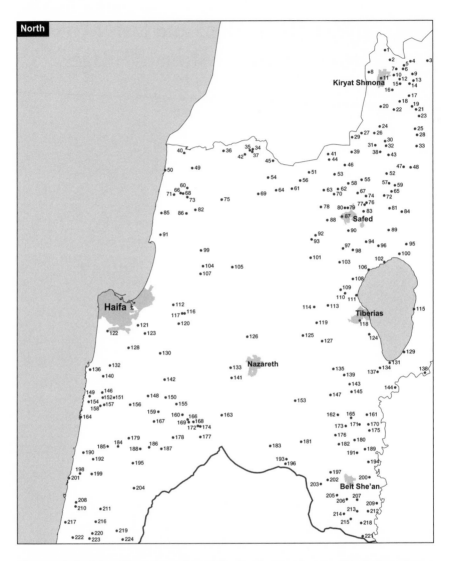

Maps 1–2. Palestinian villages depopulated following the War of 1948, within the boundaries of the State of Israel.

Source: The maps were produced by the author, with the assistance of Yuval Drier Shilo.

Notes:

· Every village is assigned a number that represents it on all of the following maps. The numbering of the villages runs from northwest eastward and southward and refers to their built-up area.

· The maps and the tables that follow include villages referred to by Khalidi (*All That Remains*): villages depopulated during the War of 1948 and its aftermath, which had permanent structures; they do not indicate areas from which Bedouins were uprooted in the South.

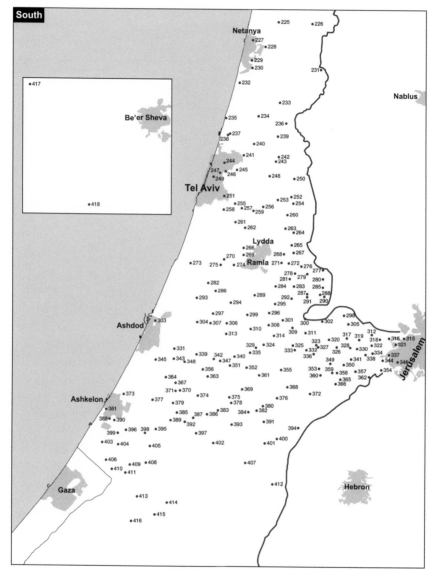

Table 1. Key to Maps 1–6.

Number in map	Village name	Number in map	Village name
1	Abil al-Qamh	37	al-Nabi Rubin
2	al-Zuq al-Fawqani	38	'Arab al-Zubayd
3	Khan al-Duwayr	39	Dayshum
4	al-Shawka al-Tahta	40	al-Bassa
5	al-Sanbariyya	41	Saliha
6	al-Khisas	42	Iqrit
7	al-Manshiyya	43	al-'Ulmaniyya
8	Hunin	44	Fara
9	al-Mansura	45	al-Mansura
10	al-Zuq al-Tahtani	46	'Alma
11	al-Khalisa	47	Tulayl
12	Lazzaza	48	al-Dirdara
13	Madahil	49	'Arab al-Samniyya
14	al-'Abisiyya	50	al-Zib
15	Qaytiyya	51	Kafr Bir'im
16	al-Na'ima	52	al-Husayniyya
17	al-Dawwara	53	al-Ras al-Ahmar
18	al-Salihiyya	54	Dayr al-Qasi
19	al-Muftakhira	55	Marus
20	al-Buwayziyya	56	Sa'sa'
21	al-Hamra'	57	Kirad al-Ghannama
22	al-Zawiya	58	Dallata
23	Khiyam al-Walid	59	Kirad al-Baqqara
24	Jahula	60	al-Kabri
25	Ghuraba	61	Ghabbatiyya
26	al-Nabi Yusha'	62	Taytaba
27	Qadas	63	Safsaf
28	al-'Urayfiyya	64	Sabalan
29	al-Malikiyya	65	Yarda
30	Baysamun	66	al-Tall
31	Harrawi	67	'Ammuqa
32	Mallaha	68	al-Nahr
33	al-Dirbashiyya	69	Suhmata
34	Suruh	70	Qaddita
35	Tarbikha	71	Umm al-Faraj
36	Khirbat 'Iribbin	72	al-Wayziyya

Number in map	Village name	Number in map	Village name
73	al-Ghabisiyya	110	Wadi al-Hamam
74	Qabba'a	111	al-Majdal
75	Khirbat Jiddin	112	Wa'arat al-Sarris
76	Mughr al-Khayt	113	Hittin
77	Fir'im	114	Nimrin
78	Mirun	115	al-Nuqayb
79	Biriyya	116	Hawsha
80	'Ayn al-Zaytun	117	Khirbat al-Kasayir
81	Khirbat al-Muntar	118	Nasir al-Din
82	'Amqa	119	Lubya
83	al-Ja'una	120	Khirbat Sa'sa'
84	Mansurat al-Khayt	121	Balad al-Shaykh
85	al-Sumayriyya	122	al-Tira
86	Kuwaykat	123	Yajur
87	al-Zahiriyya al-Tahta	124	al-Manara
88	al-Sammu'i	125	al-Shajara
89	al-Zanghariyya	126	Saffuriyya
90	'Akbara	127	Kafr Sabt
91	al-Manshiyya	128	Khirbat al-Damun
92	al-Farradiyya	129	al-Samra
93	Kafr 'Inan	130	al-Jalama
94	Jubb Yusuf	131	Samakh
95	al-Butayha	132	'Ayn Hawd
96	Khirbat Karraza	133	Ma'alul
97	al-Shuna	134	al-Manshiyya
98	al-Qudayriyya	135	Ma'dhar
99	al-Birwa	136	'Atlit
100	'Arab al-Shamalina	137	al-'Ubaydiyya
101	al-Mansura	138	al-Hamma
102	al-Samakiyya	139	Hadatha
103	Yaquq	140	al-Mazar
104	al-Damun	141	al-Mujaydil
105	Mi'ar	142	Khirbat al-Mansura
106	al-Tabigha	143	'Awlam
107	al-Ruways	144	al-Dalhamiyya
108	Ghuwayr Abu Shusha	145	Sirin
109	Khirbat al-Wa'ra al-Sawda	146	Jaba'

(continued)

Table 1. (*continued*)

Number in map	Village name	Number in map	Village name
147	al-Tira	182	al-Murassas
148	Umm al-Zinat	183	Zir'in
149	al-Sarafand	184	al-Sindiyana
150	Qira	185	Burayka
151	Ijzim	186	Khubbayza
152	Khirbat al-Manara	187	al-Butaymat
153	Indur	188	Umm al-Shawf
154	Kafr Lam	189	Zab'a
155	Abu Zurayq	190	Kabara
156	Khirbat Qumbaza	191	al-Hamidiyya
157	'Ayn Ghazal	192	Khirbat al-Shuna
158	al-Sawamir	193	Nuris
159	al-Rihaniyya	194	'Arab al-Bawati
160	Abu Shusha	195	Qannir
161	Khirbat al-Taqa	196	al-Mazar
162	Danna	197	al-Sakhina
163	Khirbat Lid	198	Barrat Qisarya
164	al-Tantura	199	Khirbat al-Burj
165	al-Bira	200	al-Ghazzawiyya
166	al-Ghubayya al-Tahta	201	Qisarya
167	Daliyat al-Rawha'	202	Tall al-Shawk
168	al-Naghnaghiyya	203	Khirbat al-Jawfa
169	al-Ghubayya al-Fawqa	204	Wadi 'Ara
170	Khirbat al-Zawiya	205	al-Ashrafiyya
171	Kawkab al-Hawa	206	Farwana
172	al-Mansi ('Arab Baniha)	207	Umm 'Ajra
173	Kafra	208	'Arab Zahrat al-Dumayri
174	'Ayn al-Mansi	209	Masil al-Jizl
175	Khirbat Umm Sabuna	210	'Arab al-Fuqara'
	('Arab al-Saqr)	211	Khirbat al-Sarkas
176	Yubla	212	'Arab al-Safa
177	al-Lajjun	213	'Arab al-'Arida
178	al-Kafrayn	214	al-Samiriyya
179	Sabbarin	215	al-Hamra
180	Jabbul	216	Raml Zayta (K. Qazaza)
181	Qumya	217	'Arab al-Nufay'at

Number in map	Village name	Number in map	Village name
218	al-Khunayzir	254	Qula
219	Khirbat al-Majdal	255	al-Khayriyya (Ibn Baraq)
220	Khirbat Zalafa	256	al-'Abbasiyya (al-Yahudiyya)
221	al-Fatur	257	Saqiya
222	Wadi al-Hawarith	258	Yazur
223	al-Manshiyya	259	Kafr 'Ana
224	al-Jalama	260	al-Tira
225	Wadi Qabbani	261	Bayt Dajan
226	Qaqun	262	al-Safiriyya
227	Umm Khalid	263	Dayr Tarif
228	Khirbat Bayt Lid	264	Bayt Nabala
229	Bayyarat Hannun	265	al-Haditha
230	Ghabat Kafr Sur	266	Sarafand al-'Amar
231	Fardisya	267	Dayr Abu Salama
232	Khirbat al-Zababida	268	Khirbat al-Duhayriyya
233	Miska	269	Abu al-Fadl (Satariyya)
234	Tabsur (Khirbet 'Azzun)	270	Sarafand al-Kharab
235	al-Haram	271	Daniyal
236	Kafr Saba	272	Jimzu
237	Ijlil al-Shamaliyya	273	al-Nabi Rubin
238	Ijlil al-Qibliyya	274	Bir Salim
239	Biyar 'Adas	275	Wadi Hunayn
240	Abu Kishk	276	Khirbat Zakariyya
241	al-Sawalima	277	Shilta
242	al-Muwaylih	278	Kharruba
243	al-Mirr (Mahmudiya)	279	Barfiliya
244	al-Shaykh Muwannis	280	al-Burj
245	al-Jammasin al-Sharqi	281	'Innaba
246	Jarisha	282	al-Qubayba
247	al-Jammasin al-Gharbi	283	al-Kunayyisa
248	Fajja	284	al-Barriyya
249	al-Mas'udiyya (Summayl)	285	Bir Ma'in
250	Majdal Yaba (Majdal al-Sadiq)	286	Zarnuqa
		287	Bayt Shanna
251	Salama	288	Khirbat al-Buwayra
252	al-Muzayri'a	289	al-Na'ani
253	Rantiya	290	'Ajanjul

(continued)

Table 1. (*continued*)

Number in map	Village name	Number in map	Village name
291	Salbit	327	Ishwa'
292	al-Qubab	328	Bayt Umm al-Mays
293	Yibna	329	Qazaza
294	'Aqir	330	Dayr 'Amr
295	Abu Shusha	331	Barqa
296	Saydun	332	Sar'a
297	al-Maghar	333	Dayr Rafat
298	Nitaf	334	Sataf
299	al-Mansura	335	Jilya
300	al-Latrun	336	'Artuf
301	Dayr Muhaysin	337	'Ayn Karim
302	Dayr Ayyub	338	Khirbat al-Lawz
303	'Arab Suqrir	339	Yasur
304	Bashshit	340	al-Khayma
305	Bayt Thul	341	'Aqqur
306	Shahma	342	al-Masmiyya al-Kabira
307	Qatra	343	al-Batani Al-Gharbi
308	Khulda	344	al-Jura
309	Bayt Jiz	345	Isdud
310	Umm Kalkha	346	al-Maliha
311	Bayt Susin	347	al-Masmiyya al-Saghira (al-Huraniyya)
312	Bayt Naqquba		
313	al-Mukhayzin	348	al-Batani Al-Sharqi
314	Khirbat Bayt Far	349	Dayr al-Hawa
315	Lifta	350	Dayr al-Shaykh
316	Qalunya	351	al-Tina
317	Saris	352	Idnibba
318	al-Qastal	353	Dayr Aban
319	Khirbat al-'Umur	354	al-Walaja
320	Bayt Mahsir	355	al-Burayj
321	Dayr Yasin	356	Qastina
322	Suba	357	Ras Abu 'Ammar
323	'Islin	358	Bayt 'Itab
324	Sajad	359	Sufla
325	Khirbat Ism Allah	360	Jarash
326	Kasla	361	Mughallis

Number in map	Village name	Number in map	Village name
362	al-Qabu	391	Kudna
363	Tall al-Turmus	392	Karatiyya
364	Bayt Daras	393	Zayta
365	'Allar	394	Khirbat Umm Burj
366	Khirbat al-Tannur	395	Kawkaba
367	al-Sawafir al-Shamaliyya	396	al-Jiyya
368	Zakariyya	397	al-Faluja
369	Tall al-Safi	398	Bayt Tima
370	al-Sawafir al-Sharqiyya	399	Barbara
371	al-Sawafir al-Gharbiyya	400	Dayr Nakhkhas
372	Bayt Nattif	401	Bayt Jibrin
373	Hamama	402	'Iraq al-Manshiyya
374	al-Jaladiyya	403	Hiribya
375	Bi'lin	404	Bayt Jirja
376	'Ajjur	405	Hulayqat
377	Julis	406	Dayr Sunayd
378	Barqusya	407	al-Qubayba
379	'Ibdis	408	Burayr
380	Dayr al-Dubban	409	Simsim
381	al-Jura	410	Dimra
382	Ra'na	411	Najd
383	Summil	412	al-Dawayima
384	Zikrin	413	Huj
385	Bayt 'Affa	414	al-Jammama
386	Jusayr	415	Kawfakha
387	Hatta	416	al-Muharraqa
388	al-Khisas	417	al-'Imara
389	'Iraq Suwaydan	418	al-Khalasa
390	Ni'ilya		

Table 2. Details on the Palestinian villages depopulated following the War of 1948, inside the State of Israel.

Village name	No. in map	No. of residents (1945) [1]	Size of village lands (1945, acres) [1] [2]	Date of depopulation [3]	Causes of depopulation [3] [4]	Village site has official name [5]	Village site in official maps	Built on an ancient settlement	Remaining buildings
Abil al-Qamh	1	330	1,140	May 10, 1948	N, F	yes	yes	yes	no
Abu al-Fadl ('Arab al-Satariyya)	269	510	709	May 9, 1948	N	no	no	no	yes
Abu Kishk	240	1,900	4,564	March 30, 1948	F, N	no	no	no	no
Abu Shusha	160	720	2,147	April 9, 1948	M, E	yes	yes	yes	no
Abu Shusha	295	870	2,329	May 14, 1948	M	no	yes	yes	no
Abu Zurayq	155	550	1,604	April 12, 1948	M, E	no	no	no	no
Ashrafiyya (al-)	205	230	1,658	May 12, 1948	F	yes	no	yes	no
'Abbasiyya (al-) (al-Yahudiyya)	256	5,650	5,076	May 4, 1948	M	no	no	yes	yes
'Abisiyya (al-)	14	1,200	3,813	May 25, 1948	N	no	no	no	no
'Ajanjul	290	n.d.	n.d.	n.d.	n.d.	yes	yes	yes	no
'Ajjur	376	3,730	14,351	October 24, 1948	M	no	yes	no	yes
'Akbara	90	390	797	May 1948	M, N	no	yes	yes	yes
'Allar	365	440	3,053	October 22, 1948	M	no	yes	no	yes
'Alma	46	950	4,818	October 30, 1948	M, E	no	yes	yes	yes
'Ammuqa	67	140	636	May 24, 1948	M, F	no	yes	yes	no
'Amqa	82	1,240	1,499	July 11, 1948	M	no	no	yes	yes

Village				Date	Cause				
'Aqir	294	2,480	3,910	May 6 (?), 1948	M, E	no	no	yes	yes
'Aqqur	341	40	1,365	July 14, 1948	M	no	no	no	yes
'Arab al-'Arida	213	150	563	May 20, 1948	N	yes	no	no	no
'Arab al-Bawati	194	520	2,629	May 16 or 20, 1948	N (?)	no	yes	yes	no
'Arab al-Fuqara'	210	310	671	April 10, 1948	E	no	no	no	no
'Arab al-Nufay'at	217	820	2,208	April 10, 1948	E	no	no	no	yes
'Arab al-Safa	212	650	3,093	May 20, 1948	N	no	no	no	no
'Arab al-Samniyya	49	~200	n.d.	October/November 1948	n.d.	no	no	no	no
'Arab al-Shamalina	100	~550	n.d.	April 4, 1948	M, E	no	no	no	no
'Arab al-Zubayd	38	~200	n.d.	April 20, 1948	F	no	no	no	no
'Arab Suqrir	303	390	9,940	May 25, 1948	M	no	no	no	yes
'Arab Zahrat al-Dumayri	208	620	341	April 10, 1948	E	no	no	yes	no
'Artuf	336	350	100	July 18, 1948	M	no	no	yes	yes
'Atlit	136	150	2,244	n.d.	n.d.	yes	yes	yes	no
'Awlam	143	720	4,583	April 6, 1948	O	no	yes	yes	no
'Ayn al-Mansi	174	90	320	mid-April 1948	M	no	no	no	no
'Ayn al-Zaytun	80	820	272	May 2, 1948	M, E	no	yes	yes	yes
'Ayn Ghazal	157	2,170	4,467	July 26, 1948	M, E	no	yes	no	yes
'Ayn Hawd	132	650	3,115	July 15, 1948	M	no	no	no	yes
'Ayn Karim	337	3,180	3,714	April 10-21, 1948; July 16, 1948	N; M	no	no	yes	yes

(continued)

Table 2. (*continued*)

Village name	No. in map	No. of residents (1945) [1]	Size of village lands (1945, acres) [1] [2]	Date of depopulation [3]	Causes of depopulation [3] [4]	Village site has official name [5]	Village site in official maps	Built on an ancient settlement	Remaining buildings
'Ibdis	379	540	1,135	July 9, 1948	M	no	yes	no	no
'Imara (al-)	417	n.d.	n.d.	May/October 1948	n.d.	no	no	no	no
'Innaba	281	1,420	3,177	July 10, 1948	M	yes	yes	yes	no
'Iraq al-Manshiyya	402	2,010	4,423	February–June 1949	E	yes	no	no	no
'Iraq Suwaydan	389	660	1,860	July 8, 1948	M	yes	yes	yes	no
'Islin	323	260	534	July 18, 1948	M	no	no	no	no
'Ubaydiyya (al-)	137	870	1,269	March 5, 1948	F	yes	yes	yes	yes
'Ulmaniyya (al-)	43	260	289	January 18, 1948; April 20, 1948	M; F	no	no	no	no
'Urayfiyya (al-)	28	n.d.	n.d.	April/May 1948	n.d.	yes	yes	no	no
Balad al-Shaykh	121	4,120	2,434	April 25, 1948	M, N	no	no	yes	yes
Barbara	399	2,410	3,454	November 5, 1948	M	yes	no	no	no
Barfiliya	279	730	1,763	mid-July 1948	M	no	yes	yes	no
Barqa	331	890	1,286	May 13, 1948	M	no	no	yes	yes
Barqusya	378	330	795	July 1948	n.d.	no	yes	yes	no
Barrat Qisarya	198	n.d.	n.d.	mid-April 1948	F, E	no	no	yes	yes

Barriyya (al-)	284	510	700	July 10–13, 1948	M	no	no	no	yes
Bashshit	304	1,620	4,585	May 13, 1948	M	no	no	no	yes
Bassa (al-)	40	~4,000	7,298	May 14, 1948	M, E	no	yes	yes	yes
Batani al-Gharbi (al-)	343	980	1,130	May 13, 1948	M (?)	no	yes	no	yes
Batani al-Sharqi (al-)	348	650	1,424	May 13, 1948/ June 11, 1948	F, M/(?)	no	yes	yes	no
Baysamun	30	20	519	May 25, 1948	P	no	no	no	no
Bayt 'Affa	385	700	1,435	July 9, 1948	F	no	yes	yes	no
Bayt 'Itab	358	540	2,164	October 21, 1948	M	no	yes	yes	yes
Bayt Dajan	261	3,840	4,282	late April1948	N	no	no	yes	yes
Bayt Daras	364	2,750	4,042	May 11, 1948	M	no	yes	yes	no
Bayt Jibrin	401	2,430	13,884	October 29, 1948	M	yes	yes	yes	yes
Bayt Jirja	404	940	2,096	October 30, 1948	n.d.	no	no	no	no
Bayt Jiz	309	550	2,065	April 20, 1948	M	yes	yes	no	yes
Bayt Mahsir	320	2,400	4,020	May 11, 1948	M	no	no	yes	yes
Bayt Nabala	264	471	3,719	May 13, 1948	O	yes	yes	yes	yes
Bayt Naqquba	312	240	736	early April 1948	M	no	no	no	yes
Bayt Nattif	372	2,150	11,018	October 22, 1948	M	yes	yes	yes	yes
Bayt Shanna	287	210	894	mid-July 1948	M (?)	yes	yes	yes	yes
Bayt Susin	311	210	1,602	April 20, 1948	M	no	no	no	no

(continued)

Table 2. (continued)

Village name	No. in map	No. of residents (1945) [1]	Size of village lands (1945, acres) [1] [2]	Date of depopulation [3]	Causes of depopulation [3] [4]	Village site has official name [5]	Village site in official maps	Built on an ancient settlement	Remaining buildings
Bayt Thul	305	260	1,144	April–June 1948 (?)	n.d.	no	yes	yes	no
Bayt Tima	398	1,060	2,726	October 18, 1948	M	yes	yes	yes	yes
Bayt Umm al-Mays	328	70	250	October 21, 1948	M (?)	no	yes	no	no
Bayyarat Hannun	229	~600 (inc. no. 230)	n.d.	early April 1948	F, E	yes	yes	no	yes
Bi'lin	375	180	1,986	July 1948	n.d.	no	yes	no	no
Bir Ma'in	285	510	2,303	July 16, 1948	M	yes	no	yes	yes
Bir Salim	274	410	840	May 9, 1948	M	no	no	no	yes
Bira (al-)	165	260	1,697	May 16, 1948	N	no	yes	yes	no
Biriyya	79	240	1,379	May 2, 1948	M	no	no	yes	yes
Birwa (al-)	99	1,460	3,346	June 11, 1948 (?)	M	no	yes	no	yes
Biyar 'Adas	239	300	1,357	April 12, 1948	M	no	no	yes	yes
Burayj (al-)	355	720	4,715	October 1948	n.d.	no	no	no	no
Burayka	185	290	2,825	May 12, 1948	M	no	no	no	no
Burayr	408	2,740	11,412	May 12, 1948	M	no	no	yes	yes
Burj (al-)	280	480	1,163	July 15, 1948	M	yes	yes	yes	yes
Butayha (al-)	95	~100	n.d.	May 1948	n.d.	yes	yes	no	yes
Butaymat (al-)	187	110	2,115	May 1948 (?)	F	no	yes	no	no
Buwayziyya (al-)	20	~400	3,613	May 11, 1948	N	no	no	no	no

Dalhamiyya (al-)	144	410	705	April/May 1948	n.d.	no	no	no	no
Daliyat al-Rawha'	167	280	2,473	late March 1948	P, M	no	yes	no	no
Dallata	58	360	2,242	May 1948 (?)	n.d.	no	yes	yes	no
Damun (al-)	104	1,310	5,030	mid-July 1948	M, E	no	yes	no	yes
Daniyal	271	410	694	July 10, 1948	M	no	no	no	yes
Danna	162	190	1,634	May 28, 1948	E	no	yes	yes	no
Dawayima (al-)	412	3,710	14,971	October 29, 1948	M	no	no	yes	no
Dawwara (al-)	17	700	1,352	May 25, 1948	P	no	no	no	no
Dayr 'Amr	330	~50	759	mid-July 1948	N, E	no	no	yes	yes
Dayr Aban	353	2,100	5,618	October 20, 1948	M	no	yes	yes	yes
Dayr Abu Salama	267	60	295	July 13, 1948	M	yes	no	no	no
Dayr al-Dubban	380	730	1,923	October 24, 1948	M	no	yes	no	no
Dayr al-Hawa	349	60	1,460	October 19, 1948	M	no	yes	yes	no
Dayr al-Qasi	54	~1,000	n.d.	October 30, 1948	M	no	no	yes	yes
Dayr al-Shaykh	350	220	1,676	October 21, 1948	M (?)	no	yes	yes	yes
Dayr Ayyub	302	320	1,490	April 1948	M	no	no	no	no

(continued)

Table 2. (continued)

Village name	No. in map	No. of residents (1945) [1]	Size of village lands (1945, acres) [1] [2]	Date of depopulation [3]	Causes of depopulation [3] [4]	Village site has official name [5]	Village site in official maps	Built on an ancient settlement	Remaining buildings
Dayr Muhaysin	301	460	2,473	April 6, 1948	M	no	no	yes	no
Dayr Nakhkhas	400	600	3,577	October 29, 1948	M	yes	no	yes	yes
Dayr Rafat	333	430	3,272	July 18, 1948	M	no	no	no	no
Dayr Sunayd	406	730	1,503	n.d.	n.d.	no	yes	no	no
Dayr Tarif	263	1,750	2,164	July 10, 1948	M	no	no	yes	yes
Dayr Yasin	321	750	706	April 9, 1948	M, E	no	no	yes	yes
Dayshum	39	590	5,694	October 30, 1948	M	no	yes	no	no
Dimra	410	520	2,098	early November 1948	F	no	yes	yes	yes
Dirbashiyya (al-)	33	310	712	May 1948 (?)	n.d.	yes	yes	no	no
Dirdara (al-)	48	100	1,572	April/May 1948	n.d.	no	no	no	no
Fajja	248	1,200	1,216	by May 15, 1948	M, P	no	no	yes	yes
Faluja (al-)	397	4,670	9,400	February–March 1949	E	yes	yes	no	yes
Fara	44	320	1,786	October 30, 1948	M	no	yes	no	yes
Fardisya	231	20	270	early April 1948 (?)	n.d.	no	yes	yes	yes

Farradiyya (al-)	92	670	4,880	February 1949	E	no	no	yes	no	yes
Farwana	206	330	1,235	May 11, 1948	M	yes	yes	yes	yes	no
Fatur (al-)	221	110	180	mid-February/May 1948	n.d.	no	yes	no	no	no
Fir'im	77	740	541	May 26, 1948	M	no	yes	yes	yes	no
Ghabat Kafr Sur	230	see no. 229	n.d.	April/May 1948	n.d.	no	no	no	no	yes
Ghabatiyya	61	60	725	October 30, 1948	n.d.	no	yes	no	no	no
Ghabisiyya (al-)	73	690	n.d.	May 21, 1948; January 1950	M, E; E	no	yes	no	no	yes
Ghazzawiyya (al-)	200	1,020	4,549	May 20, 1948	n.d.	no	no	no	no	no
Ghubayya al-Fawqa (al-)	169	see no. 166	n.d.	April 9, 1948	M	no	yes	no	no	no
Ghubayya al-Tahta (al-)	166	1,130 (inc.)	3,000	April 9, 1948	M	no	no	no	no	no
Ghuraba	25	220	853	May 28, 1948	F	yes	no	yes	yes	no
Ghuwayr Abu Shusha	108	1,240	2,990	April 21, 28, 1948	M, N	no	no	no	no	no
Hadatha	139	520	2,548	April 6, 1948	O	yes	yes	yes	yes	no
Haditha (al-)	265	760	1,757	July 12, 1948	M	no	yes	yes	yes	no
Hamama	373	5,070	10,222	November 4, 1948	M	no	yes	yes	yes	no
Hamidiyya (al-)	191	220	2,694	May 12, 1948	N	no	yes	yes	no	no
Hamma (al-)	138	290	418	1949–1956	P	yes	yes	yes	yes	yes

(continued)

Table 2. (*continued*)

Village name	No. in map	No. of residents (1945) [1]	Size of village lands (1945, acres) [1] [2]	Date of depopulation [3]	Causes of depopulation [3] [4]	Village site has official name [5]	Village site in official maps	Built on an ancient settlement	Remaining buildings
Hamra (al-)	215	730	2,844	n.d.	n.d.	no	no	no	no
Hamra' (al-)	21	n.d.	n.d.	May 1, 1948	M, F	no	yes	no	yes
Haram (al-) (Sayyiduna 'Ali)	235	520	1,993	February 3, 1948	F	no	yes	no	yes
Harrawi	31	~150	921	May 1948 (?)	n.d.	no	no	yes	no
Hatta	387	970	1,311	July 18, 1948	M	yes	yes	yes	no
Hawsha	116	400	223	mid-April 1948	M	yes	yes	yes	yes
Hiribya	403	2,300	5,513	late October–early November 1948	M, E	no	yes	yes	yes
Hittin	113	1,190	5,625	July 17, 1948	F, M	no	yes	yes	yes
Huj	413	810	5,433	May 31, 1948	E	yes	yes	yes	no
Hulayqat	405	420	1,739	May 12, 1948; October 20, 1948	N; n.d.	no	no	yes	no
Hunin	8	~1,200	3,515	May 3, 1948; September 1948	F, E	no	yes	yes	yes
Husayniyya (al-)	52	see no. 47	n.d.	March/April 1948	F/M	no	yes	no	no
Idnibba	352	490	2,002	July 10, 1948	M, E	no	yes	yes	yes

Ijlil al-Qibliyya	238	470	3,758	late March–April 3, 1948	F	yes	no	no	yes
Ijlil al-Shamaliyya	237	190	605	late March–April 3, 1948	F	no	no	no	no
Ijzim	151	2,970	11,591	July 26, 1948	M, E	no	no	yes	yes
Indur	153	620	3,075	May 24, 1948	M, N	yes	yes	yes	no
Iqrit	42	490	6,109	early November 1948	E	no	yes	yes	yes
Isdud	345	4,620	11,829	October 28, 1948	M, E	yes	yes	yes	yes
Ishwa'	327	620	1,365	July 18, 1948	M	no	no	no	yes
Ja'una (al-)	83	1,150	207	May 9, 1948; June 5, 1949	N; E	no	no	yes	yes
Jaba'	146	1,140	1,733	July 26, 1948	M, E	no	yes	yes	yes
Jabbul	180	250	3,738	May 18, 1948	F, N	yes	yes	yes	no
Jahula	24	420	956	May 1948 (?)	n.d.	no	yes	no	no
Jaladiyya (al-)	374	360	1,070	July 1948	F, M	no	no	yes	no
Jalama (al-)	130	n.d.	1,906	April/May 1948 (?)	n.d.	no	yes	yes	no
Jalama (al-)	224	70	n.d.	March 1, 1950	E	yes	yes	yes	no
Jammama (al-)	414	hundreds	n.d.	May 22, 1948	M	yes	yes	yes	no
Jammasin al-Gharbi (al-)	247	1,080	337	by March 17, 1948	F	no	no	no	yes
Jammasin al-Sharqi (al-)	245	730	88	by March 17, 1948	F	no	no	no	yes

(continued)

Table 2. (*continued*)

Village name	No. in map	No. of residents (1945) [1]	Size of village lands (1945, acres) [1] [2]	Date of depopulation [3]	Causes of depopulation [3] [4]	Village site has official name [5]	Village site in official maps	Built on an ancient settlement	Remaining buildings
Jarash	360	190	869	October 21, 1948	M	no	no	no	no
Jarisha	246	190	137	April/May 1948	N	no	no	no	yes
Jilya	335	330	2,557	July 10, 1948	M, E	no	yes	yes	no
Jimzu	272	1,510	2,392	July 10, 1948	M	no	no	yes	yes
Jiyya (al-)	396	1,230	2,102	November 5, 1948	M	no	no	yes	no
Jubb Yusuf ('Arab al-Suyyad)	94	170	2,799	April 5, 1948	n.d.	yes	yes	yes	yes
Julis	377	1,030	3,357	June 11, 1948	M	no	no	yes	yes
Jura (al-)	344	420	1,027	July 1948 (?)	n.d.	no	yes	no	yes
Jura (al-)	381	2,420	3,021	November 5, 1948	M	no	yes	no	yes
Jusayr	386	1,180	3,055	July 18, 1948	M	yes	yes	yes	yes
Kabara	190	120	2,429	April/May 1948 (?)	n.d.	no	no	no	no
Kabri (al-)	60	1,520	11,720	May 5, 21, 1948	F, M	no	no	yes	no
Kafr 'Ana	259	2,800	4,288	April 25, 1948	M	yes	yes	yes	no
Kafr 'Inan	93	360	1,440	February 1949	E	yes	yes	yes	yes
Kafr Bir'im	51	710	3,027	early November 1948	E	no	yes	yes	yes

Kafr Lam	154	340	1,690	July 16, 1948	M, N	no	yes	yes	yes
Kafr Saba	236	1,270	2,394	mid-May 1948	M	no	yes	yes	yes
Kafr Sabt	127	480	2,434	April 22, 1948	N	no	yes	yes	no
Kafra	173	430	2,266	May 16, 1948	N	no	yes	yes	no
Kafrayn (al-)	178	920	2,689	April 12, 1948	M	no	yes	yes	no
Karatiyya	392	1,370	3,388	July 18, 1948	M	yes	yes	yes	no
Kasla	326	280	1,978	July 18, 1948	M	no	yes	yes	no
Kawfakha	415	500	2,117	May 28, 1948	M, E	yes	yes	yes	yes
Kawkab al-Hawa	171	300	2,458	May 16, 1948	M	yes	yes	yes	yes
Kawkaba	395	680	2,111	May 12, 1948; mid-October 1948	N; n.d.	no	no	yes	no
Khalasa (al-)	418	n.d.	n.d.	October 1948 (?)	n.d.	yes	yes	yes	yes
Khalisa (al-)	11	1,840	2,787	May 11, 1948	N, P	no	no	no	yes
Khan al-Duwayr	3	260	1,381	April/May 1948	n.d.	yes	yes	yes	yes
Kharruba	278	170	834	mid-July 1948	M	no	yes	no	no
Khayma (al-)	340	190	1,273	July 10, 1948	M, E	no	no	no	no
Khayriyya (al-) (Ibn Baraq)	255	1,420	3,378	April 25, 1948	M	yes	yes	yes	no
Khirbat 'Iribbin	36	n.d.	n.d.	November 1948	E	yes	yes	yes	no
Khirbat al-'Umur	319	270	1,022	October 21, 1948	M (?)	no	no	no	no

(continued)

Table 2. (*continued*)

Village name	No. in map	No. of residents (1945) [1]	Size of village lands (1945, acres) [1] [2]	Date of depopulation [3]	Causes of depopulation [3] [4]	Village site has official name [5]	Village site in official maps	Built on an ancient settlement	Remaining buildings
Khirbat al-Burj	199	n.d.	1,307	by late March 1948	E (?)	no	no	yes	yes
Khirbat al-Buwayra	288	190	284	mid-July 1948 (?)	n.d.	yes	yes	yes	no
Khirbat al-Damun	128	340	691	April 1948	M, F	yes	yes	yes	yes
Khirbat al-Duhayriyya	268	100	331	July 10, 1948	M	no	yes	yes	yes
Khirbat al-Jawfa	203	n.d.	n.d.	May 12, 1948	N (?)	yes	yes	no	no
Khirbat al-Kasayir	117	n.d.	n.d.	mid-April 1948	M	yes	yes	no	no
Khirbat al-Lawz	338	450	1,112	July 14, 1948	n.d.	no	no	yes	yes
Khirbat al-Majdal	219	n.d.	n.d.	n.d.	n.d.	yes	yes	yes	no
Khirbat al-Manara	152	n.d.	n.d.	May/July 1948	n.d.	yes	yes	yes	no
Khirbat al-Mansura	142	n.d.	n.d.	April 1948 (?)	n.d.	yes	yes	yes	no
Khirbat al-Muntar	81	n.d.	n.d.	1949–1956	P	yes	yes	yes	no
Khirbat al-Sarkas	211	~400	n.d.	mid-April 1948	E	no	yes	no	no
Khirbat al-Shuna	192	n.d.	n.d.	by late May 1948	M	yes	yes	no	no
Khirbat al-Tannur ('Allar al-Sufla)	366	n.d.	n.d.	October 1948	n.d.	no	yes	yes	yes
Khirbat al-Taqa	161	n.d.	n.d.	May 1948 (?)	n.d.	yes	yes	yes	yes
Khirbat al-Wa'ra al-Sawda	109	1,870	1,739	November 2, 1948	E	no	no	no	no

Village								
Khirbat al-Zababida	232	n.d.	2,688	early April 1948 (?)	n.d.	no	no	yes
Khirbat al-Zawiya	170	n.d.	n.d.	May 1948	n.d.	yes	yes	no
Khirbat Bayt Far	314	300	1,385	April/May/June 1948	n.d.	yes	no	no
Khirbat Bayt Lid	228	460	1,319	April 5, 1948	F	yes	yes	no
Khirbat Ism Allah	325	20	140	July 1948	n.d.	no	no	yes
Khirbat Jiddin	75	1,500	1,875	July 1948	M (?)	yes	yes	yes
Khirbat Karraza	96	n.d.	n.d.	May 1948 (?)	n.d.	yes	yes	no
Khirbat Lid (al-'Awadin)	163	640	3,354	April / July 1948 (?)	n.d.	yes	no	no
Khirbat Qumbaza	156	n.d.	n.d.	May 1948 (?)	n.d.	yes	yes	no
Khirbat Sa'sa'	120	130	n.d.	April 1948 (?)	n.d.	yes	yes	yes
Khirbat Umm Burj	394	140	3,233	late October 1948 (?); March 8, 1949	n.d.	yes	yes	yes
Khirbat Umm Sabuna	175	n.d.	n.d.	May 1948	n.d.	yes	yes	no
Khirbat Zakariyya	276	n.d.	1,121	July 13, 1948	M, N	yes	yes	no
Khirbat Zalafa	220	210	1,906	April 15, 1948	P, F	no	no	no
Khisas (al-)	6	470	1,185	May 25, 1948; June 5, 1949	P, N, E	yes	yes	no
Khisas (al-)	388	150	1,549	November 5, 1948	M	yes	yes	no
Khiyam al-Walid	23	280	1,019	May 1, 1948	F	yes	no	no

(continued)

Table 2. (continued)

Village name	No. in map	No. of residents (1945) [1]	Size of village lands (1945, acres) [1] [2]	Date of depopulation [3]	Causes of depopulation [3] [4]	Village site has official name [5]	Village site in official maps	Built on an ancient settlement	Remaining buildings
Khubbayza	186	290	1,199	mid-May 1948	M	no	yes	no	no
Khulda	308	280	2,338	April 6, 1948	M	no	yes	yes	yes
Khunayzir (al-)	218	260	768	May 20, 1948	N	no	no	no	no
Kirad al-Baqqara	59	360	559	April 22, 1948; 1956	N; E	no	no	no	no
Kirad al-Ghannama	57	350	982	April 22, 1948; 1956	N; E	no	yes	no	no
Kudna	391	450	3,890	October 23, 1948	M	yes	yes	yes	yes
Kunayyisa (al-)	283	40	957	July 10, 1948	M	yes	yes	yes	yes
Kuwaykat	86	1,050	1,170	July 10, 1948	M, E	no	no	no	yes
Lajjun (al-)	177	1,103	19,087	May 30, 1948 (?)	M	yes	yes	yes	yes
Latrun (al-)	300	190	2,070	May/July 1948; April 1949	M; A	no	yes	yes	no
Lazzaza	12	230	392	May 21, 1948	P	no	no	no	no
Lifta	315	2,550	2,160	January 1948	M	yes	yes	yes	yes
Lubya	119	2,350	9,051	July 16, 1948	F, M	yes	yes	yes	yes
Ma'alul	133	690	1,161	July 15, 1948	M	no	yes	yes	yes
Ma'dhar	135	480	2,883	April 6, 1948	O	yes	yes	yes	no
Madahil	13	100+	n.d.	April 30, 1948	F	no	no	no	no

Maghar (al-)	297	1,740	3,803	May 18, 1948	M	no	yes	yes	no
Majdal (al-)	111	360	1,386	April 22, 1948	M, N	no	yes	yes	yes
Majdal Yaba (Majdal al Sadiq)	250	1,520	6,581	July 13, 1948	M	yes	yes	yes	yes
Maliha (al-)	346	1,940	1,687	April 21, 1948; mid-July 1948	N; M	yes	yes	yes	yes
Malikiyya (al-)	29	360	1,811	May 28, 1948	M	no	no	no	no
Mallaha	32	~700	n.d.	May 25, 1948	P	no	yes	no	no
Manara (al-)	124	490	n.d.	early March 1948	M	yes	yes	yes	no
Manshiyya (al-)	7	~80	n.d.	May 24, 1948	P	no	no	no	no
Manshiyya (al-)	91	810	3,678	May 14, 1948	M	no	no	yes	yes
Manshiyya (al-)	134	n.d.	n.d.	March 1948	n.d.	no	yes	no	no
Manshiyya (al-)	223	260	4,144	mid-April 1948	F	no	no	no	no
Mansi (al-) ('Arab Baniha)	172	1,220	3,033	April 13, 1948	M	no	no	no	yes
Mansura (al-)	9	360	382	May 25, 1948	P	no	no	no	no
Mansura (al-)	45	~1,200	n.d.	early November 1948	E	no	yes	yes	yes
Mansura (al-)	101	n.d.	n.d.	May/October 1948	n.d.	no	yes	no	no
Mansura (al-)	299	90	575	April 20, 1948	M	no	no	no	no
Mansurat al-Khayt	84	200	1,664	January 18, 1948; 1949–1956	M; P	yes	yes	no	no

(continued)

Table 2. (continued)

Village name	No. in map	No. of residents (1945) [1]	Size of village lands (1945, acres) [1] [2]	Date of depopulation [3]	Causes of depopulation [3] [4]	Village site has official name [5]	Village site in official maps	Built on an ancient settlement	Remaining buildings
Marus	55	80	787	May 26, 1948/ October 30, 1948	N/M	yes	yes	yes	no
Mas'udiyya (al-) (Summayl)	249	850	n.d.	December 25, 1947	F	no	no	no	yes
Masil al-Jizl	209	100	1,451	May 1948 (?)	n.d.	no	no	no	no
Masmiyya al-Kabira (al-)	342	2,520	5,112	July 9, 1948	M	yes	no	no	yes
Masmiyya al-Saghira (al-) (al-Huraniyya)	347	530	1,601	July 9, 1948	M	no	yes	no	no
Mazar (al-)	140	210	1,971	July 15, 1948	M	no	yes	yes	yes
Mazar (al-)	196	270	3,583	May 30, 1948	M	yes	yes	yes	no
Mi'ar	105	770	2,666	mid-July 1948	M	no	no	yes	no
Mirr (al-) (al-Mahmudiyya)	243	170	1,386	February/ March 1948	F	no	yes	yes	yes
Mirun	78	290	3,488	May 12, 1948	N	no	yes	yes	yes
Miska	233	880	1,996	April 15, 1948	E	no	yes	no	yes
Muftakhira (al-)	19	350	2,277	May 16, 1948	F	no	no	no	no
Mughallis	361	540	2,832	July 10, 1948	M, E	no	yes	no	no
Mughr al-Khayt	76	490	1,638	May 2, 1948	M	yes	yes	yes	yes
Muharraqa (al-)	416	580	1,200	May 28, 1948	M, E	no	no	yes	no

Village								
Mujaydil (al-)	141	1,900	4,655	mid-July 1948	M, E	no	yes	no	yes
Mukhayzin (al-)	313	200	3,101	April 20, 1948	M	no	yes	yes	no
Murassas (al-)	182	460	3,577	May 16, 1948	N	no	yes	no	no
Muwaylih (al-)	242	360	826	early 1948	n.d.	no	no	no	yes
Muzayri'a (al-)	252	1,160	2,674	July 12, 1948 (?)	n.d.	yes	yes	yes	yes
Na'ani (al-)	289	1,470	3,986	May 14, 1948	F	no	yes	yes	yes
Na'ima (al-)	16	1,030	1,768	May 14, 1948	N	no	yes	no	no
Nabi Rubin (al-)	37	~150	n.d.	early November 1948	E	no	yes	no	no
Nabi Rubin (al-)	273	1,420	7,661	June 1, 1948	E	no	yes	no	yes
Nabi Yusha' (al-)	26	70	894	May 16, 1948	M	no	yes	no	yes
Naghnaghiyya (al-)	168	see no. 166	n.d.	April 13, 1948	M	no	no	no	no
Nahr (al-)	68	610	1,300	May 21, 1948	M	no	no	yes	yes
Najd	411	620	3,355	May 12, 1948	E	yes	yes	yes	no
Nasir al-Din	118	90	n.d.	April 12, 23, 1948	M, E	no	no	yes	no
Ni'ilya	390	1,310	1,293	November 5, 1948	M	no	yes	no	yes
Nimrin	114	320	2,970	July 17, 1948	F, M (?)	no	yes	yes	no
Nitaf	298	40	346	n.d.	E	yes	yes	yes	yes
Nuqayb (al-)	115	320	3,215	May 14, 1948	E	no	yes	no	no
Nuris	193	570	1,546	May 30, 1948	M, F	yes	yes	yes	no
Qabba'a	74	460	3,414	May 26, 1948	M	yes	yes	yes	no
Qabu (al-)	362	260	940	October 22, 1948	M	yes	yes	yes	yes

(continued)

Table 2. (continued)

Village name	No. in map	No. of residents (1945) [1]	Size of village lands (1945, acres) [1] [2]	Date of depopulation [3]	Causes of depopulation [3] [4]	Village site has official name [5]	Village site in official maps	Built on an ancient settlement	Remaining buildings
Qadas	27	~300	3,494	May 28, 1948	M	yes	yes	yes	yes
Qaddita	70	240	603	May 11, 1948	N	no	yes	no	no
Qalunya	316	910	1,197	early April 1948	M	no	no	yes	no
Qannir	195	750	2,800	April 25, 1948	F, N	no	yes	no	no
Qaqun	226	1,970	10,321	June 5, 1948	M	no	yes	yes	yes
Qastal (al-)	318	90	357	April 3, 1948	M	no	yes	yes	yes
Qastina	356	890	2,970	July 9, 1948	M, N	no	no	no	no
Qatra	307	1,210	1,941	May 1948	M, E	no	no	yes	yes
Qaytiyya	15	924	1,332	May 19, 1948; June 5, 1949	E, P	no	no	no	no
Qazaza	329	940	4,653	July 10, 1948	M, E	no	yes	no	no
Qira and Qamun	150	~100	3,649	late March 1948 (?)	P	yes	yes	yes	yes
Qisarya	201	960	7,855	February 1948	E	yes	yes	yes	yes
Qubab (al-)	292	1,980	3,439	May 15, 1948	M	no	yes	no	yes
Qubayba (al-)	282	1,720	2,653	May 28, 1948	M, E	no	yes	yes	no
Qubayba (al-)	407	1,060	2,944	October 28, 1948	M	yes	yes	yes	no
Qudayriyya (al-)	98	390	3,086	April 4, 1948	M, E	no	yes	no	yes
Qula	254	1,010	1,074	July 10, 1948	M	no	yes	yes	yes
Qumya	181	440	1,210	March 26, 1948	F	no	no	no	no

Village			Date					
Ra'na	382	190	1,711	October 23, 1948	M	no	yes	no	no
Raml Zayta (K. Qazaza)	216	140	3,143	March/April 1948 (?)	n.d.	no	no	no	yes
Rantiya	253	590	1,085	April 28, 1948; July 10, 1948	M	no	no	yes	yes
Ras Abu 'Ammar	357	620	2,061	October 21, 1948	M	no	yes	no	yes
Ras al-Ahmar (al-)	53	620	1,961	October 30, 1948	M	no	no	yes	yes
Rihaniyya (al-)	159	240	477	April 1948 (?)	n.d.	no	yes	no	no
Ruways (al-)	107	330	287	mid-July 1948	M	no	yes	yes	yes
Sa'sa'	56	1,130	3,656	October 30, 1948	M, E	no	yes	yes	yes
Sabalan	64	70	444	October 30, 1948	n.d.	no	yes	no	yes
Sabbarin	179	1,700	6,254	May 12, 1948	M, E	no	yes	yes	no
Saffuriyya	126	4,330	13,684	July 16, 1948; January 1949	M, E	yes	yes	yes	yes
Safiriyya (al-)	262	3,070	3,173	April/May 1948	n.d.	no	no	yes	yes
Safsaf	63	910	1,826	October 29, 1948	M, F	no	yes	yes	yes
Sajad	324	370	691	June–July, 1948	n.d.	no	yes	yes	no
Sakhina (al-)	197	530	1,581	May 12, 1948 (?)	n.d.	no	no	no	no

(continued)

Table 2. (*continued*)

Village name	No. in map	No. of residents (1945) [1]	Size of village lands (1945, acres) [1] [2]	Date of depopulation [3]	Causes of depopulation [3] [4]	Village site has official name [5]	Village site in official maps	Built on an ancient settlement	Remaining buildings
Salama	251	6,730	1,676	April 25, 1948	M	no	no	no	yes
Salbit	291	510	1,510	July 16, 1948	M	yes	yes	yes	no
Saliha	41	1,070	2,900	October 30, 1948	M	no	yes	yes	yes
Salihiyya (al-)	18	1,520	1,386	May 25, 1948	P, F	no	no	no	no
Samakh	131	3,460	4,599	April 28, 1948	M	no	no	yes	no
Samakiyya (al-)	102	380	2,601	n.d.	n.d.	no	no	no	no
Samiriyya (al-)	214	250	957	May 27, 1948	M	yes	yes	yes	no
Sammu'i (al-)	88	310	3,740	May 12, 1948	N	yes	yes	yes	yes
Samra (al-)	129	290	3,104	April 21, 1948	N	no	yes	yes	no
Sanbariyya (al-)	5	130	626	May 1948 (?)	n.d	no	no	no	no
Saqiya	257	1,100	1,446	April 25, 1948	M	no	no	no	yes
Sar'a	332	340	1,227	July 18, 1948	M	yes	yes	yes	yes
Sarafand (al-)	149	290	1,337	July 16, 1948	M, N	no	yes	no	yes
Sarafand al-'Amar	266	1,950	3,278	May 20, 1948 (?)	n.d.	yes	yes	yes	no
Sarafand al-Kharab	270	1,040	1,360	April 20, 1948	F	no	no	yes	yes
Saris	317	560	2,644	mid-April 1948	M	no	yes	no	yes
Sataf	334	540	933	July 14, 1948	M	no	no	yes	yes
Sawafir al-Gharbiyya (al-)	371	1,030	1,859	May 18, 1948	F, N, M	no	yes	yes	no

Village									
Sawafir al-Shamaliyya (al-)	367	680	1,448	May 18, 1948	M	no	yes	yes	yes
Sawafir al-Sharqiyya (al-)	370	970	3,418	May 18, 1948	F, M	no	no	no	no
Sawalima (al-)	241	800	1,468	March 30, 1948	F, N	no	no	no	yes
Sawamir (al-)	158	n.d.	n.d.	May/July 1948	n.d.	yes	yes	yes	yes
Saydun	296	210	1,850	April 1948 (?)	n.d.	no	no	yes	yes
Shahma	306	280	1,699	May 14, 1948	N	no	no	no	no
Shajara (al-)	125	770	928	May 6, 1948	M	no	yes	yes	yes
Shawka al-Tahta (al-)	4	200	527	May 14, 1948	F	no	no	no	no
Shaykh Muwannis (al-)	244	1,930	3,947	late March 1948	M, F	no	yes	no	yes
Shilta	277	100	1,329	mid-July 1948	M	yes	yes	yes	no
Shuna (al-)	97	170	904	April/May 1948 (?)	n.d.	yes	yes	yes	no
Simsim	409	1,290	4,151	May 12, 1948	E	no	yes	yes	no
Sindiyana (al-)	184	1,250	3,749	May 12, 1948	M	no	yes	yes	no
Sirin	145	810	7,029	April 6, 1948	O	no	yes	yes	yes
Suba	322	620	1,014	July 13, 1948	M	yes	yes	yes	yes
Sufla	359	60	509	October 19, 1948	M	no	yes	yes	no
Suhmata	69	1,130	4,215	October 30, 1948	M	no	no	yes	yes
Sumayriyya (al-)	85	760	2,111	May 14, 1948	M, N	no	yes	yes	no
Summil	383	950	4,770	mid-July 1948	M	no	yes	no	no

(continued)

Table 2. (continued)

Village name	No. in map	No. of residents (1945) [1]	Size of village lands (1945, acres) [1] [2]	Date of depopulation [3]	Causes of depopulation [3] [4]	Village site has official name [5]	Village site in official maps	Built on an ancient settlement	Remaining buildings
Suruh	34	~150	n.d.	early November 1948	E	yes	no	yes	no
Tabigha (al-)	106	330	1,332	May 1948	M, N	yes	no	yes	no
Tabsur (Khirbat 'Azzun)	234	~1,000	1,317	April 3, 1948	F, E	no	no	yes	no
Tall (al-)	66	300	n.d.	May 21, 1948	M	no	no	yes	no
Tall al-Safi	369	1,290	7,148	July 10, 1948	M	yes	yes	yes	yes
Tall al-Shawk	202	120	911	May 12, 1948	N (?)	yes	yes	no	no
Tall al-Turmus	363	760	2,844	July 1948	F	yes	yes	yes	no
Tantura (al-)	164	1,490	3,588	May 21, 1948	M, E	no	yes	yes	no
Tarbikha	35	~700	n.d.	early November 1948	E	no	no	yes	yes
Taytaba	62	530	2,089	May 1948 (?)	N	no	yes	no	no
Tina (al-)	351	750	1,730	July 9, 1948	M	no	yes	no	no
Tira (al-) (Tirat Haifa)	122	5,270	11,185	July 16, 1948	M	no	no	yes	yes
Tira (al-)	147	150	2,522	April 15, 1948	P	no	yes	yes	no
Tira (al-) (Tirat Dandan)	260	1,290	1,719	July 10, 1948	M	no	yes	yes	no
Tulayl	47	430 (inc. no. 52)	n.d.	late April 1948 (?)	n.d.	yes	yes	yes	yes
Umm 'Ajra	207	260	1,592	May 1948 (?)	n.d.	no	no	no	no

Umm al-Faraj	71	800	204	May 21, 1948	M	no	no	no	no
Umm al-Shawf	188	480	1,835	May 12–14, 1948	M	yes	no	yes	no
Umm al-Zinat	148	1,470	5,436	May 1948	F	yes	yes	yes	no
Umm Kalkha	310	60	347	May 1948 (?)	n.d.	no	no	no	no
Umm Khalid	227	970	715	March 20, 1948	F	yes	yes	yes	no
Wa'arat al-Sarris	112	190	n.d.	April 1948 (?)	n.d.	yes	no	no	no
Wadi 'Ara	204	230	2,420	February 27, 1948	F	yes	yes	no	no
Wadi al-Hamam	110	n.d.	n.d.	n.d.	n.d.	no	no	no	no
Wadi al-Hawarith	222	1,330	n.d.	April 15, 1948	M, F	yes	no	no	no
Wadi Hunayn	275	~1,600	1,335	April 17, 1948	N	yes	no	no	no
Wadi Qabbani	225	320	2,425	April 1948 (?)	n.d.	no	yes	no	no
Walaja (al-)	354	1,650	4,376	October 21, 1948; April 3, 1949	M; A	yes	no	yes	no
Wayziyya (al-)	72	100	945	May 1948	n.d.	no	no	no	no
Yajur	123	610	672	April 25, 1948	M, N	yes	no	yes	no
Yaquq	103	210	2,102	May 1948 (?)	n.d.	no	yes	no	no
Yarda	65	20	338	1949–1956	P	yes	yes	yes	no
Yasur	339	1,070	4,050	June 11, 1948	M	yes	no	no	no
Yazur	258	4,030	2,918	May 1, 1948	M, N	yes	yes	yes	no
Yibna	293	5,420	14,716	June 4, 1948	M, E	yes	yes	yes	no
Yubla	176	210	1,276	May 16, 1948	N	no	yes	yes	no
Zab'a	189	170	981	n.d.	n.d.	no	no	no	no

(continued)

Table 2. *(continued)*

Village name	No. in map	No. of residents (1945) [1]	Size of village lands (1945, acres) [1] [2]	Date of depopulation [3]	Causes of depopulation [3] [4]	Village site has official name [5]	Village site in official maps	Built on an ancient settlement	Remaining buildings
Zahiriyya al-Tahta (al-)	87	350	1,674	May 10, 1948	N	no	no	no	yes
Zakariyya	368	1,180	3,786	June 1950	E	no	no	yes	yes
Zanghariyya (al-)	89	840	6,899	April 4, 1948	M, E	yes	yes	yes	no
Zarnuqa	286	2,380	1,864	May 28, 1948	M, E	yes	yes	no	yes
Zawiya (al-)	22	760	978	May 24, 1948	M, E	no	no	no	no
Zayta	393	330	2,592	July 18, 1948	M	yes	yes	no	no
Zib (al-)	50	1,910	3,115	May 14, 1948	M	yes	yes	yes	yes
Zikrin	384	960	4,249	October 23, 1948	M	yes	yes	yes	yes
Zir'in	183	1,420	5,911	May 28, 1948	M	yes	yes	yes	yes
Zuq al-Fawqani (al-)	2	160	453	May 21, 1948	P, M	no	yes	yes	no
Zuq al-Tahtani (al-)	10	1,050	2,875	May 11, 1948	N	no	yes	yes	no

Notes:

n.d. = no data

[1] The number of inhabitants and the size of the village lands are based on a survey conducted by the British Mandate government in Palestine in 1944–1945, quoted in Khalidi, *All That Remains*.

[2] The total area of the Palestinian villages includes land sold to Jews, which comprised 7 percent of the total villages' area in 1948.

[3] The sources for the date of village depopulation, and reasons behind it, are Khalidi, *All That Remains*, and Morris, *The Birth of the Palestinian Refugee Problem Revisited*. When the depopulation date of a village is not known, the date of its occupation is presented. A question mark represents a speculated date or reason of depopulation.

[4] Key of causes of depopulation:

A = Armistice agreement   E = Expulsion

F = Fear of an attack   M = Military attack

N = Occupation, attack, or   O = An Arab order

    depopulation of a nearby community   P = Psychological warfare and pressure

[5] The information in the last four columns is based on documents of the GNC; hiking maps; Khalidi, *All That Remains*; Markus and Ela'zari, *Mapa Encyclopedia*; and field observations.

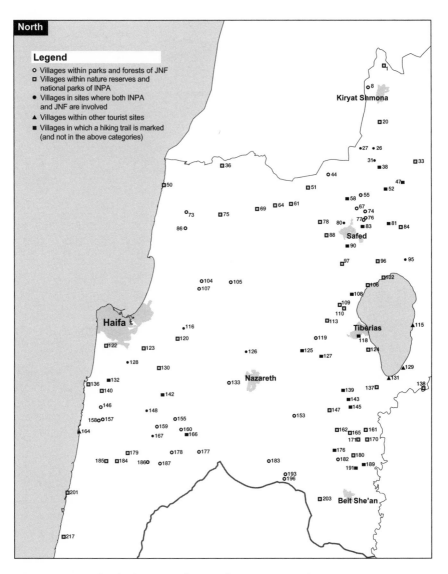

Maps 3–4. Depopulated Palestinian villages within recreation and tourism Sites.
Source of the maps and Tables 3–6: Primary material of JNF, INPA, official maps, and field observations.
Note: The maps and Tables 3–6 refer to villages whose built-up area was within recreation and tourism sites in 2007.

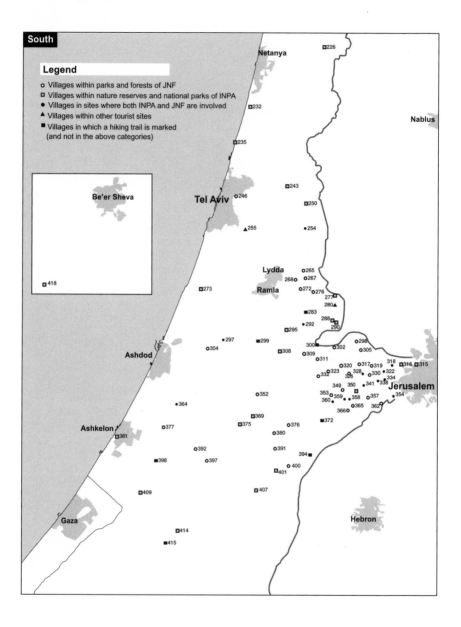

Table 3. Depopulated Palestinian villages within JNF forests and parks.

Village name	Name of park or forest [1]	Hiking trail [2]	Signs/mention of village	Brochures/mention of village	No. in map
al-Walaja*	'Aminadav Forest	yes	none	yes/no mention	354
Bashshit	'Aseret Forest	no	yes/mention	none	304
Dayr Ayub	Ayalon Canada Park [7]	yes	yes/no mention	yes/mention	302
Farra	Bar'am Forest	no	none	yes/no mention	44
Dayr Nakhkhas	Be'er Nakhash	yes	none	none	400
Ras Abu 'Ammar	Begin Park	yes	none	yes/no mention	357
al-Qabu	Begin Park	yes	none	yes/mention	362
Kuwaykat	Beit Ha'Emek Forest	no	none	none	86
Dayr Abu Salama	Ben Shemen Forest	yes	yes/no mention	yes/no mention	267
Khirbat al-Duhayriyya	Ben Shemen Forest	no	yes/no mention	yes/no mention	268
Jimzu	Ben Shemen Forest	no	yes/no mention	yes/no mention	272
Khirbat Zakariyya	Ben Shemen Forest	no	yes/no mention	yes/no mention	276
Haditha	Ben Shemen Forest	yes	yes/mention	yes/mention	265
'Ayn al-Zaytun*	Biria Forest	no	yes/mention	yes/mention	80
'Ammuqa	Biria Forest	no	yes/no mention	yes/no mention	67
Qabba'a	Biria Forest	no	yes/no mention	yes/no mention	74
Mughr al-Khayt	Biria Forest	no	yes/no mention	yes/no mention	76
Fir'im	Biria Forest	yes	yes/no mention	yes/no mention	77
Dayr al-Dubban	British Park	no	yes/no mention	yes/no mention	380
'Ajjur	British Park	no	yes/no mention	yes/mention	376
Kudna	British Park	no	yes/no mention	yes/mention	391
Jaba'	Carmel Coast Forest	yes	yes/no mention	yes/mention	146

(continued)

Table 3. *(continued)*

Village name	Name of park or forest [1]	Hiking trail [2]	Signs/mention of village	Brochures/mention of village	No. in map
Sawamir	Carmel Coast Forest	yes	yes/no mention [5]	yes/no mention [5]	158
'Ayn Ghazal	Carmel Coast Forest	yes	yes/no mention [5]	yes/mention	157
al-Qastal*	Castel N.P.	no	yes/no mention [4]	none	318
Indur	Forest near 'Ein Dor	no	none	none	153
al-Damun	Forest near Kabul	no	none	none	104
Ruways	Forest near Tamra	no	none	none	107
Nuris	Gilboa' Forest	no	none	yes/mention	193
al-Mazar	Gilboa' Forest	no	none	yes/mention	196
Umm al-Zinat*	HaCarmel Forests	no	none	yes/no mention	148
Khirbat al-Damun*	HaCarmel Forests	no	none	yes/no mention	128
Idniba	Haruvit Forest	yes	none	yes/no mention	352
al-Butayha*	HaYarden Park	no	none	yes/no mention	95
Julis	Hodaya recreation area	no	yes/mention	none	377
Ma'alul	Kfar HaHoresh Forest	no	yes/mention	yes/no mention [3]	133
Nitaf	Kfira Forest	yes	none	yes/mention	298
Bayt Thul	Kfira Forest	yes	none	yes/mention	305
Hawsha*	Kiryat Ata Forest	no	yes/no mention	yes/mention	116
Lubia	Lavi Forest	yes	none	yes/mention	119
al-Qubab*	Lehi Forest	no	none	none	292
Bayt Umm al-Mays*	Martyrs Forest	no	none	yes/no mention	328
'Aqqur*	Martyrs Forest	yes	none	yes/no mention	341
Khirbat al-'Umur	Martyrs Forest	no	none	yes/no mention	319

Village	Location				
Kasla	Martyrs Forest	no	none	yes/no mention	326
Dayr 'Amr	Martyrs Forest	no	yes/mention	yes/no mention	330
al-Lajjun	Megiddo Forest	yes	none	none	177
al-Maghar*	Merar Hills	yes	yes/mention	none	297
Marus	Merot Ruin	yes	yes/no mention [3]	none	55
Qadas*	Naftali Hills	no	yes/no mention	yes/no mention	27
al-Nabi Yusha**	Naftali Hills	yes	yes/no mention	yes/mention	26
Harawi*	Naftali Hills	yes	none	yes/no mention	31
Hunin	Naftali Hills	no	none	yes/mention	8
Karatiyya	Plugot Forest	no	none	none	392
al-Faluja	Plugot Forest	no	none	none	397
Qula*	Qula Forest	no	none	none	254
Bayt Jiz	Rabin Park	yes	yes/mention	yes/mention	309
'Islin	Rabin Park/Eshta'ol Forest	yes	yes/no mention	yes/no mention	323
Bayt Susin	Rabin Park/Eshta'ol Forest	yes	yes/mention	yes/mention	311
Saris	Rabin Park/Martyrs Forest	no	yes/mention	yes/no mention	317
Bayt Mahsir	Rabin Park/Martyrs Forest	no	yes/mention	yes/no mention	320
Daliyat al-Rawha'*	Ramot Menashe Park	yes	yes/no mention	yes/no mention	167
al-Rihaniyya	Ramot Menashe Park	yes	yes/no mention	yes/no mention	159
Abu Shusha	Ramot Menashe Park	no	yes/no mention	yes/no mention	160
Khubbayza	Ramot Menashe Park	yes	yes/no mention	yes/no mention	186
al-Butaymat	Ramot Menashe Park	no	yes/no mention	yes/no mention	187
al-Kafrayn	Ramot Menashe Park	yes	yes/no mention	yes/mention	178
Abu Zurayq	Ramot Menashe Park	no	yes/no mention	yes/no mention	155
al-Murassas	Ramot Yissachar scenic road	no	none	yes/no mention	182
Jarisha	Rosh Tzipor Forest	no	yes/no mention [6]	yes/no mention	246

(continued)

Table 3: (*continued*)

Village name	Name of park or forest [1]	Hiking trail [2]	Signs/mention of village	Brochures/mention of village	No. in map
Khirbat al-Lawz*	Sataf Forest	no	none	yes/no mention	338
Sataf*	Sataf Forest	yes	none	yes/mention	334
Mi'ar	Segev Forest	no	none	none	105
Suba*	Tel Tsova	yes	yes/mention	yes/mention	322
Zir'in	Tel Yizra'el	no	yes/no mention	yes/mention	183
Saffuriyya*	Tzipori N.P.	no	none	none	126
Sar'a	Tzor'a Forest	yes	yes/no mention	yes/mention	332
Sufla*	USA Independence Park	yes	yes/no mention	yes/no mention	359
Jarash*	USA Independence Park	yes	yes/no mention	yes/no mention	360
Bayt 'Itab*	USA Independence Park	yes	yes/no mention	yes/mention	358
Khirbat al-Tannur	USA Independence Park	yes	yes/no mention	yes/no mention	366
Dayr al-Hawa	USA Independence Park	yes	yes/no mention	yes/mention	349
Dayr Aban	USA Independence Park	yes	yes/no mention	yes/mention	353
'Allar	USA Independence Park	yes	yes/no mention	yes/mention	365
Ghabsiyya	Yehi'am Forest	no	yes/no mention	none	73
Bayt Daras*	Zmorot Pool N.P.	no	yes/mention	none	364

Notes:

*The village site is in an area where both JNF and INPA are involved in distributing information to the public.

[1] N.P. = National Park

[2] Hiking trail in the village site or next to it.

[3] The village is not mentioned in the text, but its name appears on the accompanying map.

[4] The village is mentioned in a photo and not in the text.

[5] An element of the village is mentioned, but not the village itself.

[6] The village is mentioned on signs posted by other official bodies, but not in JNF signs.

[7] Park Canada also includes the built-up area of 'Imwas and Yalu, depopulated in 1967.

Table 4. Depopulated Palestinian villages within INPA reserves and parks.

Village name	National park/Nature reserve	Hiking trail [1]	Signs/mention of village	Brochures/mention of village	No. in map
al-Zib	Achziv N.P.	no	yes/mention	yes/mention	50
Sabbarin	Alona N.R.	yes	none	none	179
al-Sindiyana	Alona N.R.	no	none	none	184
Burayka	Alona N.R.	no	none	none	185
al-Shuna	'Amud Stream N.R.	no	none	yes/no mention	97
al-Jura	Ashkelon N.P.	no	yes/no mention	yes/mention	381
'Atlit	'Atlit Antiquities N.P.	no	none	none	136
Abil al-Qamh	Avel Bayt Ma'acha N.R.	no	none	yes/no mention	1
al-Qubab*	Ayalon Valley N.P.	no	none	none	292
Kafr Bir'im	Bar'am N.P.	no	yes/no mention [2]	yes/mention	51
Bayt Jibrin	Beit Guvrin N.P.	yes	yes/mention	yes/mention	401
Bayt 'Itab*	Beit 'Itab N.P.	yes	yes/mention	yes/mention	358
Khirbat 'Iribbin	Betzet Stream N.R.	yes	none	none	36
Qisarya	Caesarea Antiquities N.P.	yes	yes/mention	yes/mention	201
al-Samakiyya	Capernaum N.P.	yes	yes/no mention	yes/no mention	102
al-Tabigha	Capernaum N.P.	yes	none	yes/no mention	106
al-Qastal*	Castel N.P.	no	yes/mention	yes/mention	318
Daliyat al-Rawha'*	Dalia Stream and Tributaries N.R.	yes	none	none	167
Sufla*	Dolev Stream N.R.	yes	none	yes/mention	359
Jarash*	Dolev Stream N.R.	yes	none	yes/no mention	360
Khirbat al-Jawfa	East Gilboa' N.R.	no	none	none	203

(continued)

Table 4. (*continued*)

Village name	National park/Nature reserve	Hiking trail [1]	Signs/mention of village	Brochures/mention of village	No. in map
al-Buwayziyya	'Ein Avazim N.R.	yes	none	none	20
Khirbat al-Zawiya	'Ein Or N.R.	no	none	none	170
Qalunya	'Einot Telem N.P.	no	none	yes/no mention	316
al-Dirbashiyya	Golan Foothills N.R.	no	none	none	33
Hawsha*	Gush Alonim N.P.	no	none	none	116
Khirbat Sa'sa'	Gush Alonim N.P.	no	none	none	120
Simsim	Gvar'am N.R.	no	yes/mention	none	409
Khirbat al-Wa'ra al-Sawda	HaArbel N.P.	no	none	none	109
Wadi al-Hamam	HaArbel N.P.	yes	none	none	110
Hittin	HaArbel N.P.	yes	none	none	113
al-Hamma	Hamat Gader N.P.	no	none	none	138
Mansurat al-Khayt	HaYarden Park N.R.	yes	none	none	84
al-Butayha*	HaYarden Park South N.R.	no	none	yes/no mention	95
Bayt Umm al-Mays*	Judean Hills N.P.	no	none	none	328
Khirbat al-Lawz*	Judean Hills N.P.	no	none	none	338
al-Walaja*	Judean Hills N.P.	yes	none	none	354
Harawi*	Keren Naftali N.P.	yes	yes/no mention	yes/no mention	31
al-Khalasa	Khalutsa Ruins N.P.	yes	none	none	418
Khulda	Khulda N.P.	no	none	none	308
Kawkab al-Hawa	Kochav HaYarden N.P.	no	yes/mention	yes/mention	171
Khirbat Karraza	Korazim N.P.	no	yes/mention	yes/mention	96
Qula*	Kula Fortress N.P.	no	none	none	254

Lifta	Lifta N.R.	yes	none	315
Khirbat al-Buwayra	Makabim N.P.	no	none	288
'Ajanjul	Makabim N.P.	no	none	290
al-Maghar*	Merar Hills N.P.	yes	none	297
Majdal Yaba	Migdal Afek N.P.	yes	none	250
al-Tira	Mt. Carmel N.P.	yes	none	122
Yajur	Mt. Carmel N.P.	no	none	123
Khirbat al-Damun*	Mt. Carmel N.P.	no	none	128
al-Jalama	Mt. Carmel N.P.	yes	none	130
al-Mazar	Mt. Carmel N.P.	yes	none	140
Umm al-Zinat*	Mt. Carmel N.P.	no	none	148
Ghabbatiyya	Mt. Meron N.R.	no	none	61
Sabalan	Mt. Meron N.R.	yes	none	64
Mirun	Mt. Meron N.R.	yes	none	78
'Ayn al-Zaytun*	Mt. Meron N.R.	no	none	80
al-Sammu'i	Mt. Meron N.R.	no	none	88
'Arab al-Nufay'at	Park HaSharon N.P.	no	none	217
Qaqun	Qaqun Fortress N.P.	no	none	226
al-Jammama	Ruhama Badlands N.R.	no	none	414
Sataf*	Sataf-Mt. Heret N.P.	yes	none	334
Khirbat al-Zababida	Sha'ar Poleg N.R.	yes	yes/no mention	232
Shilta	Shilat N.P.	no	none	277
al-Haram (Sayyiduna 'Ali)	Sidna 'Ali N.P.	no	none	235
al-Nabi Rubin	Sorek Stream N.P.	yes	none	273
'Aqqur*	Sorek Stream North N.R.	yes	yes/no mention	341

(continued)

Table 4. (*continued*)

Village name	National park/Nature reserve	Hiking trail [1]	Signs/mention of village	Brochures/mention of village	No. in map
Dayr al-Shaykh	Sorek Stream South N.R.	yes	yes/no mention	yes/mention	350
al-Tira	Tabor Stream N.R.	yes	none	yes/mention	147
Khirbat al-Taqa	Tabor Stream N.R.	yes	none	yes/no mention	161
Danna	Tabor Stream N.R.	yes	none	yes/mention	162
al-Bira	Tabor Stream N.R.	yes	none	yes/mention	165
Abu Shusha	Tel Gezer N.P.	yes	yes/no mention	yes/no mention	295
Qadas*	Tel Kadesh N.P.	no	yes/no mention	yes/no mention	27
al-Qubayba	Tel Lakhish N.P.	yes	yes/no mention	yes/mention	407
Tall al-Safi	Tel Tsafit N.P.	yes	none	yes/mention	369
Bi'lin	Tsafit N.R.	no	none	none	375
Suba*	Tsova N.P.	yes	yes/mention	yes/mention	322
Saffuriyya*	Tzipori N.P.	no	yes/mention	yes/mention	126
Suhmata	Tzuri'el Pool N.R.	no	none	none	69
al-'Ubaydiyya	Yarden South N.R.	no	none	none	137
al-Mirr (al-Mahmudiyya)	Yarkon N.P.	no	yes/mention	yes/mention	243
Khirbat Jiddin	Yehi'am Fortress N.P.	no	yes/no mention	yes/no mention [3]	75
al-Nabi Yusha'*	Yesha' Fortress N.P.	yes	none	yes/no mention	26
Jabbul	Yisaschar Stream N.R.	no	none	none	180
Bayt Daras*	Zmorot Pool N.R.	no	yes/mention	yes/mention	364

Notes:
*The village site is in an area where both JNF and INPA are involved in distributing information to the public.
[1] Hiking trail is in the village site or next to it.
[2] The village is not mentioned in signs, but is referred to in the audio information provided on the site.
[3] An element of the village is mentioned, but not the village itself.

Table 5. Depopulated Palestinian villages within other tourist sites.

Village name	Site name	Responsibility	Hiking trail	No. in map
Burj (al-)	Titora Hill	Modi'in municipality	no	280
Khayriyya (al-)	Ayalon Park	Government ministries, local councils	no	255
Nuqayb (al-)	Tziltzal Beach, Sea of Galilee	Gofra Beach (private)	yes	115
Samakh	Tsemaḥ Beach, Sea of Galilee	Tsemaḥ Beach (private)	no	131
Samra (al-)	Ha'On Beach, Sea of Galilee	Ha'On Village (private)	no	129
Tantura (al-)	Dor Beach	Dor Beach, Dor Resort, Nachsholim Hotel (private)	yes	164

Table 6. Depopulated Palestinian villages on marked hiking trails (which are not included in previous lists).

Village name	No. in map
'Akbara	90
'Arab al-Zubayd	38
'Awlam	143
'Ayn Hawd	132
Bayt Nattif	372
Bayt Tima	398
Dallata	58
al-Ghubayya al-Tahta	166
Ghuwayr Abu Shusha	108
Hadatha	139
al-Hamidiyya	191
al-Husayniyya	52
al-Ja'una	83
Kafr Sabt	127
Kawfakha	415
Khirbat al-Mansura	142
Khirbat al-Muntar	81
Khirbat Umm Burj	394
al-Kunayyisa	283
al-Latrun	300
al-Mansura	299
Nasir al-Din	118
al-Shajara	125
Sirin	145
Tulayl	47
Yubla	176
Zab'a	189

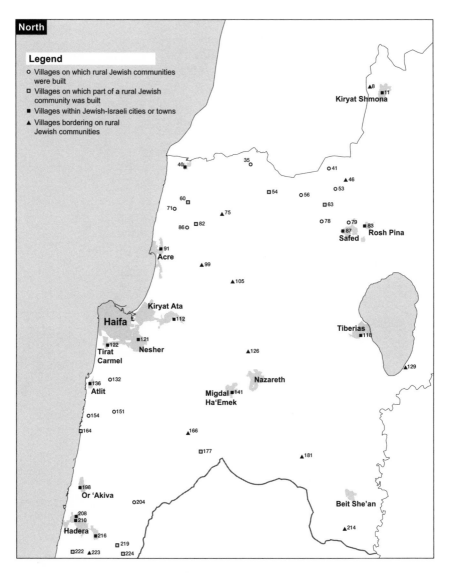

Maps 5–6. Depopulated Palestinian villages within Jewish-Israeli rural and urban communities. Sources of the maps and Tables 7–10: Official maps; field observations; Khalidi, *All That Remains*; Golan, *Wartime Spatial Changes*; Morris, *The Birth of the Palestinian Refugee Problem Revisited*; Markus and Ela'zari, *Mapa Encyclopedia*.

Notes:

· The villages are ordered by the year of establishment of the rural Jewish community or by the name of city.

· Some of the settlements have changed their locations throughout the years. The year of establishment here is the year the settlement was built in its current location.

· Tables 7–10 do not include moshavim that were built on depopulated village sites and were relocated elsewhere after a few years, nor do they include village sites within the boundaries of Israeli-Palestinian villages and towns: al-Mansura (Galilee), Wadi al-Hamam, and Fardisya.

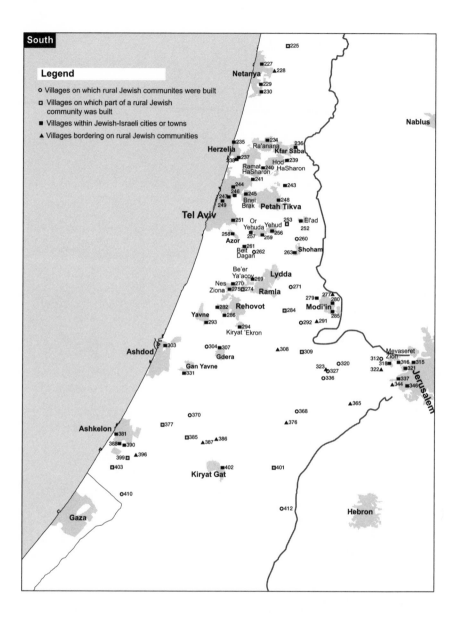

South

Legend

○ Villages on which rural Jewish communites were built

◻ Villages on which part of a rural Jewish community was built

■ Villages within Jewish-Israeli cities or towns

▲ Villages bordering on rural Jewish communities

◻225

■227
▲228
Netanya
■229
■230

Nablus

■235 ■234 236◻
Ra'anana
Herzelia **Kfar Saba**
238◻ ■237
239■
Ramat■240 Hod HaSharon
HaSharon
■241
■243
244■
246■ ■245
247◻ Bnei ■248
249◻ Brak **Petah Tikva**
Tel Aviv
251■ Or 253 ■El'ad
Yehuda Yehud 252
258■ 256■
257■ ■259
Azor ○260
261■
Beit ○262
Dagan 263■ **Shoham**

Be'er
Ya'acov 269 **Lydda**
Nes ■270
Ziona ■275◻274 **Ramla** ○271
277▲
279■ 280
282■ **Rehovot** 277▲
Yavne 286■ 284■ **Modi'in**
293■ ○292 ▲291 285
294■
Kiryat 'Ekron

■303 ○304■307 ▲308 ■309
Ashdod **Gdera** Mevaseret
312○ Zion
Gan Yavne 323 ○320 318■ ■316 ■315
331■ ○327 322▲ ■321
○336 ■337
344▲ ■346

▲365
○370 ○368
▲376
Ashkelon ■377
■381 ■385 ▲387 ▲386
388■ ■390
399◻ ▲396
◻403 ■402 ■401
Kiryat Gat

○410

○412 **Hebron**

Gaza

Table 7. Depopulated Palestinian villages on which rural Jewish communities were established.

Village name	Jewish community	Established	Affiliation	Village houses used by Jews	No. in map
al-Dawayima	Amatzya	1955	Cherut	no	412
Bashshit	'Aseret	1954	n/a	no	304
al-Tira	Bareket	1952	Po'el Mizrachi	yes	260
Wadi 'Ara	Barkay	1949	Kibbutz Artzi	yes	204
Kuwaykat	Beit Ha'Emek	1949	United Kibbutz Movement	yes	86
Bayt Mahsir	Beit Me'ir	1950	Po'el Mizrachi	yes	320
Bayt Naqquba	Beit Nekofa	1949	Moshavim Movement	yes	312
Umm al-Faraj	Ben 'Ami	1949	Moshavim Movement	yes	71
Biriyya	Biria	1949	n/a	no	79
'Ayn Hawd	'Ein Hod	1954	n/a	yes	132
Dimra	Erez	1949	United Kibbutz Movement	no	410
Ishwa'	Eshta'ol	1949	Moshavim Movement	yes	327
Kafr Lam	HaBonim	1949	United Kibbutz Movement	yes	154
al-Ras al-Ahmar	Kerem Ben Zimra	1949	Po'el Mizrachi	yes	53
Ijzim	Kerem Maharal	1949	Moshavim Movement	yes	151
al-Safariyya	Kfar Chabad	1949	n/a	yes	262
Daniyal	Kfar Daniel	1949	United Kibbutz Movement	yes	271
al-Sawafir al-Sharqiyya	Merkaz Shapira	1948	n/a	no	370
Mirun	Meron	1949	Cherut	no	78
al-Qubab	Mishmar Ayalon	1949	Moshavim Movement	yes	292
'Artuf	Naham	1950	Po'el Mizrachi	yes	336
Sa'sa'	Sasa	1949	Kibbutz Artzi	yes	56
Tarbikha	Shomera	1949	Moshavim Movement	yes	35
Saliha	Yir'on	1949	United Kibbutz Movement	no	41
Zakariyya	Zekharia	1950	Moshavim Movement	yes	368

Table 8. Depopulated Palestinian villages where rural Jewish communities exist on part of the Palestinian built-up area.

Village name	Jewish community	Established	Affiliation	Village houses used by Jews	No. in map
'Amqa	'Amka	1949	Moshavim Movement	yes	82
Bayt Jibrin	Beit Guvrin	1949	United Kibbutz Movement	yes	401
al-Barriyya	Beit Ḥashmonay/'Azaria	1972	n/a	no	284
Dayr al-Qasi	Elqosh	1949	Moshavim Movement	yes	54
Wadi al-Hawarith	Ge'ulei Teiman	1950	Po'el Mizrachi	yes	222
Wadi Qabbani	Ha'Ogen	1947	Kibbutz Artzi	no	225
Bayt Jiz	Har'el	1948	Kibbutz Artzi	yes	309
Julis	Hodaya	1949	Moshavim Movement	no	377
al-Kabri	Kabri	1949	United Kibbutz Movement	no	60
Hiribya	Karmia	1950	Kibbutz Artzi	yes	403
al-Jalama	Lehavot Ḥaviva	1949	Kibbutz Artzi	no	224
Barbara	Mavki'im	1949	Zionist Worker	no	399
al-Lajjun	Megiddo	1949	Kibbutz Artzi	no	177
al-Tantura	Nachsholim	1948	United Kibbutz Movement	yes	164
Bir Salim	Netzer Sereni	1948	United Kibbutz Movement	no	274
Rantiya	Nofech / Rinatia	1949	n/a / Moshavim Movement	no	253
Khirbat al-Majdal	Sde Yitzhak	1952	Moshavim Movement	yes	219
Safsaf	Sifsufa (Kfar Ḥoshen)	1949	Moshavim Movement	yes	63
Bayt 'Affa	Yad Natan	1953	Zionist Worker	no	385

Table 9. Depopulated Palestinian villages within the boundaries of Jewish-Israeli towns and cities.

Village name	City name	Established since 1948	Village site in built-up area	Village houses used by Jews	No. in map
al-Manshiyya	Acre	no	no	no	91
ʿArab Suqrir	Ashdod	no	no	no	303
al-Khisas	Ashkelon	yes	no	no	388
Niʿilya	Ashkelon	yes	no	no	390
al-Jura	Ashkelon	yes	no	no	381
ʿAtlit	ʿAtlit	no	no	no	136
Yazur	Azor	yes	yes	yes	258
Abu al-Fadl	Beʾer Yaʿacov	no	yes	no	269
Bayt Dajan	Beit Dagan	yes	yes	yes	261
al-Jammasin al-Sharqi	Bnei Brak	no	yes	yes	245
Muzayriʿa	Elʿad	yes	yes	no	252
Barqa	Gan Yavne	no	yes	yes	331
Qatra	Gedera	no	yes	no	307
ʿArab al-Fuqaraʾ	Hadera	no	yes	no	210
ʿArab Zahrat al-Dumayri	Hadera	no	no	no	208
Raml Zayta	Hadera	no	yes	yes	216
Ijlil al-Shamaliyya	Herzliya	no	yes	no	237
Ijlil al-Qibliyya	Herzliya	no	yes	no	238
al-Haram (Sayyiduna ʿAli)	Herzliya	no	yes	yes	235
Abu Kishk	Hod HaSharon	no	no	no	240
Biyar ʿAdas	Hod HaSharon	no	yes	no	239
Dayr Yasin	Jerusalem	no	yes	yes	321

(continued)

Table 9. (continued)

Village name	City name	Established since 1948	Village site in built-up area	Village houses used by Jews	No. in map
Lifta	Jerusalem	no	yes	yes	315
al-Maliha	Jerusalem	no	yes	yes	346
'Ayn Karim	Jerusalem	no	yes	yes	337
Kafr Saba	Kfar Saba	no	yes	yes	236
Wa'arat al-Sarris	Kiryat Ata	no	yes	yes	112
'Aqir	Kiryat 'Ekron	yes	yes	yes	294
'Iraq al-Manshiyya	Kiryat Gat	yes	yes	no	402
al-Khalisa	Kiryat Shmona	yes	yes	yes	11
Qalunya	Mevaseret Zion	yes	no	no	316
al-Qastal	Mevaseret Zion	yes	no	no	318
al-Mujaydil	Migdal Ha'Emek	yes	yes	no	141
Barfiliya	Modi'in	yes	no	no	279
al-Burj	Modi'in	yes	no	no	280
Wadi Hunayn	Nes Ziona	no	yes	yes	275
Sarafand al-Kharab	Nes Ziona	no	yes	yes	270
Balad al-Shaykh	Nesher	no	yes	yes	121
Umm Khalid	Netanya	no	yes	yes	227
Bayyarat Hannun	Netanya	no	no	yes	229
Ghabat Kafr Sur	Netanya	no	yes	yes	230
Barrat Qisarya	Or 'Akiva	yes	yes	no	198
Kafr 'Ana	Or Yehuda	yes	yes	no	259
Saqiya	Or Yehuda	yes	yes	yes	257

Fajja	Petaḥ Tikva	no	yes	no	248
al-Mirr (Mahmudiya)	Petaḥ Tikva (Kfar HaBaptistim)	yes	no	no	243
Tabsur (khirbat ʿAzzun)	Raʿanana	no	yes	no	234
al-Sawalima	Ramat HaSharon	no	no	no	241
Zarnuqa	Rehovot	no	yes	yes	286
al-Qubayba	Rehovot	no	yes	yes	282
Bir Maʿin	Reʿut	no	yes	no	285
al-Jaʿuna	Rosh Pina	no	yes	yes	83
al-Zahiriyya al-Tahta	Safed	no	no	no	87
al-Bassa	Shlomi	no	yes	yes	40
Dayr Tarif	Shoham	yes	no	no	263
Jarisha	Tel Aviv	no	no	no	246
al-Jammasin al-Gharbi	Tel Aviv	no	yes	yes	247
al-Masʿudiyya (Summayl)	Tel Aviv	no	yes	yes	249
Salama	Tel Aviv	no	yes	yes	251
al-Shaykh Muwannis	Tel Aviv	no	yes	yes	244
Nasir al-Din	Tiberias	no	yes	no	118
al-Tira	Tirat Carmel	yes	yes	yes	122
Yibna	Yavne	yes	yes	yes	293
al-ʿAbbasiyya (al-Yahudiyya)	Yehud	yes	yes	yes	256

Table 10. Depopulated Palestinian villages whose built-up area borders on a rural Jewish community.

Village name	Jewish community	Established	Affiliation	No. in map
al-Birwa	Aḥihud	1950	Moshavim Movement	99
ʿAjjur	ʿAgur	1950	Moshavim Movement	376
ʿAlma	ʿAlma	1949	Poʿel Mizrachi	46
Hatta	Aluma	1965	Agudat Israel Youth	387
Qumya	ʿEin Ḥarod Ihud	1929 (1954)	United Kibbutz Movement	181
Ishwaʿ	Eshtaʾol	1949	Moshavim Movement	323
al-Jiyya	Geʾa	1949	Moshavim Movement	396
al-Manshiyya	Givʿat Haim	1932	United Kibbutz Movement	223
al-Samra	HaʾOn	1949	United Kibbutz Movement	129
Hunin	Margaliot	1951	Moshavim Movement	8
ʿAllar	Mataʿ	1950	Moshavim Movement	365
Jusayr	Menucha	1953	Moshavim Movement	386
Khulda	Mishmar David	1949	United Kibbutz Movement	308
al-Ghubayya al-Tahta	Mishmar HaʿEmek	1926	Kibbutz Artzi	166
Khirbat Bayt Lid	Nordia	1948	Cherut-Beitar	228
al-Jura	Ora	1950	Moshavim Movement	344
al-Sumayriyya	Sdei Trumot	1951	Poʿel Mizrachi	214
Salbit	Shaʿalvim	1951	Agudat Israel Workers	291
Shilta	Shilat	1977	Zionist Worker	277
Suba	Tsuba	1948	United Kibbutz Movement	322
Saffuriyya	Tzipori	1949	Moshavim Movement	126
Miʿar	Yaʿad	1974	Moshavim Movement	105
Khirbat Jiddin	Yeḥiʿam	1946	Kibbutz Artzi	75

Appendix B: Official Names Given to Depopulated Palestinian Villages by the Government Names Committee

Table 11. Depopulated Palestinian villages whose official name is the name of the preceding ancient site.

Village name	Official name	Official name on official maps	Ancient name preserved in Arabic name	No. in map
Abil al-Qamh	Tel Avel Bet Ma'akhah	yes	yes	1
Bayt Jibrin	Beit Guvrin	yes	yes	401
Bayt Jiz	Ḥurbat Gizza*	no	yes	309
Bayt Nabala	Ḥurbat Nevalat	yes	yes	264
Hadatha	Tel 'Ein Ḥada	yes	yes	139
Hamma (al-)	Ḥamat Gader	yes	yes	138
Hawsha	Ḥurbat Usha	yes	yes	116
Huj	Ḥurbat Hoga	yes	yes	413
'Innaba	Ḥurbat Beit 'Anava	yes	yes	281
Indur	Ḥurbat Endor	yes	yes	153
Isdud	Tel Ashdod	yes	yes	345
Jabbul	Ḥurbat Gvul	yes	yes	180
Kafr 'Ana	Ono	yes	yes	259
Kafr 'Inan	Ḥurbat Kfar Ḥanania	yes	yes	93
Khalasa (al-)	Ḥurbat Ḥalutsa	yes	yes	418
Khan al-Duwayr	Ḥanot Panyas	yes	no	3
Khayriyya (al-) (Ibn Baraq)	Ḥurbat Bnei Brak	yes	yes	255
Khirbat al-Shuna	Kfar Shumi	yes	yes	192
Khirbat Karraza	Korazim	yes	yes	96
Khirbat Sa'sa'	Ḥurbat Sasay	yes	yes	120
Lajjun (al-)	Ḥurbat Kfar 'Otnay	yes	no	177
Lifta	Mei Nefto'aḥ	no	no	315

Lubya	Ḥurbat Lubya	no	yes	119
Majdal Yaba	Migdal Afek	yes	no	250
Maliha (al-)	Manaḥat	yes	no	346
Manara (al-)	Ḥurbat Menorim	no	yes	124
Marus	Ḥurbat Merot	yes	yes	55
Qabu (al-)	Ḥurbat Qovi	yes	yes	362
Qadas	Ḥurbat Kedesh	yes	yes	27
Qisarya	Ḥurbat Qesari	yes	yes	201
Qubayba (al-)	Ḥurbat Kfar Lakhish	no	yes	407
Saffuriyya	Tsippori	yes	yes	126
Salbit	Tel Sha'alvim	yes	yes	291
Sar'a	Tel Tsor'a	yes	yes	332
Sarafand al-'Amar	Ḥurbat Zrifin*	yes	yes	266
Shilta	Tel Shilat	yes	yes	277
Suba	Tsova	yes	yes	322
Tall al-Safi	Tel Tsafit	yes	yes	369
Tall al-Shawk	Tel Sokho	yes	yes	202
Zib (al-)	Tel Achziv	yes	yes	50
Zir'in	Tel Yizra'el	yes	no	183

Source for Tables 11–15: ITC hiking maps (2004–2007); Kadmon, *Toponomasticon*; Markus and Elaʾzari, *Mapa Encyclopedia*; Ziv, *A Moment of Place*; Ziv, "Neshia Ruins"; official registries and archival documents of the GNC.

Notes for Tables 11–15: The lists do not include names of rural or urban communities established on ruined villages. The official name assigned to depopulated villages often includes the prefix Ḥurbat (ruin of) or Tyei (ruins of).

Note for Table 11: *Estimated historical identification.

Table 12. Official names given to sites of depopulated Palestinian villages due to sound resemblance to the Arabic name.

Village name	Official name	Name given for*	Village on ancient site	Official name has Hebrew meaning	Official name on official maps	No. in map
Abu Shusha	Tel Shush	ancient site	yes	yes	yes	160
Ashrafiyya (al-)	Ḥurbat Shravit	ruin	yes	yes	no	205
'Ajanjul	Ḥurbat 'Agalgal	ruin	yes	yes	yes	290
'Iraq al-Manshiyya	'Iyei Neshiyya	ruin	no	yes	no	402
'Iraq Suwaydan	'Iyei Sidim	ruin	yes	no	yes	389
'Ubaydiyya (al-)	Tel 'Ovadya	mountain, hill	yes	yes	yes	137
'Urayfiyya (al-)	'Orpa	other	no	yes	yes	28
Barbara	Ḥurbat Barbarit	ruin	no	yes	no	399
Bayyarat Hannun	Honnen Wells	well	no	yes	yes	229
Bir Ma'in	'Iyei Be'er Ma'on	ruin	yes	yes	no	285
Butayha (al-)	Ḥurbat Bteiḥa	ruin	no	no	yes	95
Dayr Abu Salama	Ḥurbat Shalem	ruin	no	yes	no	267
Dayr Nakhkhas	'Iyei Naḥash	ruin	yes	yes	no	400
Dirbashiyya (al-)	Divsha	other	no	yes	yes	33
Faluja (al-)	'Iyei Plugot	ruin	no	yes	yes	397
Farwana	Ḥurbat Parva	ruin	yes	yes	yes	206
Ghuraba	Ḥurbat 'Orva	ruin	yes	yes	no	25
Ijil	Ḥurbat Galil	ruin	no	yes	no	238
Jalama (al-)	Ḥurbat Gelom	ruin	yes	no	yes	224
Jammama (al-)	Ḥurbat Gmama	ruin	yes	no	yes	414
Karatiyya	'Iyei Krattia	ruin	yes	no	yes	392
Kawafkha	Kofha	other	yes	no	yes	415

Khirbat 'Iribbin	Hurbat 'Erav	ruin	yes	yes	yes	36
Khirbat al-Damun	Hurbat Damon	ancient site	yes	no	yes	128
Khirbat al-Buwayra	Hurbat Be'erit	ruin	yes	no	yes	288
Khirbat al-Jawfa	Hurbat Gefet	ruin	no	yes	no	203
Khirbat al-Kasayir	Hurbat Kosher	ruin	no	yes	yes	117
Khirbat al-Majdal	Hurbat Migdal	ruin	yes	yes	yes	219
Khirbat al-Manara	Hurbat Nur	other	yes	yes	yes	152
Khirbat al-Mansura	Hurbat Netzora	ruin	yes	yes	yes	142
Khirbat al-Muntar	Hurbat Nator	ruin	yes	yes	yes	81
Khirbat al-Taqa	Hurbat Takka	ruin	yes	no	yes	161
Khirbat al-Zawiya	Hurbat Zevet	ruin	no	no	yes	170
Khirbat Jiddin	Gadin Fortress	ancient site	yes	no	yes	75
Khirbat Qumbaza	Hurbat Qipoz	ruin	yes	no	yes	156
Khirbat Umm Burj	Hurbat Burgin	ruin	yes	no	yes	394
Khirbat Umm Sabuna	Hurbat Zavon	ruin	yes	no	yes	175
Khirbat Zakariyya	Hurbat Zekharia	ruin	yes	yes	yes	276
Khisas (al-)	Hurbat Hatsats	ruin	no	yes	yes	388
Kudna	'Iyei Kidon	ruin	yes	yes	yes	391
Kunayyisa (al-)	Hurbat Nekhes	ruin	yes	yes	yes	283
Ma'dhar	Hurbat Ma'azer	ruin	yes	no	yes	135
Mansurat al-Khayat	Mantur	other	yes	yes	no	84
Masmiyya al-Kabira (al-)	Mashmia' Shalom	other	no	yes	no	342
Mazar (al-)	Hurbat Mezarim	ruin	yes	no	yes	196
Muzayri'a (al-)	Hurbat Mazor	ancient site	yes	yes	yes	252

(continued)

Table 12. *(continued)*

Village name	Official name	Name given for*	Village on ancient site	Official name has Hebrew meaning	Official name on official maps	No. in map
Najd	Ḥurbat Neged	ruin	yes	yes	no	411
Nuris	Nurit	other	no	yes	no	193
Qabbaʿa	Ḥurbat Qubaʿat	ruin	yes	yes	yes	74
Samiriyya (al-)	Ḥurbat Shimrit	ruin	yes	yes	yes	214
Sammuʿi (al-)	Ḥurbat Kfar Shamai	other	yes	yes	yes	88
Sawamir (al-)	Ḥurbat Shimri	ruin	yes	yes	yes	158
Suruh	Ḥurbat Serah	ruin	yes	yes	no	34
Tulayl	Ḥurbat Talil	ruin	yes	no	yes	47
Zikrin	Ḥurbat Beit Dikhrin	ruin	yes	yes	yes	384

*Other = junction, cave, fortress, a small inhabited place.

Table 13. Depopulated Palestinian villages whose original name was officially recognized by Israel.

Village name	Official name	Name given for*	Village on ancient site	Official name has Hebrew meaning	Official name on official maps	No. in map
Shuna (al-)	Ḥurbat Shuna	ruin	yes	no	yes	97
Tabigha (al-)	Tabaʿa	other	yes	no	no	106
ʿArab al-ʿArida	Ḥurbat ʿArida	ruin	no	no	no	213
ʿAtlit	ʿAtlit	ancient site	yes	no	yes	136
Bayt Nattif	Ḥurbat Beit Nattif	ruin	yes	yes	yes	372
Bayt Shanna	Ḥurbat Beit Shanna	ruin	yes	yes	yes	287
Bayt Tima	ʿIyei Beit Tema	ruin	yes	no	yes	398
Hatta	ʿIyei Hatta	ruin	yes	yes	yes	387
Nitaf	Ḥurbat Nataf	ruin	yes	yes	yes	298
Qira	Ḥurbat Ḥanot Qira	ruin	yes	no	yes	150
Tall al-Turmus	Tel Turmus	mountain, hill	yes	yes	no	363
Zarnuqa	Zarnuka	other	no	no	yes	286
Zeita	ʿIyei Zeita	ruin	no	yes	yes	393

*Other = junction, cave, fortress, a small inhabited place.

Table 14. Depopulated Palestinian villages whose official name was based on a translation of their original name.

Village name	Official name	Name given for*	Village on ancient site	Official name on official maps	No. in map
Burj (al-)	Ḥurbat Titora	ruin	yes	yes	280
Jubb Yusuf	Ḥurbat Gov Yossef	ancient site	yes	yes	94
Jusayr	Tel Gishron	ruin	yes	yes	386
Kawkab al-Hawa	Kokhav HaYarden	ancient site	yes	no	171
Khiyam al-Walid	Ḥurbat Mahal	ruin	no	yes	23
Mughr al-Khayt	'Iyei Me'arot	ruin	yes	yes	76
Zanghariyya (al-)	Ḥurbat Tsviya	ruin	yes	yes	89

*Other = junction, cave, fortress, a small inhabited place.

Table 15. Non-official names of depopulated Palestinian villages, which appear on official maps.

Village name	Name on map	Hebrew/Arabic name	Village on ancient site	No. in map
'Akbara	'Akbara	Arabic	yes	90
'Awlam	Ḥurbat Ulam	Hebrew	yes	143
'Ayn Ghazal	'Ein Ayala (Razala)	Arabic	no	157
'Ibdis	'Ibdis	Arabic	no	379
Barfiliya	Barfiliya	Arabic	yes	279
Bayt 'Itab	Ḥ. 'Itab	Arabic	yes	358
Damun (al-)	Damun	Arabic	no	104
Dayr al-Shaykh	Dayr a-Shaykh	Arabic	yes	350
Fardisya	Fardisya (deserted)	Arabic	yes	231
Fatur (al-)	Ḥ. Ḥamd al-Fatur	Arabic	no	221
Ghabbatiyya	Ghabbatiyya	Arabic	no	61
Ghuraba	Kharuba	Arabic	no	278
Haditha (al-)	Tel Ḥadid	Hebrew	yes	265
Hamidiyya (al-)	'Iyei Ḥamadia	Hebrew	no	191
Hamma (al-)	al- Ḥamma*	Arabic	yes	138
Hamra' (al-)	al- Ḥamra'	Arabic	no	21
Haram (al-) (Sayyiduna 'Ali)	Sidni 'Ali	Arabic	no	235
Hittin	Ḥurbat Ḥittim	Hebrew	yes	113
Iqrit	Iqrit	Arabic	yes	42
Jalama (al-)	Jalama	Arabic	yes	130
Kafr Bir'im	Bar'am	Hebrew	yes	51

(continued)

Table 15. *(continued)*

Village name	Name on map	Hebrew/Arabic name	Village on ancient site	No. in map
Kafr Saba	Tel Kfar Saba	Hebrew	yes	236
Kafra	'Iyei Kafra	Arabic	yes	173
Kafrayn (al-)	Kafrein	Arabic	yes	178
Kawkab al-Hawa	Kawkab al-Hawa	Arabic	yes	171
Khan al-Duwayr	Khan a-Duwayr*	Arabic	yes	3
Khirbat al-Mansura	Mansura*	Arabic	yes	142
Khirbat al-Tannur	Khirbat Tannur	Arabic	yes	366
Khirbat Bayt Far	Hurbat Beit Far	Arabic	no	314
Khirbat Lid	Lid	Arabic	no	163
Khisas (al-)	Tel Tsats	Hebrew	yes	6
Khiyam al-Walid	Khiyam al-Walid*	Arabic	no	23
Latrun (al-)	Latrun	Original (ancient)	yes	300
Lifta	Lifta	Arabic	yes	315
Maghar (al-)	Merar Hills	Hebrew	yes	297
Majdal (al-)	Majdal	Arabic	yes	111
Manshiyya (al-)	Umm Juni	Arabic	no	134
Mansura (al-)	al-Mansura	Arabic	yes	45
Mazar (al-)	Hurbat Mazar*	Arabic	yes	196
Mirun	Meron	Hebrew	yes	78
Murassas (al-)	'Iyei Murassas	Arabic	no	182
Na'ani (al-)	Tel Na'na'	Hebrew	yes	289
Nabi Rubin (al-)	Nabi Rubin	Arabic	no	273

Nimrin	Nimrin	Arabic	yes	114
Nuqayb (al-)	al-Nuqayb	Arabic	yes	115
Qaddita	H. Qaddita	Arabic	no	70
Qastal (al-)	Castel	Arabic	yes	318
Qisarya	Caesarea	Original (ancient)	yes	201
Sabalan	Sabalan	Arabic	no	64
Samra (al-)	a-Samra	Arabic	yes	129
Shaykh Muwannis (al-)	Shaykh Munnis	Arabic	no	244
Sumayriyya (al-)	al-Sumayriyya	Arabic	yes	85
Zuq (al-) al-Fawqani	al-Zuq al-Fawqani	Arabic	yes	2
Zuq (al-) al-Tahtani	al-Zuq al-Tahtani	Arabic	yes	10

Notes:
*An official Hebrew name given to the village site appears as well.
Ḥ. = Hurbat (ruin).

Appendix C: Mapping the Depopulated Palestinian Villages over the Decades

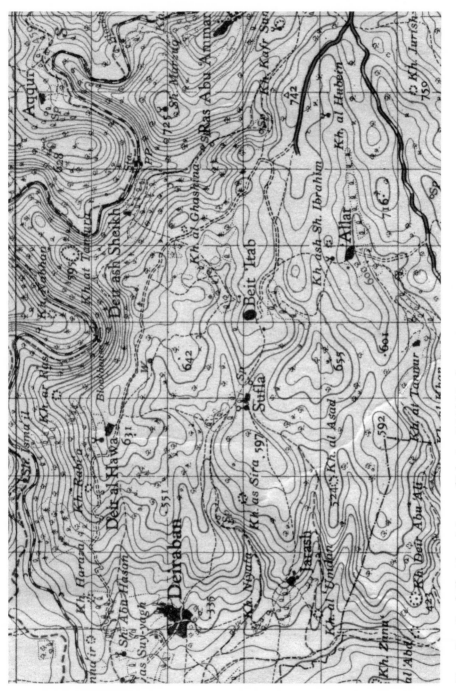

Map 7. From Ramla Sheet (no. 9), Survey of Palestine, British Mandate, 1946, 1:100,000.
Source:  © 2015. All rights reserved to the Survey of Israel. Maps 7–9 were printed by permission of the Survey of Israel.

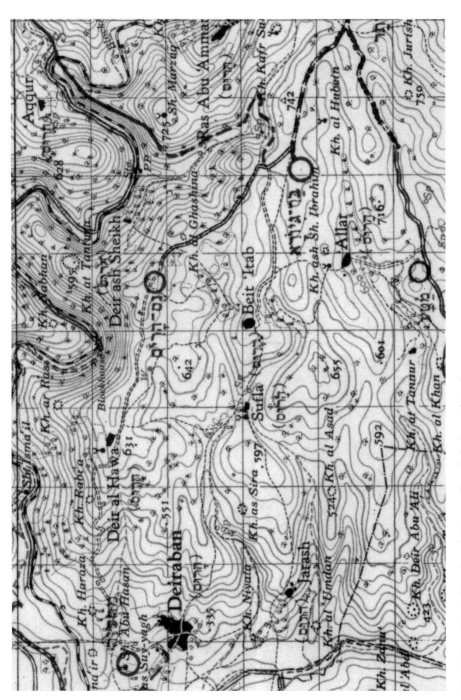

Map 8. From Ramla Sheet (no. 9), Survey of Israel, the State of Israel, 1954, 1:100,000.

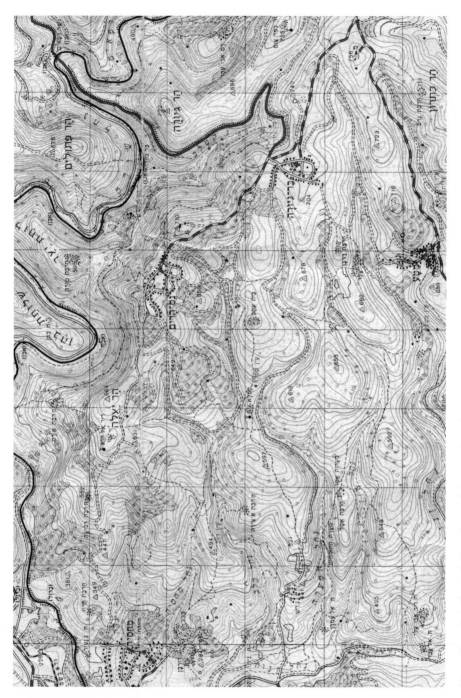

Map 9. From Beit Shemesh Sheet (no. 11-1), Survey of Israel, 2003; 1:50,000.

Notes

Foreword

1. Yizhar, *Khirbet Khizeh*, 7.

Introduction

1. The information presented in the book is based on material collected up to 2008, the year of publication of the Hebrew edition of this book.

2. Khalidi, *All That Remains*.

3. Abu Sitta, *Atlas of Palestine*; Abu Sitta, *The Return Journey*.

4. Khalidi, *All That Remains*, xviii, 582.

5. On that matter see, for example, Golan, *Wartime Spatial Changes*; Goren, *Arab Haifa in 1948*; Hasan, "The Destruction of the City and the War on the Collective Memory"; Margalit, "Jewish Haifa Denies its Arab Past"; Piroyansky, *Ramle Remade*; Rotbard, *White City Black City*; Weiss, *A Confiscated Memory*.

6. Regarding demolitions of villages in territories occupied by Israel in 1967, see Shai, "The Fate of the Abandoned Arab Villages in Israel," 166–169; Kenan, "Report on the Razing of Emmaus, Beit Nuba and Yalou in 1967"; and Zochrot, *Remembering 'Imwas*. Regarding Zochrot's activity on signing depopulated villages from 1967, see chapter 5.

7. Quote from Falah, "The 1948 Israeli-Palestinian War and Its Aftermath," 268.

8. Benvenisti, *Sacred Landscape*; Slyomovics, *The Object of Memory*; H. Cohen, *The Present Absentees*.

9. Ram, "Ways of Forgetting"; Pappe, "The Green Lungs and the Blue Box"; Bauman, "Tourism, the Ideology of Design, and the Nationalized Past in Zippori/Sepphoris"; Meishar, "Fragile Guardians"; Benjamin, "Present Absentees"; and Fenster, "Belonging, Memory, and the Politics of Planning in Israel," respectively.

10. Fenster, "Belonging, Memory, and the Politics of Planning in Israel"; Groag, "Preservation and Forgetfulness"; Peled, "The Opposition of the Historian to the Construction Plan for Lifta"; Sharon, "Planners, the State, and the Shaping of National Space in the 1950s"; Yacobi, *The Jewish-Arab City*; Amit, "The Looting of Palestinian Books"; Kletter, *Just Past?*; Weiss, *A Confiscated Memory*; and Rotbard, *White City Black City*, respectively.

11. Morris, "The New Historiography," 20; Ram, "Ways of Forgetting," 371–374.

12. Khalidi, *All That Remains*, xvii, xxxiv.

13. On that matter see, for example, Bardenstein, "Threads of Memory and Discourses of Rootedness"; Ben-Ze'ev and Aburaiya, "Middle Ground Politics and the Re-Palestinization of Places in Israel"; H. Cohen, *The Present Absentees*, 11–15; Magat, *Bir'am*; Masalha, *Catastrophe Remembered*; Slyomovics, *The Object of Memory*; and Sorek, "Cautious Commemoration."

1. Depopulation, Demolition, and Repopulation of the Village Sites

1. Morris, *The Birth of the Palestinian Refugee Problem Revisited*, 18.
2. Golan, "The 1948 War and the Transformation of Abandoned Rural Arab Areas," 231–232.
3. Benvenisti, *Sacred Landscape*, 81, 91.
4. Falah, "The 1948 Israeli-Palestinian War and Its Aftermath," 274–277.
5. Morris, *The Birth of the Palestinian Refugee Problem Revisited*, 602–604.
6. Ibid., xiv–xviii. For the exact circumstances of the depopulation of each village, see table 2 in appendix A.
7. Khalidi, *All That Remains*; Morris, *The Birth of the Palestinian Refugee Problem Revisited*.
8. H. Cohen, *The Present Absentees*. See also Kabha and Barzilai, *Refugees in Their Land*; and Masalha, *Catastrophe Remembered*.
9. UNRWA Headquarters, "UNRWA in Figures as of 1 Jan 2013," accessed February 27, 2014, http://www.unrwa.org/sites/default/files/2013042435340.pdf. Some of the refugees of 1948 were made into refugees once more in 1967, as they were among the 250,000 Palestinians who fled or were made to flee their homes in the West Bank during the war.
10. Morris, *The Birth of the Palestinian Refugee Problem Revisited*, 78.
11. Ibid., 99–125.
12. Ibid., 125–133.
13. Ibid., 130–132; Morris, "Yosef Weitz and the Transfer Committees," 106–112. For background on the JNF, see chapter 2.
14. Morris, *The Birth of the Palestinian Refugee Problem Revisited*, 67.
15. Ibid., 163–166.
16. Pa'il, "Obtaining Territorial Contiguity in the War of Independence," 12.
17. Morris, *The Birth of the Palestinian Refugee Problem Revisited*, 32, 164–166, 232–262.
18. Pappé, "Historical Truth, Modern Historiography, and Ethical Obligations," 172–185. The question whether there was a massacre in al-Tantura remained a bone of contention among historians. See Morris, *The Birth of the Palestinian Refugee Problem Revisited*, 299–301, note 671; and Confino, "Miracles and Snow in Palestine and Israel."
19. Abu Sitta, *The Palestinian Nakba 1948*, 12. See also Morris, *The Birth of the Palestinian Refugee Problem Revisited*, 222, 257–258, 289, note 427.
20. Morris, *The Birth of the Palestinian Refugee Problem Revisited*, 32, 165–169, 232–262.
21. Ibid., 181–232.
22. Ibid., 262–265.
23. Ibid., 309–315, 318–323.
24. Ibid., 415–437.
25. Ibid., 438–448.
26. Ibid., 329.
27. Morris, "The Crystallization of Israeli Policy against a Return of the Arab Refugees," 109–111.
28. Morris, "Yosef Weitz and the Transfer Committees," 144–151.
29. Morris, *The Birth of the Palestinian Refugee Problem Revisited*, 462–472, 490–491.
30. Abu Sitta, *The Palestinian Nakba 1948*, 12. See also Morris, *The Birth of the Palestinian Refugee Problem Revisited*, 469–471, 480–481.
31. Morris, *The Birth of the Palestinian Refugee Problem Revisited*, 507–517.
32. Ibid., 517–536.

33. Kubursi, *Palestinian Losses in 1948*, 4. These numbers are given in 1948 values, as are other financial estimates in this chapter, unless stated differently.

34. Kedar, "Majority Time, Minority Time," 683.

35. Morris, *The Birth of the Palestinian Refugee Problem Revisited*, 360.

36. Kedar, "Majority Time, Minority Time," 682.

37. Peretz, *Israel and the Palestine Arabs*, 145–153.

38. Granot, *Agrarian Transformations in Israel and in the World*, 88.

39. See a detailed list in table 2, appendix A.

40. Abu Sitta, *Atlas of Palestine*, 44.

41. Fischbach, *Records of Dispossession*, 372.

42. Peretz, *Israel and the Palestine Arabs*, 143.

43. Kimmerling, *Zionism and Territory*, 123; Abu Sitta, "The Feasibility of the Right of Return."

44. Abu Sitta, "The Feasibility of the Right of Return"; Abu Sitta, *The Palestinian Nakba 1948*, 44; Abu Sitta, *Atlas of Palestine*, 78.

45. Khalidi, *All That Remains*, xxxii.

46. Golan, "The 1948 War and the Transformation of Abandoned Rural Arab Areas," 222.

47. Peretz, *Israel and the Palestine Arabs*, 143.

48. Khalidi, *Before Their Diaspora*, 130.

49. Karmi, "The Question of Compensation and Reparations," 211.

50. Quoted in Segev, *1949: The First Israelis*, 69.

51. Jiryis, *The Arabs in Israel*, 78; Morris, *The Birth of the Palestinian Refugee Problem Revisited*, 353.

52. Golan, "The Transformation of Abandoned Arab Rural Areas," 100.

53. Granot, *Agrarian Transformations in Israel and in the World*, 100–105.

54. For extensive information on this issue, see Benziman and Mansour, *Subtenants*, 160; Fischbach, *Records of Dispossession;* Forman and Kedar, "From Arab Land to 'Israel Lands'"; Golan, "The Transfer to Jewish Control of Abandoned Arab Lands"; Golan, *Wartime Spatial Changes*, 201–229; Granot, *Agrarian Transformations in Israel and in the World*, 100–110; Hofnung, *Democracy, Law, and National Security in Israel*, 101–122; Jiryis, *The Arabs in Israel*, 78–79, 245; Kedar, "Majority Time, Minority Time," 682; Kimmerling, *Zionism and Territory*, 134–146; Morris, *The Birth of the Palestinian Refugee Problem Revisited*, 364–366; Ozacky-Lazar, *Ikrit and Bir'am;* and Peretz, *Israel and the Palestine Arabs*, 143–145.

55. Kimmerling, *Zionism and Territory*, 136.

56. By 1966, Israel restored some 3.6 million pounds sterling out of that money to its owners, as indicated by Fischbach, *Records of Dispossession*, 208.

57. Peretz, *Israel and the Palestine Arabs*, 146–147.

58. Kedar, "Majority Time, Minority Time," 682.

59. Morris, *The Birth of the Palestinian Refugee Problem Revisited*, 369–382.

60. Ibid., 376–377.

61. H. Cohen, *The Present Absentees*, 71; Peretz, *Israel and the Palestine Arabs*, 143.

62. Golan, *Wartime Spatial Changes*, 246–253; cf. Braverman, *Planted Flags*.

63. Morris, *Israel's Border Wars 1949–1956*, 122–123.

64. Golan, *Wartime Spatial Changes*, 230–232, 261.

65. Morris, *The Birth of the Palestinian Refugee Problem Revisited*, 394.

66. Peretz, *Israel and the Palestine Arabs*, 143. For other sources on the repopulation of depopulated Arab cities, see, for example, Golan, "Jewish Settlement of Former Arab Towns," 153–154; Tamari, *Jerusalem 1948;* Weiss, *A Confiscated Memory;* Yablonka, *Survivors of the Holocaust*, 19–28.

67. Morris, "Yosef Weitz and the Transfer Committees," 138; Morris, *The Birth of the Palestinian Refugee Problem Revisited,* 383–384.

68. Eshkol, *Land Bond,* 90.

69. Ibid., 91.

70. Yablonka, *Survivors of the Holocaust,* 29–30.

71. Stock, *Chosen Instrument,* 85.

72. Rubin, *A Decade of Immigrants Moshavim,* 48.

73. Eshkol, *Land Bond,* 91; Golan, "The 1948 War and the Transformation of Abandoned Rural Arab Areas," 221, 227–231; Golan, "The Transformation of Abandoned Arab Rural Areas," 101–102; Rubin, *A Decade of Immigrants Moshavim,* 48, 56.

74. Bein, *'Aliyah and Settlement in the State of Israel,* 81.

75. Benvenisti, *Sacred Landscape,* 167.

76. Brutzkus, "The Dreams That Became Cities," 131.

77. Morris, *The Birth of the Palestinian Refugee Problem Revisited,* 392–393; Segev, *1949: The First Israelis,* 86–90.

78. Golan, "From Abandoned Village to Urban Neighborhood," 73–75, 81.

79. Golan, *Wartime Spatial Changes,* 139–153; Benvenisti, *Sacred Landscape,* 187–188.

80. Golan, *Wartime Spatial Changes,* 172–183.

81. For up-to-date information and further deliberation on depopulated villages situated in present-day Jewish settlements, see chapter 5. For a list of those villages and their location on the map, see appendix A.

82. Morris, *The Birth of the Palestinian Refugee Problem Revisited,* 342, 360.

83. Ibid., 235–236, 342–347.

84. Benvenisti, *Sacred Landscape,* 138.

85. Ibid., 130–132.

86. Morris, "Yosef Weitz and the Transfer Committees," 131–132.

87. Morris, *The Birth of the Palestinian Refugee Problem Revisited,* 352–355.

88. Kletter, *Just Past?,* 45.

89. Shai, "The Fate of the Abandoned Arab Villages in Israel," 152; and JNF, *Shadow of the Landscape: Sataf* [in Hebrew] (Jerusalem: JNF, n.d.), respectively.

90. Morris, "Yosef Weitz and the Transfer Committees," 110–125, 131–134.

91. Golan, "The 1948 War and the Transformation of Abandoned Rural Arab Areas," 228–229; Golan, "The Transformation of Abandoned Arab Rural Areas," 103.

92. Golan, "The Politics of Wartime Demolition;" Golan, "The Transformation of Abandoned Arab Rural Areas," 104; Golan, *Wartime Spatial Changes,* 245.

93. This according to official documents cited in Rapoport, "History Erased."

94. Morris, *Israel's Border Wars 1949–1956,* 104, 137–138.

95. Kletter, *Just Past?,* 45.

96. Ozacky-Lazar, *Ikrit and Bir'am,* 17–18.

97. Cohen, *The Present Absentees,* 128; Benvenisti, *Sacred Landscape,* 140.

98. Kletter, *Just Past?,* 57–58. Cites a letter from Avraham Dotan of the Public Diplomacy [Hasbara] Department at the Foreign Office to Yitzhak Elam, director-general of the Labor Ministry, August 13, 1957.

99. Morris, *The Birth of the Palestinian Refugee Problem Revisited,* 356–359; Benvenisti, *Sacred Landscape,* 170.

100. Morris, *The Birth of the Palestinian Refugee Problem Revisited,* 351, 355–356.

101. Golan, "The 1948 War and the Transformation of Abandoned Rural Arab Areas," 230–231; Golan, "The Transformation of Abandoned Arab Rural Areas," 103–104.

102. Brutzkus, "The Dreams That Became Cities," 131; Golan, "The 1948 War and the Transformation of Abandoned Rural Arab Areas," 228, 231.

103. Quoted in Shai, "The Fate of the Abandoned Arab Villages in Israel," 152, footnote 4.

104. Ibid., 155–156. Footnote 10 cites Ben-Gurion at a cabinet meeting, January 20, 1952.

105. Kletter, *Just Past?*, 57–58. Cites a letter from Avraham Dotan of the Public Diplomacy [Hasbara] Department at the Foreign Office to Yitzhak Elam, director-general of the Labor Ministry, August 13, 1957.

106. Ibid.

107. Kletter, *Just Past?*, 62. Cites a letter from Ya'akov Yanai, secretary of the Landscape Improvement Company, to JNF, June 28, 1959. See also Sulimani and Kletter, "'Destruction That Can Be Studied,'" 211.

108. Shai, "The Fate of Abandoned Arab Villages in Israel," 86–87. See also Sulimani and Kletter, "'Destruction That Can Be Studied,'" 218–221.

109. Quoted in Benvenisti, *Sacred Landscape*, 168.

110. Shai, "The Fate of the Abandoned Arab Villages in Israel," 93.

111. Ibid., 91.

112. Ibid., 93, 105, footnote 20.

113. Ibid., 93–96; Sulimani and Kletter, "'Destruction That Can Be Studied,'" 218–221.

114. Benvenisti, *Sacred Landscape*, 168.

115. Shai, "The Fate of the Abandoned Arab Villages in Israel," 97–103.

116. Khalidi, *All That Remains*, xviii–xix.

117. Falah, "The 1948 Israeli-Palestinian War and Its Aftermath."

118. See Bardenstein, "Threads of Memory and Discourses of Rootedness," 28. The pricklypear cactus plant (*zabar* in Hebrew, *sabra* in Arabic), brought to the country after the sixteenth century, was taken up as a nickname and metaphor for the native-born Jews of the country and became among its most recognizable symbols, with disregard for its Arab context (ibid., 11; Almog, *The Sabra*, 4–5).

119. Benvenisti, *Sacred Landscape*, 288–289.

120. Ibid., 270–285.

121. Laor, *Narratives with No Natives*, 130–131.

2. National Identity, National Conflict, Space, and Memory

1. Anderson, *Imagined Communities*; Hobsbawm, *Nations and Nationalism since 1780*; Paasi, "Nationalizing Everyday Life"; Paasi, "Territorial Identities as Social Constructs."

2. Herb, "National Identity and Territory"; Paasi, "Territorial Identities as Social Constructs."

3. Jacobs, *Edge of Empire*, 95–99; cf. Herb, "National Identity and Territory."

4. Sibley, *Geography of Exclusion*, 184.

5. Herb, "National Identity and Territory," 20.

6. Yiftachel, *Ethnocracy*; Yiftachel, "Ethnocracy, Democracy and Geography"; Yiftachel and Kedar, "Landed Power."

7. Halbwachs, *On Collective Memory*; Paasi, "Territorial Identities as Social Constructs," 101; Zerubavel, *Recovered Roots*, 6–11, 214.

8. Nora, "Between Memory and History."

9. Anderson, *Imagined Communities*; Halbwachs, *On Collective Memory*; Hobsbawm, *Nations and Nationalism since 1780*; Said, "Invention, Memory and Place," 179.

10. Zerubavel, *Recovered Roots*, 11.

11. Halbwachs, *On Collective Memory.*

12. Bevan, *The Destruction of Memory.*

13. Falah, "The 1948 Israeli-Palestinian War and Its Aftermath," 256.

14. Groag, "Preservation and Forgetfulness," 33; Rotbard, *White City Black City*, 15.

15. Falah, "The 1948 Israeli-Palestinian War and Its Aftermath," 256; Katz, "Placenames and Their Political Role," 105. See also Azaryahu and Golan, "(Re)naming the Landscape," 181–182.

16. Azaryahu, "Between Two Cities," 99; Azaryahu and Cook, "Mapping the Nation," 195–200; Azaryahu and Golan, "(Re)naming the Landscape," 192; Benvenisti, *The Sling and the Club*, 136; Katz, "Placenames and their Political Role," 105.

17. Herb, "National Identity and Territory," 23–24.

18. Jacobs, *Edge of Empire*, 22.

19. Jacobs, "Shake 'im This Country,'" 103.

20. Harley, "Maps, Knowledge and Power," 291.

21. Herb, "National Identity and Territory," 24.

22. Harley, "Maps, Knowledge and Power," 278, 290, 303.

23. Bar-Tal and Salomon, "Israeli-Jewish Narratives of the Israeli-Palestinian Conflict," 26; Rabinowitz, *Overlooking Nazareth*, 15–16.

24. Said, "Invention, Memory and Place," 182–183.

25. Kimmerling, "Sovereignty, Ownership and 'Presence.'"

26. Ben-Gurion, *About the Settlement*, 73–74.

27. Benvenisti, *Sacred Landscape*, 61–62.

28. Horowitz and Lissak, *Origins of the Israeli Polity*, 16–32.

29. Raz-Krakotzkin, "Exile within Sovereignty," 48.

30. Falah, "The 1948 Israeli-Palestinian War and Its Aftermath," 257.

31. Benvenisti, *Sacred Landscape*, 63.

32. Zerubavel, *Recovered Roots*, 230–232.

33. Raz-Krakotzkin, "Exile within Sovereignty," 47–48. See also Ram, "Ways of Forgetting."

34. Yiftachel, "Ethnocracy, Democracy and Geography," 83.

35. Yiftachel, *Ethnocracy.*

36. Feige, *One Space, Two Places.*

37. Herb, "National Identity and Territory," 18.

38. Zerubavel, *Recovered Roots*, 29.

39. Morris, *The Birth of the Palestinian Refugee Problem Revisited*, 369–370; Shiran, *Points of Courage*, 25.

40. Kimmerling, "Sovereignty, Ownership and 'Presence'"; Shiran, *Points of Courage*, 14.

41. S. E. Cohen, *The Politics of Planting*, 7.

42. Rabinowitz, *Overlooking Nazareth*, 14.

43. Ibid., 81.

44. Shva, *One Day and Ninety Years.*

45. Yiftachel and Roded, "We Judaize You, Homeland."

46. JNF, "KKL-JNF—Israeli Government Covenant," accessed March 1, 2014, http://www.kkl.org.il/eng/about-kkl-JNF/kkl-JNF-id/kkl-JNF-israeli-government-covenant/.

47. Kaplan, "Government Planning Plan no. 22 for Forests and Forestation: Policy Paper," 16–17, 23; JNF, "The Afforestation Project of the JNF" [in Hebrew], accessed March 1, 2014, http://www.kkl.org.il/afforestaion-in-israel/; JNF, "Data on JNF Forests, 2012" [in Hebrew], accessed March 1, 2014, http://www.kkl.org.il/?catid=%7B78B46066-C745-4ED0-A212-1FF9

EBBE9733%7D. For extensive background on the JNF and its forestation project, see Tal, *Pollution in a Promised Land*, 69–111.

48. S. E. Cohen, *The Politics of Planting*, 62–67.

49. Quoted in ibid., 67.

50. Ibid., 49, 62–67; Braverman, *Planted Flags*, 95–98. The Triangle is a cluster of Israeli Arab towns and villages in the central area of Israel, which was transferred to Israeli hands based on the 1949 armistice agreements with Jordan.

51. JNF, *Green Land* [in Hebrew]; Kaplan, "Government Planning Plan no. 22 for Forests and Forestation," 23; cf. Braverman, *Planted Flags*, 79–83, 88–91.

52. Bardenstein, "Threads of Memory and Discourses of Rootedness," 7–8.

53. Ibid., 7; JNF, *JNF for a Prettier Israel* [in Hebrew].

54. S. E. Cohen, *The Politics of Planting*, 62–63.

55. Bardenstein, "Threads of Memory and Discourses of Rootedness," 6.

56. Ibid., 9; cf. Braverman, *Planted Flags*, 98–105.

57. Quoted in "The Right of Return of the Arabs of Israel," 3.

58. Slyomovics, *The Object of Memory*, 234.

59. Azaryahu, "Between Two Cities," 105.

60. Falah, "The 1948 Israeli-Palestinian War and Its Aftermath," 272.

61. JNF, "Afforestation in Israel," accessed March 1, 2014, http://www.kkl.org.il/eng /forestry-and-ecology/afforestation-in-israel/; JNF, "Our History," accessed March 1, 2014, http://www.kkl.org.il/eng/about-kkl-JNF/our-history/.

62. Shkolnik, *Walking the Trails of the Past*.

63. Ben-Yehuda, "The Development of Touristic Sites in JNF Forests in 1990–1999."

64. Tal, *Pollution in a Promised Land*.

65. Rabinowitz, "The Trans-Israel Highway and the Israeli Sect of Nature," 135–136.

66. INPA, "Who We Are," accessed March 1, 2014, http://www.parks.org.il/parks/Pages /WhoWeAre.aspx; INPA, *NPA Report for 2011* [in Hebrew] (Jerusalem: INPA, 2012), 6.

67. National Parks, Nature Reserves, National Sites and Commemoration Sites Law, 5758-1998, art. 1.

68. INPA, "Israel Nature and Parks Authority."

69. Benvenisti, *The Sling and the Club*, 146; cf. Braverman, *Planted Flags*, 83–88.

70. Meishar, "Fragile Guardians," 307–310, 321.

71. INPA, *NPA Report for 2011*, 5.

72. Tal, *Pollution in a Promised Land*, 345–352.

73. Kletter, *Just Past?*, 316.

74. Whitelam, *The Invention of Ancient Israel*; cf. Bowersock, "Palestine Ancient History and Modern Politics."

75. Kletter, *Just Past?*, 315.

76. Ibid., 52–56; Abassi, "The War on the Mixed Cities"; Golan, "The Politics of Wartime Demolition"; Paz, "Conservation of the Architectural Heritage of the Abandoned Urban Neighborhoods"; Sulimani and Kletter, "'Destruction That Can Be Studied,'" 210–212.

77. Kletter, *Just Past?*, 52, 58–61.

78. Shai, "The Fate of Abandoned Arab Villages in Israel," 94–96.

79. Benvenisti, *Sacred Landscape*, 168–169, 299–303, fig. 18x.

80. Ibid., 303–304.

81. Fenster, "Belonging, Memory and the Politics of Planning in Israel," 407–408; Groag, "On Conservation and Memory," 14–15.

82. Falah, "The 1948 Israeli-Palestinian War and Its Aftermath," 277.

83. Fenster, "Belonging, Memory and the Politics of Planning in Israel," 407–408.

84. Bauman, "Tourism, the Ideology of Design, and the Nationalized Past in Zippori /Sepphoris," 207–209.

85. Sharon, "Planners, the State, and the Shaping of National Space in the 1950s."

86. Paz, "Conservation of the Architectural Heritage of the Abandoned Urban Neighborhoods," 125.

87. Yacobi, *The Jewish-Arab City*, 53–57.

88. Peled, "The Opposition of the Historian to the Construction Plan for Lifta."

89. Bardenstein, "Threads of Memory and Discourses of Rootedness," 5.

90. Almog, *The Sabra*, 161–163.

91. Ibid.; Bardenstein, "Threads of Memory and Discourses of Rootedness," 3–4; Benvenisti, *Sacred Landscape*, 57–58, 223.

92. Almog, *The Sabra*, 166–168; Zerubavel, *Recovered Roots*, 120–121.

93. Aran and Gurevitch, "About the Place," 30–31.

94. Zerubavel, *Recovered Roots*, 28.

95. Benvenisti, *Sacred Landscape*, 57; Benvenisti, *The Sling and the Club*, 146.

96. Almog, *The Sabra*, 196.

3. The Depopulated Villages as Viewed by Jewish Inhabitants

1. On the Israeli discourse regarding villages annexed to Israeli cities see, for example, Benjamin, "Present Absentees"; and Golan, "From Abandoned Village to Urban Neighborhood."

2. Slyomovics, *The Object of Memory*.

3. The new village of Ayn Hawd was recognized by Israel in 1992 and connected to the power grid in July 2007.

4. Benjamin, "Present Absentees."

5. Benvenisti, *Sacred Landscape*; see also H. Cohen, *The Present Absentees*.

6. Kochavi-Nehab, *Sites in the Realms of Memory*, 14.

7. Ibid., 186–190.

8. For lack of space, this book does not look into the writings of older kibbutzim like Mishmar Ha'Emek and 'Ein Ḥarod, which had stood near Arab villages until 1948, regarding the departure and absence of their neighbors and the disappearance of the villages.

9. Morris, *The Birth of the Palestinian Refugee Problem Revisited*, xiv–xviii.

10. On the controversy around the massacre in al-Tantura see chapter 1, note 18.

11. Morris, *The Birth of the Palestinian Refugee Problem Revisited*, xiv, xvi, xvii–xviii, 168, 242, 245, 247–248, 253, 299–301, 354, 416–418, 423, 435, 438–440, 465, 468, 473, 481, 483–484, 486–487, 498, 500, 502, 516–518, 533.

12. Gil'ad, *Landmarks in the Absorption of Immigrants in Rural Settlements*; Koren, *Ingathering of Exiles in Their Settlement*; Rubin, *A Decade of Immigrants Moshavim*; Rubin, *My Road to the Moshav*; Rubin, *Workers Moshavim*.

13. Yablonka, *Survivors of the Holocaust*, 53–60.

14. Karmia, *The 35th Birthday of Kibbutz "Karmia": Memoirs, 20 April 1950–20 April 1985* [in Hebrew] (Karmia, 1985), 3, ʏʏ/ᴋᴀᴀ, (2)1.38-101.

15. Yossef Y. Halperin, *The Rabbi's Village: 50 Years of Kfar Chabad* [in Hebrew] (Kfar Chabad, 1998), 5.

16. Sasa, *Sasa Stories* [in Hebrew] (Sasa, 1985), 32.

17. Sifsufa Children, *Hemed School Book* [in Hebrew] (Sifsufa, 2001); Ziv, *A Moment of Place*, 65. In 2003 the moshav was renamed Kfar Ḥoshen, after the residents complained of the Arabic sound of the original name, Sifsufa. However, the original name is still used in official publications and in conversation.

18. Segal, *Kerem Maharal*, 125.

19. See the quote from the 'Ein Hod artists' website on pages 75–76 of this book. The author's request to 'Ein Hod for access to the art colony's documents was refused.

20. Slyomovics, *The Object of Memory*, 50–53.

21. Benvenisti, *Sacred Landscape*, 19.

22. Kabri, newsletter no. 2, October 14, 1949 [in Hebrew], kibbutz Kabri archive.

23. Lehavot Ḥaviva, papers, December 1958 [in Hebrew], YY/KAA, (3)1.43-101.

24. Moshav Ya'ad, "About Ya'ad," accessed October 13, 2013, http://www.yaad.org.il; Nishri, *Hard Beginnings*.

25. Sasa, *Identity Card* [in Hebrew] (Sasa, 1999); Karmia, *The 35th Birthday of Kibbutz "Karmia"*; HaBonim, *Boniclopedia: Encyclopedia of HaBonim Terminology, for the 35th Year* [in Hebrew] (HaBonim, 1985).

26. Segal, *Kerem Maharal*, 90–91.

27. Sasa, *A Passover Haggadah* [in Hebrew and English] (Sasa, 1949; repr., 1984), 29.

28. Yir'on, newsletter no. 1, July 22, 1949 [in Hebrew], kibbutz Yir'on archive.

29. Segal, *Kerem Maharal*, 13.

30. Sasa, *20 Years of Sasa* [in Hebrew] (Sasa, 1970); Kabri, newsletter no. 1325, April 29, 1998 [in Hebrew], kibbutz Kabri archive.

31. On the controversy around the massacre in al-Tantura, see chapter 1, note 18. According to Alon Confino in "Miracles and Snow in Palestine and Israel," the archivist of Nachsholim conducted oral interviews with soldiers about the battles in al-Tantura. One of them described to her the deportation of women, children, and elderly people from the village. A drawing he made was kept in the kibbutz archive.

32. Yir'on, newsletter no. 2, December 1949 [in Hebrew], kibbutz Yir'on archive; Rapaport, *Kabri—First Years*, 12.

33. Falah, "The 1948 Israeli-Palestinian War and Its Aftermath," 281.

34. Kochavi-Nehab, *Sites in the Realms of Memory*, 188.

35. Sasa, newsletter no. 1, November 1949 [in Hebrew], kibbutz Sasa archive.

36. HaBonim—Agricultural Cooperative Association, "The History of HaBonim," accessed October 13, 2013, http://www.m-habonim.co.il/htmls/page_604.aspx?co=13347&bsp=13175.

37. Yir'on, newsletter no. 1, July 22, 1949.

38. Yir'on, newsletter no. 2, December 1949.

39. Dvori, *Moshav Rinatya*, 43.

40. *Kerem Ben Zimra: General Overview* [in Hebrew] (Kerem Ben Zimra, n.d.).

41. Karmia, *The 35th Birthday of Kibbutz "Karmia,"* 1.

42. Megiddo, newsletter, June 1985 [in Hebrew], 23, YY/KAA, 3(3).44-101.

43. HaBonim, *Boniclopedia*.

44. Khefetz, *50 Years Lexicon: Kabri*, 8.

45. HaBonim, *Boniclopedia*; Beit Guvrin, *20th Anniversary Newsletter* [in Hebrew] (Beit Guvrin, 1969).

46. Rapaport, *Kabri—First Years*, 14.

47. Khefetz, *50 Years Lexicon: Kabri*, 37.

48. Har'el, information page no. 8, July 31, 1949 [in Hebrew], YY/KAA, (1)1.26-109.

49. Sasa, *Sasa Stories*, 15.

50. Khefetz, *50 Years Lexicon: Kabri*, 7.

51. Dvori, *Moshav Rinatya*, 56.

52. *Kerem Ben Zimra: General Overview* [in Hebrew] (Kerem Ben Zimra, n.d.).

53. Kabri, newsletter no. 3, February 2, 1950 [in Hebrew], kibbutz Kabri archive.

54. Netzer Sereni, *10th Anniversary to Netzer Sereni* [in Hebrew] (Netzer Sereni, 1958), 34.

55. Ibid., 61.

56. Har'el, information page no. 7, May 22, 1949 [in Hebrew], YY/KAA, (1)1.26-109.

57. Har'el, information page no. 8, July 31, 1949.

58. Beit Guvrin, newsletter no. 1, n.d. [in Hebrew], kibbutz Beit Guvrin archive.

59. Beit Ha'Emek, newsletter, November 26, 1994 [in Hebrew], kibbutz Beit Ha'Emek archive.

60. Beit Ha'Emek, kibbutz decision, October 23, 2006 [in Hebrew], kibbutz Beit Ha'Emek archive.

61. Segal, *Kerem Maharal*, 31–32.

62. Khefetz, *50 Years Lexicon: Kabri*, 37.

63. Rapaport, *Kabri—First Years*, 12.

64. Ibid., 13.

65. Koren, *Ingathering of Exiles in Their Settlement*, 29–30. The moshav later moved to a nearby site and its name was changed to Mazor. Today the village site of Muzayri'a lies within the city of El'ad.

66. Sasa, *The Launching: Sasa's First Year* (Sasa, 1951; new ed., 1984), 4.

67. *Tzipori Identity Card* [in Hebrew] (Tzipori, n.d.).

68. Kochavi-Nehab, *Sites in the Realms of Memory*, 163.

69. Halperin, *The Rabbi's Village: 50 Years of Kfar Chabad*, 33.

70. Rubin, *Workers Moshavim*, 382.

71. Benjamin, "Present Absentees," 88.

72. Ibid., 99.

73. Kochavi-Nehab, *Sites in the Realms of Memory*, 162, 242.

74. Barkai, newsletter, May 10, 1951 [in Hebrew], YY/KAA, (2)1.10-103.

75. Dvori, *Moshav Rinatya*, 31.

76. Nishri, *Hard Beginnings*.

77. Dvori, *Moshav Rinatya*.

78. Segal, *Kerem Maharal*, 120.

79. Slyomovics, *The Object of Memory*, 50–53, 57.

80. Nishri, *Hard Beginnings*, 36.

81. Dvori, *Moshav Rinatya*, 23.

82. Barkai, newsletter, 1950 [in Hebrew], YY/KAA, (2)1.10-101.

83. Megiddo, *Our Home: Foundation Day Newsletter* [in Hebrew] (Megiddo, 1951), kibbutz Megiddo archive.

84. Sasa, newsletter no. 1, November 1949.

85. Nachsholim, *45th Anniversary Newsletter* [in Hebrew] (Nachsholim, 1993), YT/UKA, 16-2/19/7.

86. Beit Guvrin, newsletter, November 9, 1951 [in Hebrew], Beit Guvrin archive.

87. Yir'on, newsletter no. 1408 (marking the fiftieth anniversary), February 19, 1999 [in Hebrew], kibbutz Yir'on archive.

88. Kfar Daniel, *1951–2002, 50 Years . . . and more* [in Hebrew] (Kfar Daniel, 2002), 19.

89. Karmia, *The 35th Birthday of Kibbutz "Karmia*,*"* 3.

90. Ibid.

91. *Erez Is 33 and a Half Years Old* [in Hebrew] (Erez, 1980).

92. Karmia, *The 35th Birthday of Kibbutz "Karmia,"* 3; Beit Ha'Emek, Olive Festival information page, 2001 [in Hebrew], kibbutz Beit Ha'Emek archive.

93. 'Ein Hod artist site, "'Ein Hod Artists' Village," accessed April 13, 2014, http://ein-hod .info.

94. Slyomovics, *The Object of Memory,* 50–57.

95. Yir'on, newsletter, April 27, 1951 [in Hebrew], kibbutz Yir'on archive.

96. Nachsholim, *10th Anniversary Newsletter 1948–1958* [in Hebrew] (Nachsholim, 1958), YT/UKA, 16-2/19/7.

97. Karmia, *The 35th Birthday of Kibbutz "Karmia,"* 3.

98. Yir'on, newsletter no. 1, July 22, 1949.

99. Ibid.

100. Sasa, *Sasa 50th Anniversary Newsletter* [in Hebrew] (Sasa, 2000), kibbutz Sasa archive.

101. Lehavot Ḥaviva, newsletter no. 4, January 13, 1951 [in Hebrew], YY/KAA, (3)1.43-101.

102. Yir'on, newsletter no. 1408 (marking the fiftieth anniversary), February 19, 1999.

103. Sasa, *Encyclosasa* [in Hebrew] (Sasa, 1980).

104. Segal, *Kerem Maharal,* 60.

105. Rubin, *My Road to the Moshav,* 163.

106. Ibid., 164.

107. *Kerem Ben Zimra: General Overview* [in Hebrew] (Kerem Ben Zimra, n.d.).

108. Karmia, *The 35th Birthday of Kibbutz "Karmia,"* 4.

109. Rubin, *A Decade of Immigrants Moshavim,* 466. Moshav and village names not mentioned.

110. Karmia, *The 35th Birthday of Kibbutz "Karmia,"* 7.

111. Ibid., 25.

112. Rubin, *My Road to the Moshav,* 163–164.

113. Morris, *Israel's Border Wars 1949–1956.*

114. Kochavi-Nehab, *Sites in the Realms of Memory,* 189.

115. Nishri, *Hard Beginnings,* 95.

116. Ibid.

117. Megiddo, *Home Court—Megiddo Newsletter* no. 79, April 14, 2000 [in Hebrew], kibbutz Megiddo archive.

118. Beit Guvrin, *20th Anniversary Newsletter.*

119. Yir'on, newsletter, December 1, 1950 [in Hebrew], kibbutz Yir'on archive.

120. Kochavi-Nehab, *Sites in the Realms of Memory,* 189.

121. Rubin, *A Decade of Immigrants Moshavim,* 490.

122. Ibid., 382.

123. Gil'ad, *Landmarks in the Absorption of Immigrants in Rural Settlements,* 142.

124. Yir'on, newsletter no. 1408 (marking the fiftieth anniversary), February 19, 1999.

125. Kabri, newsletter no. 1325, April 29, 1998.

126. Rapaport, *Kabri—First Years,* 12.

127. Ibid., 13.

128. Karmia, *The 35th Birthday of Kibbutz "Karmia,"* 25.

129. Ibid., 15.

130. Yir'on, newsletter no. 1, July 22, 1949.

131. Yir'on, newsletter no. 2, December 1949. According to the biblical story, Naboth was killed so that King Ahab could inherit his plot.

132. Sasa, *The Launching: Sasa's First Year,* 17–18.

133. Sasa, *Thirty-Five Years to the Establishment of Sasa* (Sasa, 1984).

134. Ibid.

135. Sasa, *A Passover Haggadah*, 29, 31.

136. Ibid., 33.

137. Megiddo, *Reflections following the 40th Anniversary* [in Hebrew] (Megiddo, 1989), YY/KAA, (3)1.44-101.

138. Netzer Sereni, *First Years: Collection from Past Newsletters* [in Hebrew] (Netzer Sereni, 1973), 22.

139. Karmia, *The 35th Birthday of Kibbutz "Karmia,"* 7, 15, 23, 28.

140. Morris, *The Birth of the Palestinian Refugee Problem Revisited*, 465.

141. Khalidi, *All That Remains*, 336.

142. Megiddo, *Home Court—Megiddo Newsletter* no. 79, April 14, 2000.

143. Rapaport, *Kabri—First Years*, 12.

144. Sasa, *The Launching: Sasa's First Year*, 18.

145. Ibid.

146. Ibid, 21.

147. Sasa, *A Passover Haggadah*, 31, 33.

148. Slyomovics, *The Object of Memory*, 57–58.

149. Sasa, *A Passover Haggadah*, 29, 31.

150. Sasa, *The Launching: Sasa's First Year*, 21.

151. Sasa, *A Passover Haggadah*, 33.

152. Sasa, *The Launching: Sasa's First Year*, 18.

153. Fenster, "Belonging, Memory and the Politics of Planning in Israel," 411–413.

4. Naming and Mapping the Depopulated Village Sites

1. Benvenisti, "The Hebrew Map," 26.

2. Ibid., 14.

3. The information on this committee and its successors is largely based on Minutes of the Government Names Committee (GNC) First Meeting, April 8, 1951, GNC, ISA, GL-12415/1; Benvenisti, "The Hebrew Map." See also Azaryahu and Golan, "(Re)naming the Landscape," 184–189.

4. Overview by the Names Committee, April 4, 1952, GNC, ISA, GL-22712/8.

5. Statement by Ben-Gurion to the Negev Committee, October 20, 1949, ISA, GL-22171/6.

6. Benvenisti, *Sacred Landscape*, 23.

7. Statement by Ben-Gurion to the Negev Committee, September 6, 1950, ISA, GL-5550/6.

8. Kadmon, *Toponomasticon*, 8.

9. Adler and Gavish, *50 Years of Mapping Israel 1949–1998*, 8.

10. Overview by the Names Committee, April 4, 1952, GNC, ISA, GL-22712/8.

11. SOI, "Map of Israel—South Sheet," October 1950, partial correction and reprint February 1955, 1:500,000. Mentioned in Ziv, "Neshia Ruins," 184.

12. Kadmon, *Toponomasticon*, 8.

13. Protocol of GNC meeting, April 8, 1951, GNC, ISA, GL-12415/1.

14. Ya'akov A. Aricha, secretary of the Committee on Settlement Names within the GNC, to the committee of moshav Kerem Maharal, n.d., quoted in Segal, *Kerem Maharal*, 20.

15. Benvenisti, "The Hebrew Map," 25.

16. Bitan, *Fifty Years of Settlement*.

17. Benvenisti, *Sacred Landscape*, 20.

18. Protocol of Negev Committee meeting, August 19, 1949, ISA, GL-22171/6.

19. Benvenisti, *Sacred Landscape*, 39.

20. Protocol of GNC meeting, July 13, 1952, GNC, ISA, GL-12415/11.

21. Overview by the Names Committee, April 4, 1952, GNC, ISA, GL-22712/8.

22. Avraham Biran (chairman of GNC), foreword to Bitan, *Fifty Years of Settlement.*

23. Benzion Eshel, secretary of the GNC, to writers and poets including Asher Barash, David Shimoni, S. Shalom, Anda Pinkerfeld, and Zalman Shneor, December 20, 1951, GNC, ISA, GL-22166/5.

24. Bitan, *Fifty Years of Settlement.*

25. Azaryahu, "Between Two Cities," 104; see also Azaryahu, "The Power of Commemorative Street Names"; Weiss, *A Confiscated Memory*, 35–36, 115–119.

26. Press to Yitzhak Grinboim, Interior Minister, December 15, 1948, Brawer collection, ISA, G-2613/1.

27. Protocol of Negev Committee meeting, December 17, 1950, ISA, GL-22166/8.

28. Eshel to Biran, June 14, 1951, GNC, ISA, GL-22166/8.

29. Nehemia Argov, adjutant to Prime Minister Ben-Gurion, to Ehud Avriel, director-general of the prime minister's office, June 25, 1951, GNC, ISA, G-3782/5550.

30. Protocol of GNC meeting, July 1, 1951, GNC, ISA, GL-22171/3; Benvenisti, *Sacred Landscape*, 18.

31. Eshel to Biran, July 10, 1951, GNC, ISA, GL-22171/6.

32. Protocol of GNC meeting, July 15, 1951, GNC, ISA, G-12428/3.

33. Eshel to Biran, September 9, 1951, GNC, ISA, GL-22166/5.

34. Protocol of GNC meeting, March 9, 1952, GNC, ISA, GL-22171/6.

35. Protocol of GNC meeting, May 4, 1952, GNC, ISA, GL-22171/6.

36. Yeshayahu Press, "On the Question of Names for Ruins," memorandum, May 5, 1952, GNC, ISA, GL-22166/8.

37. Aricha to the JA, March 27, 1952, GNC, ISA, GL-22166/8.

38. Protocol of Subcommittee on Historical Names meeting, January 11, 1955, Brawer Collection, ISA, G-2613-1.

39. Kletter, *Just Past?*, 318.

40. Protocol of Subcommittee on Historical Names meeting, January 11, 1955, Brawer Collection, ISA, G-2613-1.

41. Aricha to Arieh Eliav, director of the Lakhish Region at the JA, May 22, 1955, Brawer Collection, ISA, G-2613/1.

42. Ziv, "Neshia Ruins," 188–189.

43. Benvenisti, "The Hebrew Map," 23.

44. See, for example, "Registry of Geographical Names in the Map of Israel, 1:250,000, sheet 2, part 3: Geographical Items and Historic Sites," in Government of Israel, *Government Annual, 1952–1953*, 250–256.

45. Kadmon, *Toponomasticon.*

46. Bitan, *Fifty Years of Settlement;* Ziv, *A Moment of Place;* Ziv, "Neshia Ruins"; Markus and Ela'zari, *Mapa Encyclopedia.*

47. The information on the history of the site of every village in this context, and in other contexts through the book, is based on Markus and Elazari, *Mapa Encyclopedia;* and Khalidi, *All That Remains.* For a list of villages established on ancient sites, see table 2, appendix A.

48. For a detailed list of these villages, see table 2, appendix A.

49. Aricha to the prime minister's office, July 7, 1949, GNC, ISA, G-5596/16.

50. Benvenisti, *Sacred Landscape*, 35. Regarding Sifsufa, see chapter 3, note 17.

51. Falah, "The 1948 Israeli-Palestinian War and Its Aftermath," 273–274.

52. Preparatory notes of the Subcommittee on Settlement Names, August 12, 1952, GNC, ISA, GL-22171/6. Today this is an industrial zone.

53. Slyomovics, *The Object of Memory*, 66.

54. Overview for a meeting of the Settlement Names Committee, November 22, 1953, Brawer Collection, ISA, G-2613/3.

55. Bitan, *Fifty Years of Settlement*, 207.

56. Ibid., 65, 80, 111, 35, accordingly.

57. Aricha to the committee of Kerem Maharal, n.d., quoted in Segal, *Kerem Maharal*, 21.

58. Protocol of GNC meeting, April 8, 1951, GNC, ISA, GL-12415/11.

59. Eshel to the Immigration Absorption Department of the JA, October 31, 1951, GNC, ISA, 22165/5.

60. GNC to the JA, January 4, 1952, GNC, ISA, GL-22166/6.

61. For example, GNC to the UKM, October 11, 1951, GNC, ISA, GL-22166/6.

62. Protocol of GNC meeting, March 26, 1953, GNC, ISA, GL-22167/2.

63. Protocol of GNC meeting, May 8, 1951, GNC, ISA, GL-22166/8.

64. Eshel to the secretary of Tel Aviv Municipality, March 27, 1953, GNC, ISA, GL-22167/2.

65. For example, Eshel to the secretary of the Jerusalem Workers Council, September 11, 1951, GNC, ISA, GL-22166/5; GNC to Ra'anana Municipality, March 27, 1953, GNC, ISA, GL-22167/2; Eshel to the Secretary of Petaḥ Tikva Municipality, April 8, 1953, GNC, ISA, GL-22167/3.

66. Eshel to the chief of staff, September 7, 1953, GNC, ISA, GL-22167/5.

67. GNC to the JA, January 12, 1954, Brawer Collection, ISA, G-2613/1. The name Shafrir was later changed to Kfar Chabad.

68. Eshel to moshav Beit El'azari, November 12, 1952. Similar letters were sent to moshav Nurit (January 20, 1953), moshav Shoresh (July 10, 1953), and others. GNC, ISA, GL-22177/6.

69. Eshel to the Education Department of the Jerusalem Municipality, June 18, 1952, GNC, ISA, GL-22166/9.

70. Such requests can be found, among other places, in GNC, ISA, GL-22177/6, 22166/5, 22166/6.

71. Eshel to the Culture and Public Diplomacy Center, July 14, 1953, GNC, ISA, GL-22167/5.

72. GNC to *Davar Le'yeladim* Magazine, September 9, 1953, GNC, ISA, GL-22167/5.

73. Eshel to Egged, November 4, 1953, GNC, ISA, GL-22167/7.

74. Ziv, *A Moment of Place*, 196.

75. Survey Department, "Maps of Israel," 1955–1960, 16 sheets, 1:100,000, printed on maps of the Survey of Palestine, 1946–1947. For a sample of such a map and the Mandate map it is based on, see appendix C.

76. Benvenisti, "The Hebrew Map," 22.

77. Ibid., 22–23.

78. Protocol of GNC meeting, February 7, 1960, quoted in Benvenisti, "The Hebrew Map," 22.

79. Ibid.

80. Quoted in Benvenisti, "The Hebrew Map," 22.

81. SPNI, "Trails Marking and Israel National Trail," SPNI website [in Hebrew], accessed January 11, 2014, www.teva.org.il/?CategoryID=279.

82. Ohad Kochavi, Israel Trail Committee, phone conversation with author, August 16, 2007.

83. Uri Dvir, ed. "Hiking Maps and Trail Marks," ITC, SOI and SPNI, 1:50,000: No. 1: Mt. Hermon, Golan, and the Galilee Panhandle, 2006; No. 2: Upper Galilee, Western Galilee,

and the Galilee Coast, 2007; No. 3: Lower Galilee, the Valleys, and the Gilbo'a Ridge, 2006; No. 4: The Carmel Ridge, 2005; No. 5–6: Jordan Valley and Eastern Samaria; No. 7: The Sharon and Western Samaria; No. 9: Approaches to Jerusalem ("The Corridor"), 2006; No. 10: Gush Dan and Philistia Coastline, 2005; No. 12: Southern Coastal Plain and Slopes of Mt. Hebron, 2006; No. 13: Negev Coastal Plain, 2005; No. 16: The Sands and the Ridge of the Negev, 2004. An example of an SOI map that served as a basis for the trail map is in appendix C. Villages appearing on the map and omitted from the map are listed in table 2, appendix A.

84. Benvenisti, *Sacred Landscape*, 196.

85. Markus and Ela'zari, *Mapa Encyclopedia*, 37.

86. A list of informal names of the village sites that appear on the maps is in table 15, appendix B.

87. Ohad Kochavi, Israel Trail Committee, phone conversation with author, August 16, 2007.

88. Ibid.

89. Kochavi-Nehab, *Sites in the Realms of Memory*, 162–163.

5. Depopulated Villages in Tourist and Recreational Sites

1. Abu Sitta, *From Refugees to Citizens at Home*, 18.

2. Bar'on and Shkolnik, *The Green Guide*.

3. JNF, *Shadow of the Landscape: Ramot Menashe Park* [in Hebrew].

4. JNF, "British Park" [in Hebrew]. Accessed January 29, 2014, http://192.114.182.161/KKL/advanced_template.aspx?id=18341.

5. JNF, *Shadow of the Landscape: The Gilbo'a*.

6. Khalidi, *All That Remains*, 338–340.

7. Bar'on and Shkolnik, *The Green Guide*, 208.

8. Ibid., 26.

9. JNF, *Shadow of the Landscape: Naftali Mountains Forest*; JNF, "Hiking Trail: Oak and Olive in Tsuba" [in Hebrew], accessed January 29, 2014, http://192.114.182.161/kkl/hebrew/nosim_ikaryim/letayelkkl/ezim/.

10. INPA, *Tel Lachish* [in Hebrew] (INPA, 2000).

11. Bar'on and Shkolnik, *The Green Guide*, 186; JNF, *Shadow of the Landscape: Burma Road*.

12. JNF, INPA, ministry of tourism, Jezreel Valley regional council, and the governmental society for tourism, JNF, sign in Kfar HaHoresh forest in the site of Ma'alul. Observed December 16, 2006.

13. JNF, *Fighter's Path in Biria Forest* [in Hebrew].

14. INPA, *Rubin Stream National Park—Sorek Stream Estuary* (2003).

15. INPA, "Bar'am National Park and Mount Meron Reserve" [in Hebrew], accessed January 13, 2014, http://www.parks.org.il/ParksAndReserves/baram/Pages/Bram.aspx.

16. INPA, *Tabor Stream and Tributaries Nature Reserve* (2003).

17. The site contains an audio installation that allows visitors to listen for several minutes to information on the place. Only those who listen all the way to the end will also hear some information on the Arab village, which is missing from the sign.

18. Boyarin, *Palestine and Jewish History*, 249–251.

19. JNF, *Shadow of the Landscape: Sataf*.

20. Tamir, "Tsuba: Abstraction and Blindness."

21. Cf. Falah, "The 1948 Israeli-Palestinian War and Its Aftermath," 277.

22. JNF, *Shadow of the Landscape: Ben Shemen Forest*.

23. Bar'on and Shkolnik, *The Green Guide*, 200.

24. Benvenisti, *Sacred Landscape*, 303.

25. JNF, "Park Rabin—Honoring Yitzhak Rabin & Independence Day," accessed January 25, 2014, http://www.kkl.org.il/eng/tourism-and-recreation/forests-and-parks/rabin-park.aspx.

26. JNF, "JNF Inaugurates Rosh Tzipor Project" [in Hebrew], accessed January 29, 2013, http://www.kkl.org.il/?catid=%7B6947ECA6-A886-4FFD-8240-1799AAC6A977%7D&itemid=%7B85BAAF60-9BC9-433E-B7FE-D0D34D879E07%7D.

27. Benvenisti, *Sacred Landscape*, 303.

28. JNF, "Naftali Hills (Ramim Ridge)" [in Hebrew], accessed September 14, 2013, http://www.kkl.org.il/KKL/hebrew/nosim_ikaryim/yeharot/parkimveyearot/north/naftali.x.

29. Bar'on and Shkolnik, *The Green Guide*, 170.

30. JNF, *Shadow of the Landscape: Biria Forest.*

31. Ibid.

32. See Pappé, "The Green Lungs and the Blue Box," 97.

33. JNF, *Fighter's Path in Biria Forest.*

34. JNF, "Biria Forest—Magic & Mysticism in the Upper Galilee," accessed January 29, 2014, http://www.kkl.org.il/eng/tourism-and-recreation/forests-and-parks/biriya-forest.aspx.

35. See Braverman, *Planted Flags*, 68–70.

36. Bar'on and Shkolnik, *The Green Guide*, 196.

37. INPA, *Achziv National Park and the Northern Coastline* (2003).

38. Cf. Bauman, "Tourism, the Ideology of Design, and the Nationalized Past in Zippori/Sepphoris," 222.

39. Bar'on and Shkolnik, *The Green Guide*, 208.

40. Pappé, "The Green Lungs and the Blue Box," 97.

41. Tamir, "Tsuba: Abstraction and Blindness."

42. JNF, "Hiking with JNF in the Carmel Coast Forests" [in Hebrew], accessed January 21, 2014, http://192.114.182.161/KKL/trip_template.aspx?id=19882.

43. Bar'on and Shkolnik, *The Green Guide*, 110.

44. See Pappé, "The Green Lungs and the Blue Box," 98.

45. Bar'on and Shkolnik, *The Green Guide*, 104; INPA, *Tabor Stream and Tributaries Nature Reserve* (2003); JNF, "British Park" [in Hebrew], accessed January 25, 2014, http://192.114.182.161/KKL/advanced_template.aspx?id=18341.

46. Boyarin, "Ruins on the Road to Jerusalem," 11.

47. INPA, *Sorek Stream, Ktalav Stream Hiking Trail* (2001).

48. INPA, *Dolev Stream Reserve, Cave Stream and Twins Cave Trail* (2001).

49. Bar'on and Shkolnik, *The Green Guide*, 186.

50. Ibid., 167; JNF, *Wells and Cisterns Trail in British Park* [in Hebrew].

51. JNF, *Shadow of the Landscape: Biria Forest.*

52. JNF, *Fighter's Path in Biria Forest.*

53. JNF, "Hiking Trail—Hiking with JNF on the Sculptures Trail in the Tzora'a-President Forest" [in Hebrew], accessed September 14, 2013, http://www.kkl.org.il/KKL/hebrew/nosim_ikaryim/letayelkkl/hamlaza/nosafot/center/zorha.x.

54. JNF, "Ayalon-Canada Park," accessed January 29, 2014, http://www.kkl.org.il/eng/tourism-and-recreation/forests-and-parks/ayalon-canada-park.aspx.

55. JNF, *Shadow of the Landscape: Canada-Ayalon Park.*

56. Bar'on and Shkolnik, *The Green Guide*, 224.

57. INPA, *Halilim Stream Nature Reserve and Telem Springs National Park* (2002).

58. INPA, *Tel Lachish* (2000).

59. Laor, *Narratives with No Natives*, 130.

60. JNF, *Shadow of the Landscape: Lavi Forest.*

61. JNF, sign in the site of Bashshit, within moshav 'Aseret. Observed February 19, 2007.

62. Morris, *The Birth of the Palestinian Refugee Problem Revisited*, 245–246.

63. Ibid., 439–440.

64. Bar'on and Shkolnik, *The Green Guide*, 105.

65. Morris, *The Birth of the Palestinian Refugee Problem Revisited*, xiv–xx.

66. Ibid.

67. Ibid., 130.

68. INPA, *Caesaria* (1998).

69. Cf. Morris, *The Birth of the Palestinian Refugee Problem Revisited*, 258.

70. INPA, "Kfar Bar'am National Park" [in Hebrew], accessed January 29, 2014, http://www
.parks.org.il/ParksAndReserves/baram/Pages/default.aspx.

71. See Boyarin, *Palestine and Jewish History*, 251; Ozacky-Lazar, *Ikrit and Bir'am.*

72. INPA, sign in Korazim National Park, in the site of Khirbat Karraza. Observed December 2, 2006; INPA, *Tel Lachish*; INPA, "Hiking Trail in Mt. Tsuba and 'Ein Ḥemed" [in Hebrew], accessed January 29, 2014, http://www.parks.org.il/ParksAndReserves/enHemedAquaBella
/Pages/Ein-hemd.aspx, respectively.

73. Bar'on and Shkolnik, *The Green Guide*, 206.

74. INPA, sign in Gvar'am Nature Reserve in the site of Simsim. Observed December 17, 2006; INPA, *Tzipori* (2005).

75. Morris, *The Birth of the Palestinian Refugee Problem Revisited*, 258, 440, respectively.

76. INPA, *Achziv National Park and the Northern Coastline* (2003).

77. INPA, "Castel National Park" [in Hebrew], accessed April 29, 2014, http://www.parks
.org.il/ParksAndReserves/castel/Pages/default.aspx.

Conclusion

1. Morris, *The Birth of the Palestinian Refugee Problem Revisited*, 417.

2. Ibid., 469.

3. Ram, "Ways of Forgetting," 374–375; cf. Shapira, "Hirbet Hizah," 53–54.

4. See Rouhana and Sabbagh-Khoury, "Dominance, Tolerance Space and the Privileged Situation," 72–73; Shapira, "Hirbet Hizah," 53–54; Sorek, "Cautious Commemoration."

5. See also Sorek, "Cautious Commemoration."

6. Groag, "On Conservation and Memory," 15.

7. Shapira, "Hirbet Hizah," 54.

8. S. Cohen, *States of Denial*, 278.

9. See Bar-Tal and Salomon, "Israeli-Jewish Narratives of the Israeli-Palestinian Conflict," 36–39; Lederach, *Building Peace: Sustainable Reconciliation in Divided Societies*; Pappé, "A Historiography of Reconciliation."

10. Said, "Invention, Memory and Place," 192.

11. S. Cohen, *States of Denial*, 139.

12. Zochrot, "Who We Are," accessed May 11, 2014, http://zochrot.org/en/menu/%
D7%96%D7%95%D7%9B%D7%A8%D7%95%D7%AA/%D7%9E%D7%99-%D7%90%D7%
A0%D7%97%D7%A0%D7%95.

13. Gardi, Kadman, and Al-Ghubari, *Once upon a Land.*

14. Eitan Bronstein, "Position Paper on Posting Signs at the Sites of Demolished Palestinian Villages," Zochrot, last modified January 2002, accessed March 18, 2014, http://zochrot.org/en/content/position-paper-posting-signs-sites-demolished-palestinian-villages.

15. Lentin, "The Memory of Dispossession, Dispossessing Memory;" cf. Ram, "Ways of Forgetting," 389.

16. Eitan Bronstein, "A Restless Park: On the Latrun Villages and Zochrot," in Zochrot, *Remembering Imwas, Yalu, and Bayt Nuba,* 18–36. See also Pappé, "The Green Lungs and the Blue Box." Since the signs were put up in the park, they have been repeatedly vandalized and removed.

17. Eitan Bronstein from Zochrot, meeting with the author, August 21, 2008.

18. Zochrot, "Hearing on the Building Plan in Miʿar (Yaʿad)," accessed March 19, 2014, http://www.zochrot.org/en/content/hearing-building-plan-mi%E2%80%99ar-yaad.

19. Fenster, "Belonging, Memory and the Politics of Planning in Israel," 404; Fenster, "Memory, Belonging and Spatial Planning in Israel," 190.

20. "Bimkom, "Lifta: Objection" [in Hebrew], last modified November 2004, accessed March 19, 2014, http://bimkom.org/2004/11/%D7%9C%D7%99%D7%A4%D7%AA%D7%90/. A tender (public announcement for companies to submit their candidacy to build in a project) issued by ILA for building the luxury neighborhood in Lifta was canceled on technical grounds in February 2012 by the court, following a petition by refugees from the village and Israeli activists. The general plan, however, is still valid.

21. Peled, "The Opposition of the Historian to the Construction Plan for Lifta," 50.

22. Groag, "Preservation and Forgetfulness," 34–36.

23. Benvenisti, *Sacred Landscape,* 338–339.

24. Markus and Elaʾzari, *Mapa Encyclopedia.*

Bibliography

Abbasi, Mustafa. "The War on the Mixed Cities: The Depopulation of Arab Tiberias and the Destruction of its Old, 'Sacred' City (1948-9)." *Holy Land Studies: A Multidisciplinary Journal* 7, no. 1 (2008): 45–80.

Abu Sitta, Salman H. *Atlas of Palestine.* London: Palestine Land Society, 2004.

———. "The Feasibility of the Right of Return." In *The Palestinian Exodus, 1948–1998,* edited by Eugene Cotran and Ghada Karmi, 171–196. London: Ithak Press, 1999.

———. *From Refugees to Citizens at Home.* London: Palestinian Return Center, 2001.

———. *The Palestinian Nakba 1948: The Register of Depopulated Localities in Palestine.* London: Palestinian Return Center, 2000.

———. *The Return Journey: A Guide to the Depopulated Villages and Present Palestinian Towns and Villages and Holy Sites.* London: Palestine Land Society, 2007.

Adler, Ron, and Dov Gavish. *50 Years of Mapping Israel 1949–1998* [in Hebrew]. Tel Aviv: Survey of Israel, 1999.

Almog, Oz. *The Sabra: The Creation of the New Jew.* Translated by Haim Watzman. Berkeley: University of California Press, 2000.

Amit, Gish. "Ownerless Objects?: The Story of the Books Palestinians Left Behind in 1948." *Jerusalem Quarterly* 33 (2008): 7–20.

Anderson, Benedict. *Imagined Communities: Reflections on the Origin and Spread of Nationalism.* London: Verso, 1983.

Aran, Gideon, and Zali Gurevitch. "About the Place: Israeli Anthropology" [in Hebrew]. *Alpayim* 4 (1991): 9–44.

Azaryahu, Maoz. "Between Two Cities: The Commemoration of the War of Independence in Tel Aviv and Haifa" [in Hebrew]. *Cathedra* 68 (1993): 98–125.

———. "The Power of Commemorative Street Names." *Environment and Planning D: Society and Space* 14, no. 3 (1996): 311–330.

Azaryahu, Maoz, and Rebecca Cook. "Mapping the Nation: Street Names and Arab-Palestinian Identity: Three Case Studies." *Nations and Nationalism* 8, no. 2 (2002): 195–213.

Azaryahu, Maoz, and Arnon Golan. "(Re)naming the Landscape: The Formation of the Hebrew Map of Israel 1949–1960." *Journal of Historical Geography* 27, no. 2 (2001): 178–195.

Bardenstein, Carol. "Threads of Memory and Discourses of Rootedness: of Trees, Oranges and the Prickly-Pear Cactus in Israel/Palestine." *Edebiyat* 8 (1998): 1–36.

Bar'on, Chava, and Yaacov Shkolnik, *The Green Guide: Hikes to Blossoms and Hidden Corners in Israel's Parks and Forests* [in Hebrew]. Tel Aviv: Zofit/JNF, 2006.

Bar-Tal, Daniel, and Gavriel Salomon. "Israeli-Jewish Narratives of the Israeli-Palestinian Conflict: Evolution, Contents, Functions, and Consequences." In *Israeli and Palestinian Narratives of Conflict: History's Double Helix,* edited by Robert I. Rotberg, 19–46. Bloomington: Indiana University Press, 2006.

Bauman, Joel. "Tourism, the Ideology of Design, and the Nationalized Past in Zippori/ Sepphoris, an Israeli National Park." In *Marketing Heritage: Archaeology and the Consumption of the Past,* edited by Yorke Rowan and Uzi Baram, 205–228. Walnut Creek, Calif.: Rowman and Littlefield, 2004.

Bein, Alex. *'Aliyah and Settlement in the State of Israel* [in Hebrew]. Tel Aviv: Am Oved, 1982.

Ben-Gurion, David. *About the Settlement: Compilation 1915–1956* [in Hebrew]. Edited by Menachem Dorman. Tel Aviv: Hakibbutz Hameuchad, 1986.

Benjamin, Shlomit. "Present Absentees: The Case of Qubayba/Kfar Gvirol" [in Hebrew]. *Teoria Uvikoret* 29 (2006): 81–102.

Benvenisti, Meron. "The Hebrew Map" [in Hebrew]. *Teoria Uvikoret* 11 (1997): 7–29.

———. *Sacred Landscape: The Buried History of the Holy Land since 1948.* Berkeley: University of California Press, 2000.

———. *The Sling and the Club: Territories, Jews and Arabs* [in Hebrew]. Jerusalem: Keter, 1988.

Ben-Yehuda, Liora. "The Development of Touristic Sites in JNF Forests in 1990–1999: Motives and Implications" [in Hebrew]. MSc diss., Bar Ilan Geography Department, 2000.

Ben-Ze'ev, Efrat, and Issam Aburaiya. "Middle Ground Politics and the Re-Palestinization of Places in Israel." *International Journal of Middle East Studies* 36 (2004): 639–655.

Benziman, Uzi, and Atallah Mansour. *Subtenants: The Arabs of Israel, Their Status and the Policy toward Them* [in Hebrew]. Jerusalem: Keter, 1992.

Bevan, Robert. *The Destruction of Memory.* London: Reaktion Books, 2006.

Bitan, Hanna, ed. *Fifty Years of Settlement: Atlas of Communities and Places Names in Israel* [in Hebrew]. Jerusalem: Carta, 1999.

Bowersock, Glen W. "Palestine Ancient History and Modern Politics." In *Blaming the Victims,* edited by Edward Said, 181–191. London: Verso, 1988.

Boyarin, Jonathan. *Palestine and Jewish History: Criticism at the Borders of Ethnography.* Minneapolis: University of Minnesota Press, 1996.

———. "Ruins on the Road to Jerusalem" [in Hebrew]. *Studio* 37 (1992): 10–11.

Braverman, Irus. *Planted Flags: Trees, Land, and Law in Israel/Palestine.* New York: Cambridge University Press, 2009.

Brutzkus, Eliezer. "The Dreams That Became Cities." In *Immigrants and Transit Camps 1948–1952* [in Hebrew], edited by Mordechai Naor, 127–140. Jerusalem: Yad Ben Zvi, 1986.

Cohen, Hillel. *The Present Absentees: The Palestinian Refugees in Israel since 1948* [in Hebrew]. Jerusalem: Institute for Israeli Arab Studies, 2000.

Cohen, Shaul E. *The Politics of Planting: Israeli-Palestinian Competition for Control of Land in the Jerusalem Periphery.* Geography Research Paper no. 236. Chicago: University of Chicago Press, 1993.

Cohen, Stanley. *States of Denial: Knowing about Atrocities and Suffering.* Cambridge: Polity Press, 2001.

Confino, Alon. "Miracles and Snow in Palestine and Israel: Tantura, a History of 1948." *Israel Studies* 17, no. 2 (2011): 25–61.

Dvori, Bilhah, ed. *Moshav Rinatya 1949–1999* [in Hebrew]. Rinatya, 2001.

Eshkol, Levi. *Land Bond* [in Hebrew]. Tel Aviv: Culture and Education Press, 1969.

Falah, Ghazi. "The 1948 Israeli-Palestinian War and Its Aftermath: The Transformation and De-Signification of Palestine's Cultural Landscape." *Annals of the Association of American Geographers* 86, no. 2 (1996): 256–285.

Feige, Michael. *One Space, Two Places: Gush Emunim, Peace Now and the Construction of Israeli Space* [in Hebrew]. Jerusalem: Magnes Press, 2002.

Fenster, Tovi. "Belonging, Memory and the Politics of Planning in Israel." *Social and Cultural Geography* 5, no. 3 (2004): 403–417.

———. "Memory, Belonging and Spatial Planning in Israel" [in Hebrew]. *Teoria Uvikoret* 30 (2007): 189–212.

Fischbach, Michael. *Records of Dispossession: Palestinian Refugee Property and the Arab-Israeli Conflict*. New York: Columbia University Press, 2003.

Forman, Geremy, and Alexandre (Sandy) Kedar. "From Arab Land to 'Israel Lands': The Legal Dispossession of the Palestinians Displaced by Israel in the Wake of 1948." *Environment and Planning D: Society and Space* 22 (2004): 809–830.

Gardi, Tomer, Noga Kadman, and Umar Al-Ghubari, eds. *Once upon a Land: A Tour Guide* [in Hebrew and Arabic]. Tel Aviv: Zochrot-Pardes, 2012.

Gil'ad, Gershon. *Landmarks in the Absorption of Immigrants in Rural Settlements* [in Hebrew]. Tel Aviv: Center for Culture and Education of the General Federation of Labor in Israel, 1950.

Golan, Arnon. "From Abandoned Village to Urban Neighborhood: Kafr Salama 1948–1950" [in Hebrew]. *Merhavim* 4 (1991): 71–85.

———. "Jewish Settlement of Former Arab Towns and Their Incorporation into the Israeli Urban System (1948–50)." *Israel Affairs* 9, no. 1–2 (2002): 149–164.

———. "The 1948 War and the Transformation of Abandoned Rural Arab Areas in the Landscape" [in Hebrew]. *Ha-Zionut* 20/21 (1996): 221–242.

———. "The Politics of Wartime Demolition and Human Landscape Transformation." *War in History* 9, no. 4 (2002): 431–445.

———. "The Transfer to Jewish Control of Abandoned Arab Lands during the War of Independence." In *Israel: The First Decade*, edited by Ilan S. Toren and Noah Lucas, 403–440. Albany: State University of New York Press, 1995.

———. "The Transformation of Abandoned Arab Rural Areas." *Israel Studies* 2, no. 1 (1997): 94–110.

———. *Wartime Spatial Changes: Former Arab Territories within the State of Israel 1948–1950* [in Hebrew]. Sde Boker: Ben-Gurion Heritage Center, Ben-Gurion University, 2001.

Goren, Tamir. *Arab Haifa in 1948: The Intensity of the Struggle and Scope of the Collapse* [in Hebrew]. Be'er Sheva: Ben-Gurion University/Ministry of Defense Publications, 2006.

Granot, Avraham. *Agrarian Transformations in Israel and in the World* [in Hebrew]. Tel Aviv: Dvir, 1954.

Groag, Shmuel. "On Conservation and Memory: Lubya—Palestinian Heritage Site in Israel." MSc diss., London School of Economics and Political Science, 2006.

———. "Preservation and Forgetfulness" [in Hebrew]. *Block* 4 (2007): 33–36.

Halbwachs, Maurice. *On Collective Memory*. Chicago: University of Chicago Press, 1992.

Harley, John B. "Maps, Knowledge and Power." In *The Iconography of Landscape: Essays on the Symbolic Representation, Design, and Use of Past Environments*, edited by

Denis Consgrove and Stephen Daniels, 277–312. Cambridge: Cambridge University Press, 1988.

Hasan, Manar. "The Destruction of the City and the War on the Collective Memory: The Victorious and the Defeated" [in Hebrew]. *Teoria Uvikoret* 27 (2005): 197–207.

Herb, Guntram. "National Identity and Territory." In *Nested Identities: Nationalism, Territory, and Scale,* edited by Guntram Herb and David Kaplan, 9–30. Oxford: Rowman and Littlefield, 1999.

Hertzberg, Avraham. *The Zionist Idea: Compilation of Early and Late Writings* [in Hebrew]. Jerusalem: Keter, 1970.

Hobsbawm, Eric J. *Nations and Nationalism since 1780.* Cambridge: Cambridge University Press, 1990.

Hofnung, Menachem. *Democracy, Law, and National Security in Israel.* Aldershot, England: Dartmouth, 1996.

Horowitz, Dan, and Moshe Lissak. *Origins of the Israeli Polity: Palestine under the Mandate.* Translated by Charles Hoffman. Chicago: University of Chicago Press, 1978.

Jacobs, Jane M. *Edge of Empire: Postcolonialism and the City.* London: Routledge, 1996.

———. "'Shake 'im This Country': The Mapping of the Aboriginal Sacred in Australia; The Case of Coronation Hill." In *Constructions of Race, Place and Nation,* edited by Perter Jackson and Jan Penrose, 100–120. Minneapolis: University of Minnesota Press, 1994.

Jiryis, Sabri. *The Arabs in Israel.* New York: Monthly Review Press, 1976.

Kabha, Mustafa, and Ronit Barzilai. *Refugees in Their Land: The Internal Refugees in Israel 1948–1996* [in Hebrew]. Givat Haviva: Institute for Peace Research, 1996.

Kadmon, Naftali. *Toponomasticon: Geographical Gazetter of Israel; Hebrew and Romanized Name Lists.* Jerusalem: Carta, 1994.

Kaplan, Motti. "Government Planning Plan no. 22 for Forests and Forestation: Policy Paper" [in Hebrew]. Jerusalem: JNF, 1999.

Karmi, Ghada. "The Question of Compensation and Reparations." In *The Palestinian Exodus, 1948–1998,* edited by Eugene Cotran and Ghada Karmi, 197–219. London: Ithak Press, 1999.

Katz, Yossi. "Placenames and Their Political Role: Zionist Struggle to Preserve Hebrew Names during the British Mandate" [in Hebrew]. *Studies in the Geography of Israel* 15 (1998): 105–116.

———. "Reclaiming the Land: Factors in Naming the Jewish Settlements in Palestine during the Era of the British Mandate." In *These Are the Names: Studies in Jewish Onomastics,* vol. 2, edited by Aaron Demsky, 63–112. Ramat-Gan: Bar-Ilan University Press, 1999.

Kedar, Sandy. "Majority Time, Minority Time: Land, Nationality and Adverse Possession in Israel" [in Hebrew]. *Iyuney Mishpat* 21, no. 3 (1998): 665–746.

Kenan, Amos. "The First." In *Under Your Skin* [in Hebrew], edited by Amnon Birman, 66–67. Jerusalem: Keter, 1988.

———. "Report on the Razing of Emmaus, Beit Nuba and Yalou in 1967." In *Israel, a Wasted Victory,* translated by Miriam Shimoni, 18–21. Tel Aviv: Amikam, 1970.

Khalidi, Walid, ed. *All That Remains: The Palestinian Villages Occupied and Depopulated by Israel in 1948.* Washington, D.C.: Institute for Palestine Studies, 1992.

———. *Before Their Diaspora.* Washington, D.C.: Institute for Palestine Studies, 1984.

Khefetz, Aharon, ed. *50 Years Lexicon: Kabri 1949–1999: from A to Z, What There Was and What There Is* [in Hebrew]. Kabri, 2000.

Kimmerling, Baruch. "Sovereignty, Ownership and 'Presence' in the Jewish Arab Territorial Conflict: The Case of Bir'im and Ikrit." *Comparative Political Studies* 10, no. 2 (1977): 156–174.

———. *Zionism and Territory: The Socio-territorial Dimensions of Zionist Politics.* Berkeley: University of California, Institute of International Studies, 1983.

Kletter, Raz. *Just Past? The Making of Israeli Archeology.* London: Equinox, 2006.

Kochavi-Nehab, Ronnie. *Sites in the Realms of Memory: Half-Centenarian Books of Kibbutzim* [in Hebrew]. Ramat Efal: Yad Tabenkin, 2006.

Koren, Yitzhak. *Ingathering of Exiles in Their Settlement: A History of the Immigrant Moshavim in Israel* [in Hebrew]. Tel Aviv: Am Oved, 1964.

Kubursi, Atif. *Palestinian Losses in 1948: The Quest for Precision.* Washington, D.C.: Center for Policy Analysis on Palestine, 1996.

Laor, Yitzhak. *Narratives with No Natives: Essays on Israeli Literature* [in Hebrew]. Tel Aviv: Hakibbutz Hameuchad, 1995.

Lederach, John P. *Building Peace: Sustainable Reconciliation in Divided Societies.* Washington, D.C.: U.S. Institute of Peace Press, 1997.

Lentin, Ronit. "The Memory of Dispossession, Dispossessing Memory: Israeli Networks Commemorising the Nakba." In *Performing Global Networks,* edited by Karen Fricker and Ronit Lentin, 206–227. Newcastle, England: Cambridge Scholars, 2007.

Magat, Ilan. *Bir'am: A Mobilized Community of Memory* [in Hebrew]. Giv'at Haviva: Institute for Peace Research, 2000.

Margalit, Gilad. "Jewish Haifa Denies Its Arab Past." *Rethinking History: The Journal of Theory and Practice* 18, no. 2 (2014): 230–243.

Markus, Menachem, and Yuval Ela'zari, eds. *Mapa Encyclopedia: All the Communities and Places in Israel* [in Hebrew]. Tel Aviv: Mapa, 2000.

Masalha, Nur, ed. *Catastrophe Remembered: Palestine, Israel and the Internal Refugees.* London: Zed Books, 2005.

Meishar, Naama. "Fragile Guardians: Nature Reserves and Forest Facing Arab Villages." In *Constructing a Sense of Place: Architecture and the Zionist Discourse,* edited by Haim Yacobi, 303–325. Aldershot, England: Ashgate, 2003.

Morris, Benny. *The Birth of the Palestinian Refugee Problem Revisited.* Cambridge: Cambridge University Press, 2004.

———. "The Crystallization of Israeli Policy against a Return of the Arab Refugees: April–December 1948." *Studies in Zionism* 6 (1985): 85–118.

———. *Israel's Border Wars 1949–1956: Arab Infiltration, Israeli Retaliation, and the Countdown to the Suez War.* Oxford: Clarendon Press, 1993.

———. "The New Historiography: Israel Confronts its Past." *Tikkun* 3, no. 6 (1988): 19–23, 99–102.

———. "Yosef Weitz and the Transfer Committees 1948–1949." In *1948 and After: Israel and the Palestinians,* edited by Benny Morris, 101–158. Oxford: Clarendon Press, 1990.

Nishri, Yitzhak. *Hard Beginnings: Kibbutz Erez 1949–1959* [in Hebrew]. Erez: Nishri, 1993.

Nora, Pierre. "Between Memory and History: *Les Lieux de Memoire*." Translated by Marc Roudebush. *Representations* 26 (1989): 7–24.

Ozacky-Lazar, Sarah. *Ikrit and Bir'am: The Full Story* [in Hebrew]. Givat Haviva: Institute of Arab Studies, 1993.

Paasi, Ansi. "Nationalizing Everyday Life: Individual and Collective Identities as Practice and Discourse." *Geography Research Forum* 19 (1999): 4–20.

———. "Territorial Identities as Social Constructs." *Hagar* 1, no. 2 (2000): 91–113.

Pa'il, Meir. "Obtaining Territorial Contiguity in the War of Independence" [in Hebrew]. *Ma'arachot* 225 (1972): 8–17.

Pappé, Ilan. "The Green Lungs and the Blue Box" [in Hebrew]. *Mita'am* 4 (2005): 89–102.

———. "Historical Truth, Modern Historiography, and Ethical Obligations: The Challenge of the Tantura Case." *Holy Land Studies* 3, no. 2 (2004): 171–194.

———. "A Historiography of Reconciliation" [in Hebrew]. *Mit'an* (Winter 1997): 34–36.

Paz, Yair. "Conservation of the Architectural Heritage of the Abandoned Urban Neighborhoods Following the War of Independence" [in Hebrew]. *Cathedra* 88 (1998): 95–134.

Peled, Kobi. "The Opposition of the Historian to the Construction Plan for Lifta" [in Hebrew]. *Zmanim History Quarterly* 96 (2006): 48–57.

Peretz, Don. *Israel and the Palestine Arabs*. Washington, D.C.: Middle East Institute, 1958.

Piroyansky, Danna. *Ramle Remade: The Israelisatoin of an Arab Town 1948–1967*. Haifa: Pardes, 2014.

Rabinowitz, Dan. *Overlooking Nazareth: The Ethnography of Exclusion in Galilee*. Cambridge: Cambridge University Press, 1997.

———. "The Trans-Israel Highway and the Israeli Sect of Nature." In *Knowledge and Silence: On Mechanisms of Denial and Repression in Israeli Society* [in Hebrew], edited by Hanna Herzog and Kinneret Lahad, 133–144. Jerusalem: Van Leer Institute, 2006.

Ram, Uri. "Ways of Forgetting: Israel and the Obliterated Memory of the Palestinian Nakba." *Journal of Historical Sociology* 22, no. 3 (2009): 366–395.

Rapaport, Ziama. *Kabri—First Years: Stories of the Place* [in Hebrew]. Kabri, 1994.

Rapoport, Meron. "History Erased." *Haaretz*, July 5, 2007, http://www.haaretz.com /weekend/magazine/history-erased-1.224899.

Raz-Krakotzkin, Amnon. "Exile within Sovereignty: Toward a Critique of the 'Negation of Exile' in Israeli Culture" [in Hebrew]. *Teoria Uvikoret* 4 (1993): 23–55.

"The Right of Return of the Arabs of Israel Begins at 'Park Ayalon Canada,' Sponsored by the Jewish National Fund" [in Hebrew]. *Eretz Israel Shelanu* 38 (2008).

Rotbard, Sharon. *White City, Black City* [in Hebrew]. Tel Aviv: Babel, 2005.

Rouhana, Nadeem N., and Areej Sabbagh-Khoury. "Dominance, Tolerance Space and the Privileged Situation." In *Knowledge and Silence: On Mechanisms of Denial and Repression in Israeli Society* [in Hebrew], edited by Hanna Herzog and Kinneret Lahad, 62–74. Jerusalem: Van Leer Institute, 2006.

Rubin, Yosef, ed. *A Decade of Immigrants Moshavim* [in Hebrew]. Tel Aviv: Workers Moshavim Movement in Israel, 1959.

———. *My Road to the Moshav* [in Hebrew]. Tel Aviv: Workers Moshavim Movement in Israel, 1964.

————. *Workers Moshavim: An Anthology* [in Hebrew]. Tel Aviv: Workers Moshavim Movement in Israel, 1970.

Said, Edward. "Invention, Memory, and Place." *Critical Inquiry* 26 (2000): 175–192.

Sasa I.D. [in Hebrew]. Sasa, 1999.

Segal, Shalom, ed. *Kerem Maharal 1949–1979: 30 Years to the Moshav* [in Hebrew]. Haifa: Zemed, 1979.

Segev, Tom. *1949: The First Israelis*. Translated and edited by Arlen Neal Weinstein. New York: Free Press, 1986.

Shai, Aron. "The Fate of Abandoned Arab Villages in Israel, 1965–1969." *History and Memory* 18, no. 2 (2006): 86–106.

————. "The Fate of the Abandoned Arab Villages in Israel before and after the Six-Day War" [in Hebrew]. *Cathedra* 105 (2002): 151–170.

Shapira, Anita. "Hirbet Hizah: Between Remembrance and Forgetting." *Jewish Social Studies* 7, no. 1 (2000): 1–62.

Sharon, Smadar. "Planners, the State, and the Shaping of National Space in the 1950s" [in Hebrew]. *Teoria Uvikoret* 29 (2006): 31–57.

Shiran, Osnat. *Points of Courage: The Policy of Settlement and Its Affinity with Political and Security Goals before the Establishment of the State and in its Aftermath* [in Hebrew]. Tel Aviv: Center for Defence Studies, 1998.

Shkolnik, Ya'acov. *Such Fun! Guidebook to Hikes and Active Recreation in JNF Forests* [in Hebrew]. Jerusalem: JNF, 1995.

————. *Walking the Trails of the Past: Archeology, History and Heritage in JNF Forests* [in Hebrew]. Jerusalem: JNF, 2007.

Shva, Shlomo. *One Day and Ninety Years: The Story of the Jewish National Fund* [in Hebrew]. Jerusalem: JNF, 1991.

Sibley, David. *Geography of Exclusion*. London: Routledge, 1995.

Slyomovics, Susan. *The Object of Memory: Arab and Jew Narrate the Palestinian Village*. Philadelphia: University of Pennsylvania Press, 1998.

Sorek, Tamir. "Cautious Commemoration: Localism, Communalism, and Nationalism in Palestinian Memorial Monuments in Israel." *Comparative Studies in Society and History* 50, no. 2 (2008): 337–368.

Stock, Ernst. *Chosen Instrument: The Jewish Agency in the First Decade of the State of Israel*. New York: Herzl Press, 1988.

Sulimani, Gideon, and Raz Kletter. "'Destruction That Can Be Studied': Israeli Archeology and the Abandoned Palestinian Villages" [in Hebrew]. *Teoria Uvikoret* 42 (2014): 207–235.

Tal, Alon. *Pollution in a Promised Land: An Environmental History of Israel*. Berkeley: University of California Press, 2002.

Tamari, Salim, ed. *Jerusalem 1948: The Arab Neighborhoods and Their Fate in the War*. Jerusalem: Institute of Jerusalem Studies, 1999.

Tamir, Tali. "Tsuba: Abstraction and Blindness." In *Larry Abramson: Tsooba* [in Hebrew], edited by Tali Tamir. Exhibition catalog. Tel Aviv: HaKibbutz Art Gallery, 1995.

Weiss, Yfaat. *A Confiscated Memory: Wadi Salib and Haifa's Lost Heritage*. Translated by Avner Greenberg. New York: Columbia University Press, 2011.

Whitelam, Keith. *The Invention of Ancient Israel: The Silencing of Palestinian History*. New York: Routledge, 1996.

Yablonka, Hanna. *Survivors of the Holocaust: Israel after the War.* New York: New York University Press, 1999.

Yacobi, Haim. *The Jewish-Arab City: Spatio-Politics in a Mixed Community.* New York: Routledge, 2009.

Yiftachel, Oren. "Ethnocracy, Democracy and Geography" [in Hebrew]. *Alpayim* 19 (2000): 78–105.

———. *Ethnocracy: Land and Identity Politics in Israel/Palestine.* Philadelphia: University of Pennsylvania Press, 2006.

Yiftachel, Oren, and Alexander Kedar. "Landed Power: The Making of the Israeli Land Regime" [in Hebrew]. *Teoria Uvikoret* 16 (2000): 67–100.

Yiftachel, Oren, and Batya Roded. "We Judaize You, Homeland: The Inferiority of Israeli Patriotism in Songs and Landscape." In *Patriotism: We Love You, Homeland* [in Hebrew], edited by Avner Ben-Amos and Daniel Bar-Tal, 239–274. Tel Aviv: Hakibbutz Hameuhad, 2004.

Yizhar, S. *Khirbet Khizeh.* Translated by Nicholas de Lange and Yaacob Dweck. Jerusalem: Ibis Editions, 2008.

———. *Stories of a Plain* [in Hebrew]. Tel Aviv: Zmora Bitan, 1990.

Zerubavel, Yael. *Recovered Roots: Collective Memory and the Making of Israeli National Tradition.* Chicago: University of Chicago Press, 1995.

Ziv, Yehuda. *A Moment of Place: Stories Behind Places' Names* [in Hebrew]. Jerusalem: Tziv'onim, 2005.

———. "'Neshia Ruins': On the Indication of Abandoned Villages in the Map of Israel" [in Hebrew]. *Moreshet Israel* 6 (2009): 180–205.

Zochrot. *Remembering 'Imwas, Yalu, and Bayt Nuba* [in Hebrew and Arabic]. Tel Aviv: Zochrot, 2007.

Index

Page numbers in *italics* indicate material in photographs. Note that the article "al-" in Arabic words is not alphabetized at the beginning of a word.

NOGA KADMAN is a researcher in the field of human rights and the Israeli-Palestinian conflict. She holds a master's degree in Peace and Development Studies from Gothenburg University and is a licensed tour guide in Israel. She is co-editor of *Once Upon a Land: A Tour Guide to Depopulated Palestinian Villages and Towns* (in Hebrew and Arabic).